NIGHTS IN HAUNTED HOUSES

Peter Underwood has long been regarded as 'Britain's number one ghost hunter', and for over thirty years he was President and Chief Investigator of the Ghost Club of Great Britain (founded 1862), the earliest investigative society into parapsychology. He is a long-standing member of the Society for Psychical Research, Vice-President of the Unitarian Society for Psychical Studies and a former Member of the Research Committee of the Psychic Research Organisation. He has made numerous radio and television broadcasts and lectured extensively on psychic matters both in Britain and abroad. His many books include *A Gazetteer of British Ghosts*, *Exorcism!*, *A Ghost Hunter's Almanac*, and his acclaimed autobiography *No Common Task*. He was elected a Fellow of the Royal Society of Arts in 1987.

Also by Peter Underwood

A Ghost Hunter's Almanac
Ghosts – And How to See Them
This Haunted Isle
The Ghost Hunter's Guide
Queen Victoria's Other World
Dictionary of the Supernatural
The Ghost Hunters
Haunted London
Into the Occult
Deeper Into the Occult
Gazetteer of British Ghosts
Gazetteer of Scottish and Irish Ghosts
Hauntings: New Light on Ten Famous Cases
A Host of Hauntings
A Ghost Hunter's Handbook
Ghosts of Cornwall
Ghosts of Devon
Ghosts of Somerset
Ghosts of Dorset
Ghosts of Wiltshire
Westcountry Hauntings
Mysterious Places
Ghosts and Phantoms of the West
Ghosts of Wales
Ghostly Encounters
Ghosts of North West England
Ghosts of Kent
Ghosts of Hampshire and the Isle of Wight
The Ghosts of Borley: A critical history of 'the most haunted
house in England' (*with Dr Paul Tabori*)
The Vampire's Bedside Companion
The Complete Book of Dowsing and Divining
Lives to Remember: A Casebook on Reincarnation
(*with Leonard Wilder*)
Jack the Ripper: One Hundred Years of Mystery
Death in Hollywood
No Common Task: The Autobiography of a Ghost Hunter
Thirteen Famous Ghost Stories

Nights in Haunted Houses

Peter Underwood

HEADLINE

First published in 1994
by HEADLINE BOOK PUBLISHING

First published in paperback in 1994
by HEADLINE BOOK PUBLISHING

10 9 8 7 6 5 4 3 2 1

ISBN 0 7472 4258 5

Typeset by Keyboard Services, Luton

Printed and bound in Great Britain by
Cox & Wyman Ltd, Reading, Berks

HEADLINE BOOK PUBLISHING
A division of Hodder Headline PLC
338 Euston Road
London NW1 3BH

This book is dedicated to all the Ghost Club Society Members who have spent nights with me in haunted houses but especially to my wife who has done so much in so many ways.

Contents

Acknowledgements

I am deeply indebted to members of the Ghost Club societies who have accompanied me on nights in haunted houses and allowed me to reproduce their recollections, their photographs and their comments. I also owe a debt of gratitude to many other people including Stephen Bowen, British Tourist Authority, Tony Broughall, John and Sandra Bruce, Daphne Caruthers, D. J. Chapman, Arthur J. Chapple, Geoffrey Cole, Norman and Joy Cooke, *Daily Express*, J. Davis, James Wentworth Day, Rev. John Dening, Downing, the Earls of Strathmore, The Forbes Foundation, Wilfred Granville-Grey, Edward Griffiths, Rev. R. W. Hardy, Charles and Sandra Hill, Rev. and Mrs Christopher Johnson, Mary Knox-Johnston, Brigadier J. A. MacKenzie, Alasdair Alpin MacGregor, Dita Mallet and daughter, Patricia McCaldin, Maureen G. Moore, Daniel O'Sullivan, Bob Parsons, Len Sewell, Deryck Seymour, Margery Skinley, Robert Stepsis and the University of Evansville, *Suffolk Free Press*, Brian Tremain, Peter Watt, Anne Weston and L. Woodgate.

In all instances every effort has been made to locate the

Introduction

Here, for the first time, I reveal details of some of the nocturnal and investigative visits carried out under the auspices of the Ghost Club societies. In a number of instances I have asked club members who took part for their views, opinions and impressions, and these are included in the appropriate chapters. In these difficult regions it is always preferable to have the conviction and judgement of more than one person.

Of course these are not the only nights I have spent seeking the truth in these difficult spheres; indeed I long ago lost count of the number of nights I have spent waiting for ghosts – those elusive but well-documented ethereal entities from another world, perhaps existing in another dimension.

Since this is by no means a complete record, I have tried to include a representative and varied selection. Thus I have included a cottage, a council house, a mansion, a manor house, a church, castles, country inns, a vicarage, a royal palace, an RAF museum and a farmhouse. Although I am no spiritualist, on occasions we have attempted 'communication' when it seemed appropriate, and in one or two instances I have detailed the seances held where they seemed to throw light on some of the reported happenings or on the people concerned. But in the main, these accounts are scientifically orientated and carried out with the object of establishing that ghosts and hauntings, reported from every part of the world and in every civilisation since the beginning of recorded history, do indeed exist and that responsible people do sometimes experience ghosts and ghostly activity.

Many of the photographs included were taken at the time of the investigation and therefore have the status of evidence. All too often, memory plays tricks and afterwards events and happenings such as those I describe seem shadowy and unreal when viewed in retrospect; not unlike a dream that seems so real and solid and unforgettable but which slips away like quicksilver upon waking. Fortunately I have contemporaneous notes covering all the visits and investigations enabling me to present the events in the context of the circumstances at the time.

In the investigation of haunted houses it has always been my prime endeavour to establish that what is happening is objective – i.e. it is not all in the mind of the person concerned – and then to seek to establish scientifically whatever may be happening by means of careful personal investigation and the use of selected apparatus.

I have come to realise that there are many difficulties in using the highly sophisticated equipment that is available these days because it is so efficient that it records or registers the very slightest sound, movement or effect; so I tend to use the less highly developed, simpler equipment.

In any case I have long believed that results every bit as convincing and scientific can be obtained with quite simple apparatus. It is the integrity of the investigating team that is of paramount importance.

The preliminary procedures I go through include writing to the owner of the house or property for the necessary permission and then advising selected participants of the possibility of the event. Frequently the number of participants is strictly limited and this has tended to result in many of the same tried and trusted investigators being chosen time and time again.

Once the team taking part has been agreed by myself and the owner of the premises, then a mutually convenient date is settled and everyone concerned is reminded that all such visits are strictly confidential until after the event to protect the owner's privacy. I then prepare a tentative itinerary which details the exact geographical locality of the property and the earliest time of arrival or exactly where we will meet before we descend as discreetly as possible on the house.

Thereafter the programme will largely depend on the reported manifestations, but usually we meet the owner who will describe in full the disturbances or manifestations and we will then tour the whole house under the guidance of the owner who will point out any relevant areas. The owner then leaves us for the night. At the request of the owner we may agree to parts of the property (perhaps sleeping quarters or 'unhaunted' areas) being considered out of bounds and these areas will be sealed and clearly indicated.

A Base Room will then be selected from where the whole

of the investigation will be supervised. Various apparatus will be distributed in strategic places (for example where manifestations have been reported) and also 'trigger' objects (articles that might attract the attention of any haunting entity). Moveable objects may be ringed with chalk so that any subsequent movement is registered. A rota of regular patrols and checking of instruments, and quiet periods and possible seances will also be drawn up and meticulously carried out with immediate and detailed reports being compiled of instrument readings and *anything*, however trivial, that may be of relevance to the case in hand.

The schedule will be flexible and may be varied in the event of reported happenings – such as several experiences in one area. At the end of the investigation care will be taken to collect the apparatus, thoroughly look for and remove all signs of our visit and generally ensure that everything is as it should be. After an inspection to ensure that all is satisfactory we will, if circumstances permit, enjoy a snack breakfast before thanking the owner and leaving as quietly as possible to prepare a detailed report of the visit, a copy of which will usually be sent to the owner with our renewed thanks for all his or her co-operation.

I have to say that the Ghost Club as depicted in this book no longer exists. The Ghost Club Society, of which I am Life President, now holds meetings, discussions and events, issues a regular Society News and conducts similar scientific investigations in haunted houses countrywide. Membership is normally by invitation only.

Over the last half-century I've had an incredible time, a 'darn good time' as my American friends would say, visiting some truly wonderful and magnificent places and meeting and talking with some fascinating people and all in the company of some quite remarkable friends and club members who have joined me in these never-to-be-forgotten nights in haunted houses. I hope my readers will enjoy these journeys into the unknown.

Peter Underwood

Savage Club
1 Whitehall Place
London SW1A 2HD

November 1993

Borley Cottage

Borley Rectory, a dark and rambling, grim and secluded building situated at the top of a hill facing the church, was known far and wide from the 1920s onwards as 'the most haunted house in England'. It was built in 1863 by the Rev. H. D. E. Bull, who added a wing as his large family increased. The typical Victorian rector, who knew all about the Borley ghosts, died in 1892 in the Blue Room and was succeeded by his son, the Rev. Harry Bull who in turn died in the same room at the rectory in 1927. The living then passed to a cousin, the Rev. L. A. Foyster, who served the parish for five years, sharing the house with his much younger and fun-loving wife, Marianne. Then came the Rev. G. E. Smith, an Anglo-Indian and his peculiar English wife; and finally the Rev. A. C. Henning, during whose incumbency the rectory passed out of ecclesiastical hands and was eventually gutted by fire in 1939. The point is that *everyone* who lived there – five successive rectors, their wives and families, together with servants and neighbours and scores of visitors – all asserted that the place was haunted. There were many stories of the appearance of a phantom nun, of a ghostly coach and horses, of inexplicable fires, voices, bell-ringing, loud bangs and crashing sounds and a score of other happenings that puzzled, bewildered and frightened the inhabitants.

Harry Price, a popular ghost hunter of the time, became obsessed with the case and spent many hours there, visiting the various incumbents, inhabitants, neighbours and local people; eventually he rented the place for a year and organised investigations and vigils that were carried out under controlled conditions. He wrote two books on the subject and lectured, broadcast, talked and discussed the ghosts of Borley with enthusiasm for the rest of his life.

By the time I became seriously interested in the scientific investigation of ghosts, hauntings and other spontaneous phenomena, the rectory had gone. Only the cottage that had once adjoined the rectory, comprising living accommodation above stables and carriage space, and the old rectory garden remained to remind those interested of the house that had once seen so much happiness and unhappiness and above all so many strange happenings.

This cottage – known variously as Borley Rectory Cottage, The Coachhouse, Borley Priory, Priory Cottage and simply The Cottage – was occupied before and after the fire by Captain W. H. Gregson and his family; later he sold the property and grounds to a local builder who demolished what remained of the rectory and sold the bricks and rubble to a contractor who used them in commercial construction throughout the area. Gregson, incidentally, purchased the rectory and grounds in December 1938 for £500 and managed to insure the property and his effects for £10,000. After the fire, Gregson's claim for 'accidental loss by fire' was rejected by the insurance company and the matter was eventually settled out of court for £750 and costs. While at Borley, Captain Gregson and his two sons claimed to experience a number of curious incidents. After selling the cottage and rectory site, Gregson lived for a time at Malden in Suffolk and then he went to Tasmania where he died. The cottage changed hands two or three times and then I heard that it had been purchased by a poet and author who planned to grow mushrooms there. The then rector, the Rev. Alfred Henning, whom I already knew, informed me that the new owner was named James Turner and he and his wife, Cathy, had just moved into the cottage.

I lost no time in writing to the Turners requesting permission to spend a night on the site of the haunted rectory and I was delighted to receive a favourable reply. It was the beginning of a friendship that spread into other parts of Essex, Suffolk and three places in Cornwall before the untimely and sudden death of James in 1975 and the quiet passing of Cathy in 1992.

Accompanied by my friend and Ghost Club Society life member Thomas Brown of Weston, I journeyed by rail – including a wonderful Victorian train that ran in those days from Marks Tey – to Long Melford, the nearest station to Borley. I remember us so well walking up the long hill to Borley and viewing for the first time the scene of so much reported psychic activity. We met the new owners whom we found charming but perhaps a little out of their depth; they had been in residence only three weeks and we were the first 'ghost hunters' to visit Borley during their ownership. Sadly we were by no means the last and after a few years the Turners moved three miles to The Mill

House, Belchamp Walter. Three years at Borley had been more than long enough to convince James and Cathy that they did not need the continual harassment and inconvenience of unannounced visitors at all times of the day and night, continually trespassing on their ground and intruding into their lives. Once, returning from an evening meal in Sudbury, they found a party of 'ghost hunters' occupying the grounds, one of them carrying a shotgun and determined to shoot at the first sight of the ghost nun – or anything that moved! Another time they watched from an upstairs window as a smartly dressed gentleman calmly turned over with his rolled umbrella the sign that read 'Private – No Admittance' and walked into the garden!

With nostalgic excitement on that first visit to Borley we examined and explored the rectory site where gaping holes revealed the once hidden cellars; the enormous old pump wheel that had once stood under the arches in the courtyard over the main well; and the so-called Nun's Walk, the little grass path bordered by short yew hedges where, it was said, the phantom nun had been seen on many occasions. We found some bell-pulls and wires, a few ancient bottles and pieces of crockery and, beneath a hedge, the intact skull of a cow! Soon James Turner was to make a sunken garden of the gaping, rubble-filled cellars and outline the site of the vanished rectory with a low brick wall.

Already the Turners, no strangers to haunted houses, had odd happenings and experiences to relate. Both, at different times, had noticed strange and inexplicable smells, especially of lavender, the origins of which they were never able to discover. Then there was the smell of food being cooked in the middle of the night, the smell of incense, a curious sickly smell, and other more pleasant odours such as old-fashioned roses but completely out of season.

On that first meeting with the Turners, Tom Brown and I formed the opinion that they had little time for supernatural disturbances; certainly that was the impression they gave us. Already the garden was beginning to take shape and they had plans for fruit-farming in addition to the mushroom-growing. Yet during the few brief years they were to spend at Borley the Turners were destined to experience a wealth of curious and varied happenings which they found difficult to explain. Perhaps somewhat insignificant when viewed individually, collectively the Turners' experiences represent an impressive array of 'odd' incidents. It is perhaps important to bear in mind that I received details of these occurrences at the time they were taking place.

There was the sound of excited whispering emanating from the former rectory orchard, an area that was patently deserted. On one occasion James threw down the bill-hook he was using and ran into the undergrowth towards the direction of the voices but the loud whispering fled before him and he found nothing to account for the sounds he had heard not once but many times. Sometimes Cathy would stand near him and hear the whispering too. When the orchard area was eventually cleared and the main part of the Nun's Walk completely clear again, the whispering stopped but still they heard footsteps.

Once, on a beautiful summer morning, Cathy thought she would sit in the garden and she placed a deckchair inside the site of the old rectory, picked out a book and settled down to read. After a few moments she heard footsteps approaching her from behind; James, as usual, was working in the garden in front of her and visible. As she wondered who it could be, the footsteps came nearer and Cathy looked round the side of the deckchair – there was no one in sight! But still she could hear footsteps, distinct and deliberate, and as she sat, wondering what on earth was happening and almost holding her breath, the footsteps seemed to walk close to her side, move in front of her in an arc and pass her on the other side, finally fading and disappearing behind her again. What was especially puzzling was the fact that, although the footsteps appeared over earth and lawn that now occupied the site of the rectory, the footsteps sounded as though they were on floorboards – almost as though they were inside the vanished rectory! It was an experience Cathy was never to forget. Some forty years later I asked her which experience at Borley had most impressed her and she said she could never forget those footsteps, sounding and echoing as on floorboards but emanating from grass and earth apparently from nowhere, walking round her and disappearing to nowhere.

Both James and Cathy Turner heard footsteps that had no natural origin on open ground at the back of the cottage. They also both saw a 'spectral' cat in the same area; it was seen by Ronnie Blythe in the bathroom too. A few months later they heard a loud squeal, as of a cat in pain, close by, seemingly from the next bedroom in the cottage, when both their own cats were outside. They found nothing to account for the sound. After that the phantom cat was not seen again.

They became used to various thuds and crashing sounds that had no rational explanation. Once some workers in the yard came to the door to inquire what had happened after a particularly loud crashing sound, as though a pile of crockery had smashed. They were astonished to learn that nothing could be found to have caused the sound and looked, bewildered, around the neat kitchen from where the sound had appeared to emanate. Another time the same workmen were amazed to hear a loud report, almost like a pistol shot, when they were both in the kitchen; the noise appeared to have been produced within the room in which they stood. As always there was no explanation.

The nearby church seemed to attract paranormal activity after the destruction of the rectory and there have been many, many reported incidents for which no explanation has been discovered: footsteps, movement of objects, phantom forms, sensations of coldness, whispering, music, heavy dragging sounds, rustling noises, in fact all sorts of sounds; and once James Turner heard footsteps in circumstances that convinced him that odd things did indeed happen at Borley.

He had strolled over to the church on an exceptionally still moonlit night soon after midnight and he sat on the step of the priest's door for about a quarter of an hour. He remembered thinking to himself that he was completely happy – and then suddenly he became aware of footsteps approaching up the main path, although nothing was visible. He told me that he plainly heard 'somebody or something with a lame leg and a swishing skirt' pass along the church path in front of him and continue towards the church door – something that was completely invisible.

Those footsteps were a constant puzzle to James Turner, as were the distinct footsteps that Tom Brown and I heard in the grounds of the former Borley Rectory. I was puzzled at the time and I am still puzzled. Not once but twice during our night in the haunted garden, at 3.15 a.m. and again at 3.40 a.m. we both heard footfalls, apparently emanating from the direction of the bend in the Nun's Walk, where the little path entered some shrubbery, but on immediate silent investigation on each occasion all was quiet, nothing was visible, and no explanation was discovered for the 'footsteps'. In my notebook at the time I state: 'We are satisfied that the footsteps were not of human origin.'

The controlled investigations carried out that night, the first at Borley for a number of years, involved thermometer and atmospheric recordings and a number of controls were carefully placed and ringed with chalk, the easier to check possible movement or interference, in and around the rectory site, on the Nun's Walk, around the cottage entrance and in the church porch, just across the road. A piece of painted metal, part of the old ornamental verandah, we placed directly over the notorious 'cold spot' that had been reported by so many investigators. A large curtain ring, found among the debris on the rectory site, we placed as near as we could judge to the spot where 'wall messages' had been written by an unseen entity appealing for 'light, mass and prayers'; and using old bricks from the rectory we formed a rough cross over the place where human remains had been found. These and other controls and our apparatus were checked regularly throughout the night and we even made a few raps here and there hoping for answering ones, but all was quiet at Borley that night – except for the footsteps. None of the controls was moved and our thermometer readings showed no abnormality. But it was interesting that we heard apparently paranormal footsteps that night at Borley; 'footsteps' were the first recorded phenomena at Borley in 1886 and they have been reported repeatedly in the vicinity ever since. The area from where the sounds we heard appeared to originate was plainly visible in the bright moonlight and nothing was ever discovered that might account for those footsteps.

On subsequent visits, Tom Brown and I spent a number of nights in the haunted cottage and experienced a number of unexplained happenings. Unfortunately it was usually impossible to control the place satisfactorily for people were always calling or staying or ringing or turning up unexpectedly. None of the people who visited Borley was gullible or easily deceived but they all accepted that things were happening at the cottage at Borley that defied explanation.

There was the occasion when I came out of the upstairs bathroom and thought I glimpsed, out of the corner of my eye, a grey cat going into the bathroom. Downstairs I said to Cathy, 'Your grey cat has gone into the bathroom, is that all right?' She looked at me a little strangely for a second. 'We don't have a grey cat any more,' she said slowly. 'Both our cats are in the garden and have been all morning; look, Holly is up the tree there and Fred is lying on the lawn.' Both cats were indeed in the garden. I went up to the bathroom. There was no cat there or anywhere else in the cottage such as I had seen. In the months that followed a 'phantom' cat was seen on many occasions inside the cottage by the Turners themselves and by various visitors including Ronnie Blythe.

Then there was the whispering. I recall so plainly sitting with the Turners one evening, chatting, all four of us completely relaxed, when quite suddenly it seemed there was the sound of whispering from the room above. We looked at each other, puzzled. We all heard the same sounds at the same time. The whispering was quite loud and at any moment you felt you would catch a word or two but you never did; it was a loud yet indistinct whispering that continued for several minutes. After a couple of minutes I signalled to the Turners not to move and Tom Brown and I carefully and quietly opened the door leading to the stairs – whereupon the whispering abruptly ceased. We froze in our tracks but not a single sound now reached our ears. Very quietly we walked up the stairs and entered the room above where we had been sitting. Of course it was completely deserted. Nothing alive was in the room or had come out of it after the whispering ceased. During the following months the Turners heard similar whispering on several occasions. Always it was quite loud, always it started suddenly, always it was when they were relaxed and quiet, always the whispering was blurred and no words were distinguishable and there was never any explanation.

The cottage at Borley was haunted but not by a disruptive influence or entity, nothing was ever harmed or broken and it was almost as though whatever was there were echoes of the past. This cottage has seen inexplicable happenings over many years, it could well have harboured some of the frustration and unhappiness that pervaded Borley Rectory over the years and, as with other haunted houses, structural alterations may have placated whatever ghosts there were for I understand that nothing of a psychic nature has happened there for many years now. The whole long story of the hauntings at Borley is contained in the book I wrote with Dr Paul Tabori, entitled *The Ghosts of Borley* (1973).

In the years that followed, after the Turners left, a great deal of wasted time was spent digging and excavating the Borley site, with virtually no results. Later occupants of the cottage – the Bacons, the Williamses, the Martins and Len Sewell, who lived for a time in a caravan in the rectory garden – all reported happenings they were unable to explain, including sightings of the ghost nun. Reports of inexplicable happenings in the immediate vicinity of the much-altered cottage at Borley and in the nearby church and churchyard continue to this day but the variety of the happenings and the quality of the alleged witnesses pale into insignificance in comparison with the Borley haunting in its heyday.

Bovey House

Bovey House, near Beer in East Devon, is now an hotel. It stands at the head of two valleys near Seaton which run inland from the sea at Branscombe and Beer. Once it was probably an Elizabethan manor house but in fact it is so old that it is not possible even to estimate exactly when it was built.

In 1086, Domesday Book records the manors of Beer and Seaton being held by the Abbey of Horton in Dorset and in 1122 Horton was united with Sherborne. From then until the dissolution of the monasteries in 1539 Bovey House belonged to the Abbey of Sherborne. About 1160, Abbot Clement granted Bovey to Guy Dagville and in 1270 his descendant Alan Dagville married Amisia, daughter of John Walrond of Bradfield and on her death Bovey House passed into the possession of the Walrond family with whom it remained for many centuries.

At the dissolution, Bovey House was taken over by the Crown and at the time of his marriage to Catherine Parr in 1542, Henry VIII gave her a life interest in the house as part of her dowry and after her death the property reverted to the Walronds.

The oldest part of the present house is the large drawing room, originally the medieval hall, altered to its present state in 1592. Between 1660 and 1700, a coffered ceiling was inserted in a first-floor bedroom, now known as the King Charles Room, reputedly once occupied by Charles II. In the centre of the ceiling there is a large oak tree in relief and through the branches a man's face can clearly be discerned, surrounded by small figures depicting Cromwell's troops. The whole scene is thought to represent Boscobel Wood where Prince Charles, later King Charles II, hid in an oak tree during his flight to France after his defeat at the Battle of Worcester. During the course of his escape, through Staffordshire, Worcestershire, Warwickshire and Somerset to Charmouth in Dorset, he reputedly sheltered at Bovey House; and a number of visitors have seen a ghostly Cavalier in this room.

In the early eighteenth century, William Walrond, the last of his direct line to live at Bovey House, commemorated his marriage to Elizabeth, daughter of Sir William Drake of Ashe, with a stone representation of his coat of arms above the present front door. He died in 1762 leaving a daughter who married John Rolle in 1778 and after the Rolles the property passed to Lord Clinton whose family still own the estate.

There have been periods when the house stood empty and during these times Bovey House was in all probability used by smugglers; and there is evidence of a secret passage within the house leading to Beer cliffs. There was also a secret chamber or priests' hiding place which was discovered in one of the chimneys (perhaps also used by the royal guest) and now sealed off, while at the back of the house there is a raised Monks' Walk, reminding us of the ecclesiastical origins of the house. Here, it has been repeatedly noticed, there is a sense of peace and serenity that has perhaps remained in this particular area for several centuries.

There is a ghost story at Bovey House, handed down over the centuries, that tells of a lady resident who always dressed in black and was heavily veiled. She is said to have associated with a priest or monk and together they eloped. Such figures, a female figure in black and a priest or monk, have reportedly been seen here in recent years as has the ghostly Lady in Blue.

Bovey House has many lovely rooms, among them Room I; tastefully furnished in blue and haunted to this day, it is said, by a tall but headless lady dressed in blue. She was seen by Duncan Pierce whose sister Frances recorded the event in her diary which seems to date from about 1870, and is still preserved at Bovey House. Frances records the event in matter-of-fact terms:

Behind his door the staircase descended to another landing, and here was a side door and the window, already alluded to, in the romantic episode of the eloping couple; from thence it descended again to the drawing-room.

One bright, sunny morning, we had almost finished dressing, when Duncan, whistling cheerfully, came briskly rushing up the two steps, on his way along the corridor and so to the front stairs en route for breakfast. Suddenly we heard his footsteps abruptly stop at the door of the unoccupied room into which he hastily dived. Of course we ran out to investigate this most unusual proceeding and discovered Duncan gazing at us with a most puzzled expression.

'What is it?' we cried. 'Well, I'm hanged,' he elegantly replied, staring at *me*! Then he explained that on passing the door, which was open, his eye was caught by a wonderful gleam of blue and he saw, standing before the mirror of the dressing table, which was across the window and immediately opposite the door, a figure, which, because of the height, he thought was the tallest of his sisters.

'I wondered where you got that rich blue brocade; but,' he added, 'you didn't seem to have any head that I could see, and no sooner did I stop, than you quickly moved round to the other side of the room, and as I followed, quite disappeared. What the dickens was it?'

Now, there was no imagination about this, as Duncan was the most practical creature I ever knew; so absolutely healthy and cheerful, and he used to tell us that he had never had a dream in his life, waking or sleeping. This old Manor had been the Dower House of one of Henry VIII's wives, so one might have suggested the ghost was, perhaps, one of those unfortunately situated ladies whose fate it was to go out of life minus a head! But second thoughts repudiated this idea for Catherine Parr who once owned this property had the good luck to survive her husband! Anyway, we soon forgot about the ghost but it was recalled to us suddenly one day when our groom, who slept in the house, came tearing down from the top storey, where the servants' rooms were, with a face deathly white and fell almost fainting onto a chair. As soon as he could speak, he cried out that he had seen the ghost. At first he, like Duncan, 'thought it was Miss Frances,' because of the height, and she rustled past him in the dim light, wearing a rich silk gown. Then he saw the figure had no head and he nearly broke his neck getting downstairs to human companionship again.

Later the same figure was seen by a no-nonsense army captain who promptly packed his belongings and hurriedly left the house, never to return.

The same room in which the mysterious Lady in Blue appears has occasionally become inexplicably impregnated with the scent of lavender and this perfume-like smell has been reported by several visitors in recent years.

A few years ago my wife and I visited Bovey House for a few days accompanied by our old friend Steuart Kiernander, an active and valued member of the Ghost Club for more than forty years, together with his charming wife Freda. My wife and I occupied the allegedly haunted Blue Room and Freda and Steuart occupied the King Charles Room.

My wife and I thought the 'haunted' room had a distinct and disquietening atmosphere, a stillness not apparent elsewhere in that interesting and quiet house; it was something we noticed immediately on entering the room for the first time and subsequently, at various times throughout the following several days and nights, we always had the same feeling. It was almost as though someone was about to appear or as though someone invisible was already there, watching. And once, at 4.30 a.m., as I entered the room, I noticed a faint but distinct odour of lavender. I called my wife and she noticed it too.

It has long been common knowledge that Bovey House is haunted, according to a local historian Arthur J. Chapple, and that 'common knowledge' may well have been made good use of by the smuggling fraternity, secure in the knowledge that no one would be likely to interfere with their coming and goings when the manor house was empty, especially at night time.

'A few years ago,' Arthur Chapple, author of *Beer in Time and Tide* (1987, 1989, 1991 and 1993) tells me, 'I visited some friends of mine who were guests at Bovey House and stayed in the Blue Room. In the course of conversation the lady remarked that she loved the smell of fresh lavender but could not understand why she could not smell it all the time. This put me in an awkward position for had I told my friends that the smell of lavender denoted that the lady ghost was astir, they might have departed and sought shelter elsewhere! And yet I wonder for the ghostly scent has a considerable ancestry and the story has been handed down from one owner to the next for generations. My youngest daughter worked as a cook in the house for three summer seasons and frequently heard about the Lavender Lady.'

In the King Charles Room, Steuart and Freda Kiernander slept undisturbed, although once, just for a second, Freda thought she glimpsed the shape of a Cavalier standing by the bedroom door with a hand that seemed to rest on the doorknob. The form, if form it was, had disappeared within seconds but it did seem very real while it lasted and Freda felt very frightened.

There are other ghosts hereabouts too. Arthur J. Chapple has also been kind enough to send me details of a sighting of the phantom coach that has long been reputed to haunt the lanes about Bovey House. 'Some years ago,' he tells me, 'probably soon after the last war, a local man visited some friends in the village of Beer and taking his leave of them about 10 o'clock in the evening, he drove up Hollyhead Hill and out to Bovey Cross. On approaching the crossroads to Bovey he was amazed at having to brake sharply to avoid colliding with an old-fashioned coach and horses that were diagonally stationary across the road and blocking his way.

'He considered himself a tolerant man but he thought this "high-spirited prank" to be ill-conceived at that time of night and he decided to telephone the owners of Bovey House the next day and tell them what he thought of such behaviour by their guests. Occupied by such thoughts he was more than a little astonished to see a liveried postilion descend from his riding position and open the door of the coach. Next he saw a lady and then a gentleman, both dressed in early Georgian finery, alight from the coach and, arm in arm, walk towards Bovey House – and then disappear into a hedge! Meanwhile the coach and its driver sped off down the road and into oblivion. The man who witnessed this manifestation always maintained that it was "gospel truth", even to his dying day.'

'Dear old Bovey Manor,' wrote Frances Pierce. 'What joys it held . . . that wide low building of grey stone, dark ivy clinging round the stone mullioned windows whose leaded panes blinked in the wintry sunshine . . .' She might have been speaking of Bovey House today for it retains many of its former glories and it is a lovely place . . . and the ghosts are interesting too!

Bramshill House

A night in the most haunted house in Hampshire sounded good to me! It arose through my friendship with Dorothea St Hill Bourne, that enthusiastic collector of ghost lore who knew the glorious Jacobean mansion of Bramshill and its various occupants over many years.

Briefly, the original 'Broomshill' of Domesday Book has completely vanished but its replacement, built in the fourteenth century, is incorporated into the present building which was designed by the builders of Holland House in London for Lord Zouche of Harringworth between 1605 and 1612.

There is a story that Lord Zouche intended the house as a gift for James I's eldest son, Henry, Prince of Wales, but after the Prince's tragic death, Zouche took over for himself what is generally considered to be one of the most beautiful houses of the period, and he lived there until his death in 1625. Bramshill was then the seat of the Cope family from the end of the seventeenth century until 1935 when it was bought by Lord Brocket who lived there until 1953 when it was bought by the Home Office and became a Police Staff College.

Dorothea St Hill Bourne knew Lieutenant-Colonel the Hon. E. Gerald French, DSO, who in turn had known Bramshill in the time of the thirteenth baronet, Sir Anthony Cope, from whom he had heard the story of the old oaken chest, immortalised by Haynes Bailey in his 1828 poem, *The Mistletoe Bough*. Whether the great carved chest, admittedly labelled to this day 'The Bride's Chest', has anything to do with the Grey Lady or any of the other ghosts that undoubtedly walk at Bramshill is open to question. Former owner Lord Brocket had no doubt, however; he not only believed the gruesome event had indeed taken place at Bramshill but he was determined to do everything in his power to ensure that the chest remained at Bramshill. 'This house is the chest's spiritual home,' he said in 1935. 'Whoever buys the house must buy the Mistletoe Bough Chest.' And the chest stands today in the entrance hall of Bramshill House.

The usual story – there are many variations – concerns the wedding of the beautiful daughter of the family one Christmas Eve, the mansion decked with holly and the bride carrying a sprig of mistletoe. After the ceremony and wedding breakfast the bride challenges her husband to find her in a game of hide-and-seek. The bridegroom, the family and the guests are said to have searched high and low with growing concern but hours, and days later the bride had not been found. The distressed family left Bramshill and went to live in France. A few years later they decided to return to their ancestral home and in preparing for the return of the family a servant, looking for some sheets, lifted the lid of a long-disused chest which had a lock that could only be opened from the outside. Inside lay the mouldering form of the once-fair bride, still clutching a sprig of mistletoe. The ghost of the girl, dressed in her white bridal gown and carrying a sprig of mistletoe, is said to have haunted her former home ever since.

Whatever the truth of the story, and several other historic houses claim the story as their own, that the ghostly form of a beautiful young lady dressed in a flowing white gown has been seen in the lonely corridors of Bramshill seems indisputable. This ghost has reportedly been seen for the best part of 100 years and witnesses include various members of the Cope family, servants and visitors of long ago and in recent years, and even the Romanian royal family. Some time after the Second World War, King Michael, his Queen and their two children stayed at Bramshill for a time and a few days after their arrival the King asked that the royal children be given another room where they would not be disturbed by 'a young lady in white' who walked through their bedroom at night carrying a sprig of mistletoe.

Shortly after this wish had been complied with the Romanian Queen asked the identity of the beautiful young lady who was staying at Bramshill. 'There isn't one,' she was told, but the Queen insisted. 'She was sitting in the King's chair while I was watching television. When I looked again she had gone. I neither heard nor saw her come or go.' But her description resembled that of the so-called White Lady.

In 1982, a security guard was patrolling the reception hall one night when he felt a cold gust of wind and when he looked round he saw the shadowy figure of a lady in a white robe or shroud.

Another ghost here is the Grey Lady whose appearance is frequently associated, after her disappearance, with the fragrant aroma of lilies. The Copes saw the ghost frequently and indeed it is thought to be a Cope ancestor. Mrs Denzil Cope, the mother of little Penelope Cope who left a record of the ghosts she saw at Bramshill, awakened one morning to see a beautiful but sad-looking woman with golden hair and wearing a grey dress leaning over her bed; the next moment there was no sign of the Grey Lady but the room was filled with the fragrance of lilies – completely out of season.

The same figure, and always accompanied on her departure by the scent of lilies, appeared on a number of occasions to the Cope children in their respective bedrooms and often the form seemed to pass through solid wooden doors. She most often appeared, it was noted, around 3 o'clock in the morning. The descriptions of the figure, supplied by each of the children, were very similar to those of Mrs Denzil Cope and other witnesses of the Grey Lady.

A titled lady from County Wicklow wrote to me recently, after attending one of my lectures, saying, 'I was particularly interested to hear what you had to say about Bramshill. I grew up not far away and I knew Joan Penelope Cope and her young brother Anthony. The former was an exact contempory of mine and we became great friends. I often went to tea at Bramshill ... and I remember her telling me in a very matter of fact way that almost every night a beautiful young girl came and sat on the end of her bed. She had a very sad face and there was a faint smell of flowers when she was in the room. Joan felt she had come to make sure that all was well... The Copes were so miserable when Bramshill was sold. Someone asked Anthony, years later, whether he missed living there and he replied, "Very much, but most of all we miss our ghosts – they must be very lonely without us." Certainly bad luck seemed to dog the Copes after they left their home. Anthony threw himself out of a train when he was still a young man. Joan married Sir Duncan Grant who shot himself, and Joan moved to Dublin after his death with her five children. I saw her several times but soon she became ill with Alzheimer's disease and died...'

The Grey Lady ghost often appears to have teardrops on her cheeks and her dark eyes have 'a kind of dead light' in them. A senior police officer, now serving in Hampshire, saw the Grey Lady at Bramshill when he was a constable. At the time that he saw the form pass him without making a sound and disappear into a solid wall opposite, he had no idea that Bramshill was haunted. A footman once reported seeing 'a lovely young lady in grey' pass through his bedroom several nights in succession and when he eventually followed her and tried to grasp hold of her, she dissolved in his arms. Another employee, there for over forty years, never believed in ghosts until he saw the Grey Lady.

Staff member Fred Cook always said to people who claimed to have seen the Grey Lady, or any of the other reported ghosts at Bramshill, that it was a trick of the moonlight, or condensation, or imagination. It was hard enough to keep maids at the isolated and rambling building without people saying there were ghosts; but then, making a tour of the house one evening with his faithful Labrador, they both saw the Grey Lady. 'I opened the door of the Long Gallery (now used as part of the Library and twice the length of a cricket pitch) and there was the Grey Lady – seemingly staring at me. If I was mistaken, my dog wasn't. She gave a howl of terror and fell over backwards in her hurry to get away. There was no stopping her, she raced out of the house – and I wasn't far behind her!'

After he caught up with the dog and they had both recovered somewhat, Fred Cook went back to the Long Gallery but nothing would persuade his dog to go anywhere near the room again. Fred looked in; it was completely empty. No sign of a soul but the lingering scent of lilies filled the air.

A similar figure was seen by Sir William Cope and members of his family. Practically the whole household were on the terrace one lovely summer evening when suddenly they all saw a grey-robed woman leaning over the balustrade at the far end of the terrace. Thinking that one of the housemaids must be sleepwalking or unwell, Sir William sent for the butler to deal with the situation. At first the man could see no one in the gathering gloom but as he advanced down the terrace, he saw a robed figure start to climb the balustrade and the next moment she had completely disappeared. No explanation was ever found for this appearance witnessed by upwards of twenty people, family, friends and servants.

Then there is the ghostly little old man with a long beard who peers in at a window in the hall; the bedroom where the ghost of a woman in the dress of the time of Charles I has been seen not once but several times; the man in armour seen in the Chapel Drawing Room also haunted on different occasions by the figure of a woman dressed in the days of Queen Anne. There is also the man dressed in green, often seen by children near the lake, and thought to be a Cope ancestor who committed suicide. And what are we to make of the figure, seen by a former Commandant and a serving police officer, standing on a little bridge in the drive? The whole length of the drive was in view of the two men and, knowing that no one had any right to be there, the Commandant sent the officer off to warn the intruder that he was trespassing. The Commandant watched for a moment and then turned to other things. When the officer returned he said that when he reached the bridge no one was anywhere in sight, nor was there any nearby cover where anyone could have hidden.

The Commandant, members of the Cope family, senior civil servants at Bramshill – all were known to Dorothea St Hill Bourne and all claimed to have experienced paranormal happenings at Bramshill. More recently there was the night guard on duty in 1985 who suddenly noticed the air in the entrance hall seemed to be filled with the perfume of lilies and as he looked round he saw the figure of a young woman in a long white or grey gown who seemed to exude sadness; after he had watched for what he said was a full minute, the seemingly solid form faded and disappeared. PC Dennis Moore is one policeman, formerly a sceptic, who encountered an unmistakable floral perfume one November afternoon; it suddenly wafted through an office at the top of the Queen Anne Staircase, a perfume noticed and remarked upon by others in the room at the time.

Then there are the two male ghosts, one believed to be the husband of the Grey Lady who died at Bramshill in the seventeenth century. His presence has been noticed in the corridor used by administrative staff and also in the stable block, perhaps his place of death; while the modern phantom form of a young man, dressed for a game of tennis, walks into the reception area through a wall, crosses the hall and disappears into the opposite wall. Descriptions resemble a young man, the son of a previous owner of the house, who died in the 1930s.

When I was there in 1980, I talked with several women clerks who said they had experienced the 'lovely smell' more than once. One of them said it seemed to move around the room, almost like a person walking about. I also talked with some of the administrative staff who told me they were sceptical of some of the ghost stories related, but three of them had walked into the Chapel Drawing Room one spring evening and found it full of people in period costumes. As they looked more closely they were astonished to see that everyone in the room seemed to be floating a foot or more above the level of the floor! A moment later the room was deserted and the three administrators could hardly believe what they had seen until subsequent inquiries revealed that the flooring of that part of the house had been lowered during alterations and the phantom forms, if phantoms they had seen, were appearing where the flooring would have been in their time.

I visited the haunted Fleur de Lys Room where more than one visitor has, inexplicably, found themselves hand-in-hand with an invisible child. Almost as soon as they are aware of the small hand nestling its way into theirs, the sensation disappears and everything is normal. But it is interesting that this experience has been reported by a considerable number of visitors who have, of course, no idea that other people have reported a similar experience. Nearby there is a room where the sound of a crying child has been heard; a room that is unoccupied. Another room, according to the Librarian, Sue King, although centrally heated and comfortable, has caused more than one senior civil servant to leave when an icy atmosphere or a sudden whistling wind invades its draught-proof confines.

I was accompanied on my first all-night visit to Bramshill by Dr Sidney Scott, the authority on Joan of Arc. Once during the night, as we entered the splendid Long Gallery that must bear comparison with any gallery in any house in England, Sidney suddenly touched my arm and pointed. I could see nothing but he said, just for a second, he had seen something white moving at the far end of the Gallery. I immediately went to the spot he indicated and stood there but felt nothing; he then went out of the door and came in again but this time he only saw me. I half hoped he would see the White Lady by my side but it was not to be. A second night was completely uneventful but a third, in the company of a much-respected scribe, was a little more successful. Both he and I heard sounds we could not account for and momentarily we both thought we saw a shadowy form in one of the reputedly haunted areas of the house. But it was all tame and feeble fare for Hampshire's most haunted house and the Ghost Club endeavoured to organise a concentrated full-scale and scientific investigation one night in 1993. Unfortunately, in the present climate the authorities responsible felt that security would be a problem (even in Britain's foremost police college!) and we were unable to proceed.

However, perhaps one day ... for in December 1992 I received a letter from Mr P. Phipps of Reading who told me he used to deliver goods to Bramshill House and on one occasion he experienced a smell of perfume near the old Bride's Chest in the entrance hall. There was no rational explanation. In a subsequent letter dated 21 January 1993, he tells me: 'My first experience was in the foyer where the security guard sits. I had a close look at the old chest and smelled what seemed to be lily-of-the-valley perfume ... no explanation ... some time later I was in the bar, delivering tobacco and confectionery, when I had the feeling that someone was standing behind me and I shouted down the cellar steps and the bar manager said he would be up in a second. I moved from where I was standing and seemed to move into an invisible column of perfume so strong it made my eyes water...'

So I have visited Bramshill House on my own, with Dr Sidney Scott, and with my grandson Toby. Now I would like to go there with the Ghost Club Society's skilled and resourceful Investigations Officer and a party of seasoned and experienced investigators and then maybe it will be decided whether or not the most haunted house in Hampshire lives up to its reputation.

Bretforton Manor

In 1985, I distributed to Ghost Club members a brief note that stated: 'There is likely to be the opportunity of spending a night at an allegedly haunted manor house near Evesham in May.' In the event, nineteen members made up the investigative party.

Bretforton Manor nestles in the mellow village of Bretforton, hidden away in the very heart of England. It is a village whose documented history goes back more than 1,250 years to a Saxon deed of 714 AD. Those Teutonic people called the hamlet Brotforton – the ford with planks; probably a reference to a footbridge alongside the ford. The village is still set in a rich patchwork of fields and orchards and is situated halfway between Evesham and the steep western edge of the Cotswold Hills: hills that for centuries supplied the honey-coloured stone for many buildings in the area, including the 450 year old Manor.

A published leaflet on the history of the property reveals that the Manor was built by the Ashwin family of Bretforton, soon after the dissolution of the monasteries by Henry VIII, and it remained in the hands of the Ashwin family until it passed to Derek J. Chapman in 1984. Building is reputed to have been started in 1539 and been completed in 1604 in more or less its present size. The Ashwin family never opened the house to the public.

Queen Elizabeth I is said to have stayed at the manor but there does not appear to be any concrete evidence for this; the Ashwin family always claimed that it was so. One definite 'royal' visitor was the Duc d'Orléans who certainly stayed at Bretforton Manor with his not inconsiderable retinue.

The pleasant seven-and-a-half-acre grounds of the Manor (which take on a sombre atmosphere during the hours of darkness) contain the original village stocks, dated 1360, a black and white thatched barn with a large horse-drawn cider mill, an artificial lake and a brook, and many fine trees among the old stables and former paddocks and carriageways.

A wide path leads past the Manor's private graveyard, on past the village churchyard to St Leonard's Church which has stood at the northern end of the village square, known as The Cross, for nearly 800 years. Inside are medieval piers with capitals carved in fantastical designs and many monuments to the Ashwin family.

Elizabeth I may have given the original manor to her favourite courtier, the Earl of Leicester, for parts of the handsome, gabled mansion go back to the sixteenth century; in any case rebuilding was completed in the early 1600s. It is a property, like the village, full of atmosphere and almost breathing history. From the grounds you descend ancient stone steps, pass through a large oaken gate in the grey stone wall and there is the time-honoured

Fleece Inn, a quaint old hostelry that was originally a farmhouse, also believed to date back to the fourteenth century and one of the few inns owned by the National Trust. Inside on the stone floor there are 'witch marks' designed to keep away evil spirits and a reminder of the inn's medieval past, while among the antiques preserved there is a forty-eight-piece set of Stuart pewter. Nearby ancient Byrd's Cottage has walls that lean at gravity-defying angles and a carved face guards one of its doors.

The Manor itself, extensively renovated in 1871 by W. H. Ashwin, has a reception hall heavily carved in black oak, some of which is reputed to have been part of a chapel from a Spanish ship which was driven aground during the Spanish Armada debacle, with carvings dedicated to St Monica, a wife and mother who was still made a saint in 387 AD.

Other features of the Manor include the dining room with its fourteen-seater dining suite in oak and its walls two-thirds panelled in oak – a part of the 1871 restoration – although it still retains the beautiful seventeenth-century black oak overmantle. There is a passageway leading to the library which contains a long half-panel of carved oak, also probably put there in 1871. The library itself has a fine seventeenth-century carved black oak overmantle and on the right-hand side there is an excellently preserved priest hole from Cromwellian days. There is also a banqueting hall with a huge open fireplace and ancient kitchens, interesting wine cellars, several eighteenth- and nineteenth-century iron fireplaces and remarkable nineteenth-century bathrooms. The official *Brief Notes on Bretforton Manor*, from which much of this information is taken, ends with four simple words: 'The house is haunted.'

A few months before I organised this visit, I received a letter from a correspondent in the Midlands who was kind enough to say she had enjoyed reading some of my books and her letter continued: '. . . I would like to pass on a little information that may be of interest to you and members of the Ghost Club . . . Yesterday I came across a newspaper item concerning a large, rambling, sixty-roomed house near Evesham that has just been bought by a man who is living there alone in one downstairs room. He lives during the day in the room he sleeps in at night and says he repeatedly hears footsteps walking the floors upstairs, doors opening and closing by themselves, and a woman's voice addressing someone. All these happenings take place between 2 a.m. and 4.30 a.m. and it sounds quite a haunting!

'I would imagine it would make an interesting investigation for your team and there is not too much time to be lost as I hear the new owner intends to open the place to the public.

'There is supposed to be a ghostly funeral procession, black-plumed horses and all, which winds its way through the garden en route to the church close by . . . I was in Bretforton some years ago and had a look at the Manor. It was getting on for dusk at the time but I remember thinking then that it looked a very eerie place . . . Hope you won't think all this a waste of time . . .'

Subsequently the same correspondent was kind enough to send me a newspaper cutting headed: 'Mr Derek Chapman opens his new home . . .' The article stated that the Manor had been purchased in 1984 for £180,000, after the last surviving member of the Ashwin family, whose home the house had been for 400 years, had died.

The house was stated to have sixty-six rooms and Derek Chapman is quoted as saying that he intended to open the place to the public, 'It is such an interesting house – although at the moment, because it is so large, I am virtually camping in the house. I just could not resist buying it because of all the interesting features it contains.'

I lost no time in writing to Mr Chapman who, in reply, kindly invited our explorers to stay the night at Bretforton Manor to carry out an investigation. Soon there were reports of a wealth of supernatural happenings at Bretforton Manor. One newspaper stated that 'businessman Derek Chapman inherited more than the title of Squire when he bought Bretforton Manor. "There are ghosts all over the place", he reportedly stated. "They occur in both the grounds and the mansion itself."' The previous week, it was stated, he had shown some women over the old house and afterwards one of the party asked who was the man with short, dark hair, lying on one of the beds? The woman concerned led the party back upstairs and into the bedroom where she had seen the man but he was no longer there. 'Since then,' said Derek Chapman, 'there have been more sightings of the same strange man with the short, dark hair. People say they have seen him and then he has vanished, just like that.'

Derek Chapman himself saw forms he could not explain. One was 'the ghostly figure of an elderly lady stalking about the rooms of the Manor,' he said. 'Another was a tall butler; and on a few occasions, at night, I have seen a figure in a bell-shaped cloak walking in the grounds,' he added. 'It all shook me at first but now I'm used to it. Now when I glimpse that figure, I watch, and it simply glides into the trees and disappears.'

It was also reported that Mr Chapman believed the apparitions were members of the Ashwin (or Ashwyn) family who resent an outsider buying their ancestral home. Not that the spectres are confined to Bretforton Manor itself and Mr Chapman reported that the figure of an old woman was regularly seen crossing the main street in the village and a vicar, the Rev. Wilfred Bates, had been called in to exorcise a troublesome ghost in another house in Bretforton; but the new owner had no intention of having the Manor exorcised. 'They all seem to be quite nice ghosts,' he said. 'Not wicked ones at all . . . I suppose you might call it a happy haunting ground!' I began to look forward to spending a night at Bretforton Manor.

On the appropriate evening, participating members congregated quietly in the forecourt of Bretforton Manor, having come from their homes all over the country. We were met by the genial Derek Chapman who welcomed us to his wonderful home and showed us all round the house and garden and then we settled down in the banqueting hall and he told us about his personal experiences of ghosts and ghostly happenings in the short time he had owned the Manor.

We were interested to learn that six months previously Derek Chapman knew nothing of any alleged haunting at Bretforton Manor but since moving in he had seen apparitions or inexplicable shapes; found himself awake regularly between 3 and 4 a.m. whenever he occupied the front bedroom; had discovered unexpected notes in passages; and had heard doors opening and closing by themselves at least a dozen times. He had seen one apparition beside the front door on three occasions and always just before midnight; a grey, indistinct, bell-like shape that he thought might be a cloaked figure, possibly male and possibly a monk.

Just before 3 o'clock one afternoon he had encountered a man in an upstairs room; he appeared to be a butler or manservant of some kind – a figure that was there one minute and gone the next. Later he discovered that thirty years before a butler, known as Bertie, had died in that particular room.

When he first moved into Bretforton Manor, Derek Chapman had occupied a first-floor bedroom (which he had pointed out to us) and while sleeping there he had found himself inexplicably awake in the early hours almost every night. He had seen nothing and he had heard nothing but something had awakened him – and it was not anything very pleasant. His first thought on awakening each time was he must get out of the room, but he was determined not to be told what to do in his own house and he stayed, but in the end whatever it was won and he never slept in that room afterwards and he would never allow anyone else to sleep there.

In several of the rooms and passageways, we were told, there were doors that opened and closed by themselves. This was not imagination. For security reasons he was particularly careful about closing all doors and windows at night but on many occasions he had heard the sound of a door opening and on going to investigate had found a door had indeed opened by itself. On other occasions he would hear a door he had purposely left open, close, and again this was found to have happened. There did seem to be certain doors in the house that would not stay shut and others that would not stay open. On the other hand there were occasions when he distinctly heard the *sound* of a door opening or closing but he could discover nothing that could have caused the sounds, there having, apparently, been no movement of any doors in the house.

A room on the top floor, known as the Schoolroom, sometimes seemed to light up of its own accord. This had been witnessed by people inside the house and also by other people outside the house. Six months previously a housekeeper had been put in this room but she had quickly asked to be moved to another room; she would give no reason – she just said she didn't like the Schoolroom. As far as is known she had no knowledge of the mysterious lights. Derek Chapman told us he had noticed that it was difficult to get dogs to enter that room; even the postmaster's great dane – who seemed to be familiar with every room in the house – couldn't be persuaded to go inside the Schoolroom.

In another bedroom, a guest, just the week before our visit, had seen the ghost of an elderly lady standing beside a bed. Here, ten years previously, but unknown to the visitor, a lady had been sleeping in the room and had awakened in the middle of the night to see an elderly lady leaning over the bed. When she screamed, the figure vanished. Derek Chapman told us he felt this apparition was the same one he had encountered in other parts of the house.

There had been several violent deaths at Bretforton Manor over the years and for a considerable period of time a stain on a red carpet was said to mark the scene of a murder, a mark that for years if not centuries could not be eradicated. The carpet was eventually replaced. There was also the case of a servant girl, years ago, who had been found dead at the bottom of the stairs. At first it was thought she had fallen but subsequently it was established that she had been murdered by another servant who had fetched the police but at length was found to be guilty of the crime and paid the penalty.

The library was haunted too and a male figure had been seen there by lots of witnesses. It was an unmoving figure that was always seen in exactly the same place. He seemed to be wearing 'old-fashioned' clothes; he seemed to be watching or waiting for something or someone, but who he was and why he waited no one now seemed to know. The library had been largely unaltered for many years.

There were many witnesses too for figures seen in the garden – male and female figures. Usually they seemed to be in a hurry and most of those who saw them did so out of the corner of their eyes and when they turned to fully face the figure or figures, they saw nothing. These figures had been seen in various parts of the garden, usually fairly close to the house, and at various times of the night and early morning. A number of objects had been moved in different parts of the house and also in the garden, and a few unidentified objects had mysteriously appeared, but unfortunately nothing of value!

During the night we spent at Bretforton Manor we instituted our usual rota of investigators who checked thermometers, patrolled haunted areas (inside and outside

47

the house), spent periods alone in specific parts of the house, attempted 'communication' and quietly, but I think efficiently, had the whole house and grounds under surveillance for all the hours of darkness.

Our efforts on this occasion had few rewards. Three times, by different members of the investigating team, a 'shadowy form' was glimpsed in the garden – always at the same spot, interestingly enough – but invariably the 'form' had vanished by the time other members arrived on the scene to corroborate the sighting. Nothing was discovered that might have accounted for the sightings. Nevertheless there were three independently reported sightings on three different occasions by three different witnesses and their descriptions corresponded, as did the exact locations. And twice, in one of the reputedly haunted bedrooms, experienced and cool-headed members reported experiencing distressing and uncomfortable feelings which immediately ceased once they left that bedroom. We could not discern any regularity or cyclic element or any fluctuation of temperature or atmospheric pressure in the room.

One of the participating and long-standing members, Godfrey Goolden, spent a lot of time in the so-called Boot Room, where in former days the boys who looked after the boots slept. The room had a curious atmosphere and there were stories of inexplicable forms being seen there, we learned, and of dark deeds long ago . . . Godfrey, who has joined us on many investigations, definitely felt Bretforton Manor to be haunted; especially he thought the upper regions.

A number of seances were attempted in the dining room,

in the Schoolroom and in the Boot Room. During his vigil in the Boot Room, Godfrey Goolden heard two thuds which seemed to come from the landing outside the room, at 2.49 a.m. and again at 3.04 a.m. No cause or reason or explanation for these sounds was ever discovered. Nothing of real interest transpired at any of the seances, but at one in the dining room at 3.28 a.m., after repetitive and seemingly meaningless jumbled messages, one sitter asked in a loud voice for the communicator to slow down – whereupon the communicator did indeed slow down, but still did not make sense. Sitters did report an icy coldness in one area of the dining room, and at 3.45 a.m. it was established that the temperature was 2°F colder in the corner of the room where the seance was being conducted.

Also during a seance in the dining room, this one at 3.15 a.m., the letters V R came up again and again and Mary Hartshorn, a long-standing and valued member who was in charge of the seance, had the distinct impression that Queen Victoria was being referred to. Much later, when we were talking and she said she could not imagine that the old Queen could have any connection with Bretforton Manor or with anyone present, I told her that in fact I was deeply involved in the life and times of Queen Victoria and I was taking time off to make this investigative visit from working on my book concerning *Queen Victoria's Other World* (published in 1986).

Other incidental experiences in the records show that at 5.20 a.m. member Keith Morbey heard a curious sound by the front door that did not seem to have any obvious explanation. Paddy Hughes heard a clicking sound, rather

49

like a tap dripping, in one of the upper corridors, for which there was no obvious explanation and the clicking ceased as she searched for some reason for the noise and recommenced when she was about to leave the corridor. When she turned back it stopped again. The time was 5.25 a.m. Oddly enough a similar sound was reported by several members around the same time outside the room we were using as a Base Room.

Two members of the investigating team reported, independently, that furniture had been moved in one bedroom and on the same floor, at approximately the same time, a very loud 'crash' or 'bang' was heard by three members of our team. The same noise was reported from the same area an hour later. The times were just before 3 a.m. and just before 4 a.m. One member, an experienced and very level-headed individual, was quite terrified when the sound occurred, seemingly very close.

Vigils were organised in the Schoolroom, the dining room, the Boot Room and elsewhere, while outside the house seven separate vigils were organised through the night using different pairs of investigators; mostly between 11.30 p.m. and 3 a.m. During this period we had thermometers and sound recording apparatus situated in the dining room, the 'haunted' passage, the Boot Room, the Schoolroom and outside the front door.

Talking to the members participating in the visit afterwards I learned that all the members present had been impressed by the fact that, during one seance in the dining room, they had all felt 'an icy coldness sweep through the room'. A curious whistling sound had been heard in the vicinity of the front door; immediate investigation had revealed that no one was anywhere near the front door at the time and the sound was not repeated. Two members had had no personal experiences of any kind and one member, spending his first night in a haunted house, was not convinced that the house was in fact haunted. One lady member, who has experienced psychical activity of various kinds over a period of many years, felt that some of the seances were interesting and had potential but more 'sympathetic power' was needed and there was not much that could be regarded as evidential as things stood; however, she did think the house was probably haunted.

Ghost Club Society Council members, Marilyn and Trevor Kenward, no strangers to haunted houses, took part in the Bretforton Manor convergence and I asked them whether they would like to let me have their thoughts about that visit. Marilyn Kenward was impressed immediately by the Manor when she explored the grounds on that early summer evening. When she saw the stocks she felt, 'There was definitely a sense of transportation back in time . . . in the vicinity of those stocks.' She couldn't help feeling that the whole house, with its fixtures and fittings, was steeped in the past, and leaving the Manor the next morning to return to the present was something of a jolt. She asked, 'Was the whole experience we had taken part in a "ghostly happening"? Certainly, those few hours spent at Bretforton Manor were not part of present life as we know it.'

Trevor Kenward, Marilyn's husband, arrived at Bretforton hoping to conduct his own research ideas as well as taking part in the routine procedures of the rest of the Ghost Club participants. Among his other investigation equipment, he had two cameras. He recalls, 'One of the things I hoped to try was the use of very high-speed film without a flash during the course of the night. So, armed with some 1500 ASA film and other equipment and apparatus, we arrived at the Manor.' It was after the initial introductions that 'I remembered the high-speed film that I had purchased specially and wished to use during the night, so I quickly used up the remaining few shots of 200 ASA film already loaded in one of the cameras with shots of the front of the Manor. This done I inserted the new fast film and joined the rest of the group inside.'

Trevor was impressed by the size of the Manor and quite rightly pointed out that 'the layout of the building was such that it was possible to go from the main hall up the front stairs, through the upper floors and return by the rear staircase to the ground floor and thence by the main rooms back to the front hallway. This made the task of the recording teams (for such procedures as temperature reading and objects control) very easy as there was no backtracking or interference with other investigators working in other areas of the building.'

After the rotas had been drawn up and duties allocated, Trevor took the opportunity of exploring the areas of the house that interested him. First he investigated the cellars but found nothing unusual there. Then, as other members were proposing to hold a seance, he felt he should be elsewhere: 'Now while I normally am very enthusiastic to be present at such events, for some reason on this occasion some unknown power seemed to be calling me to other regions. So, was it the grounds that needed my attention in those dark hours? Wandering along the church path with the overhanging trees one could sense an essence of, perhaps, Victoriana; an unhurried time, an unshakable empire... I used up some of the high-speed film and then took a stroll over the rest of the grounds, including a thorough search of the old barn. During all this time that same feeling of a resting, powerful nation and contented middle and upper classes prevailed and enveloped me.'

In the house itself, Trevor was interested in several rooms as a result of our initial guided tour. In particular he decided to investigate the Schoolroom and the adjoining teacher's room. Trevor wanted to spend some time in silent observation, which meant sitting in the dark with a tape recorder running and his camera to hand, and just taking in the atmosphere and noting any feelings or odd phenomena that could be felt, heard, seen or smelt. In the Schoolroom he experienced nothing whatsoever, but, 'upon returning to the teacher's room I immediately experienced a cold, clammy, fearful sensation. I had noticed something odd when I had first entered the room but now there was no mistaking it. A sort of chilling coldness oozed from the very room itself. Just to reassure myself that I was not imagining it I returned to the passageway and at once it had gone. Everywhere was dark, all the lights were of course out, and apart from some moonlight coming in through the passageway windows, not a light anywhere; and not a sound was to be heard on that top floor. No other members of the team were in the upper reaches of the building at that time: I was alone of all earthly beings.

'Returning to the teacher's room once again, whatever it was chilled my very bones. Casting fear aside, I remained for a further ten minutes or so in the room to satisfy myself that it was not imagination. And although nothing further occurred, that presence remained all the time; something chilling and calling.'

Disappointingly, nothing was recorded on Trevor's tape to corroborate his impressions scientifically, but it was later discovered that a female member of the team had visited the Schoolroom and teacher's room later in the night and was unable to stay in either room! She described her experience as 'something like a cloud engulfing her body . . . a freezing cold wet suit slowly drawn over oneself – in a snow storm.' The feeling had such an effect on her that she didn't venture into the upper parts of the house for the rest of the investigation.

Trevor's next port of call was the Boot Room with another investigator. They sat in silent meditation for twenty minutes, but neither of them experienced anything unusual. Finally, nearing dawn, he paid a visit to the Gold Lounge which was on the first floor directly beneath the Boot Room because he felt 'For me, I still felt something was there, something I had missed; it was not malevolent, far from it, but why could I not get close?' Trevor actually recorded his impressions of the Gold Lounge that night:

These impressions were received in that Gold Lounge between the hours of 5 a.m. and 8.30 a.m. on the Saturday morning. I was seated alone and was so observed at least twice during this time by other researchers making their rounds, in accordance with the agreed rota. None of them did more than enter the room and just look round the open door. There were no lights on but of course daylight had by this time arrived. There was no wind and no outside noise. I had entered the lounge and seated myself in a comfortable position in an armchair facing the door at an angle somewhere about the middle of the room. The door I was facing was on my left and the window to my right. I then entered into a state of self-trance, i.e. the semi-conscious state or twilight zone between being awake and being asleep. At no time was awareness lost to the surrounding room and events.

The following observations were made or impressions felt. It would seem that either the father or grandfather of a previous owner of the Manor had a relation, possibly a brother or maybe a cousin, who went to South Africa and this particular relative, whatever his profession was in South Africa, be it mining, farming, or whatever, was very sympathetic to the Boer cause and during the time of the Boer War he was engaged in active hostility against the British Government working on the side of the Boers, or Dutch Afrikaans.

During this time he was engaged in a number of military campaigns and ultimately died during a very fierce encounter (the date and place of the battle was not made clear to me). During the fighting this man received serious injuries in a heavy artillery attack which was inflicted by the British against the Boers (this was rather unusual, incidentally, as heavy artillery was not used to a great extent in the Boer War). However, he did not die at once. The British Infantry then went through the Boer positions mopping up as was the normal procedure. They came across this man, very badly hurt but not dead and in fact conscious. The British army was not in the habit of taking prisoners nor wasting bullets and they often garrotted the enemy, using a rifle strap round the neck and giving it a vicious twist . . . that blue face looking up . . . eyes bulging . . . could this be the ghost of Bretforton Manor . . . I was awake now and put the tape off but the above is on record.

Trevor felt unable to rationalise his experiences at Bretforton Manor that night, and when he got home, another mystery awaited him. He had all the films he had taken that night developed, including the low-speed films he had used up before reloading the camera with high-speed film for the night's investigations. The last frames of the low-speed film showed unusual markings that he couldn't account for: 'They might be described as "ecto-plasmic formations" for they were much like some of the results of so-called "psychic photography". Had the spirits sensed the arrival of a research team and decided to vacate the Manor for the duration of our visit? If so, was this the reason I was unable to pinpoint something in the Manor . . . why I kept having the sensation that "something" was near and should be perceived?'

So, what has happened to Bretforton Manor today? Some years after the Ghost Club visit, the Kenwards returned to the house and found it empty and semi-derelict. And what of the ghosts? For Trevor Kenward, his lasting impression was that 'whatever earthbound spirits there may be, something lurks within those walls; "something" calls . . . beckons . . . cries out . . . and something will see me back there someday.'

Bromfield Manor

One of the valued members of the Ghost Club Society is that explorer extraordinaire Colonel John Blashford-Snell, MBE. During his army career he organised and led expeditions to many parts of the world, most notably the Great Abbai Expedition of the Blue Nile, the British Trans-Americas Expedition, the Zaire River Expedition, the Jade Venture and the Southern Ocean Mountaineering Expedition. He has also been the leading light and director-in-chief of such adventures as Operation Drake and Operation Raleigh and he is currently Chairman of the Scientific Exploration Society and also Chairman of the British Chapter of the Explorers' Club. Holder of the prestigious Livingstone Medal and of the Segrave Trophy, he has spent much of his life pushing back the frontiers in unknown regions, including the world of the paranormal; and he has met many mysteries that defy explanation at our present level of knowledge.

In his book *Mysteries* (1983), he deals with ghostly encounters and says that although he does not claim to have seen a ghost he knows sensible and honest people who certainly think they have and, until proved otherwise, he is prepared to believe they have indeed seen something that cannot today be explained but, in common with most Club members, he believes there will be a rational explanation one day. In the meantime he keeps an open mind and even indulges in a spot of seeking from time to time . . .

In his book, John Blashford-Snell reveals that his father and mother, 'pretty down-to-earth people' frequently held him spellbound with their tales of the unexplained, for they had had a marvellous life of adventure and excitement as Parson/Army Chaplain and his wife all around the world.

Then, in the 1930s, his father took the living of a parish in Shropshire and, together with their three Alsatian dogs, they moved into a spacious old rectory standing in its own grounds in that beautiful part of England.

One night, while sleeping in a spare room at the front of the house to enable his father, who was suffering from a heavy cold, to get some rest, and with her favourite dog on the floor beside her, Mrs Blashford-Snell found herself suddenly awakened by the dog in the middle of the night. He kept staring, seemingly terrified, at the window. When Mrs Blashford-Snell got out of bed and looked out of the window she saw nothing unusual but the dog was still very agitated and when the bedroom door was opened the animal flew out in a flash, its hackles raised and its fangs bared. Out onto the landing it went and down the stairs and into the kitchen where it disturbed the other dogs and in a moment they were all barking and howling in a way they had never done before. Once the back door was open they all catapulted out into the garden and chased round the rectory for some ten minutes before eventually returning indoors but they were still uneasy, casting repeated furtive glances at the back door. Mrs Blashford-Snell went back to bed and slept undisturbed until the morning.

Next day, thinking poachers must have been in the garden, she decided to check the pheasant rearing pens situated at the bottom of the garden, but all was well. That night Mrs Blashford-Snell was again awakened about 2 o'clock in the morning by the pressure of the dog's front paws on the bed and its low growling. Again the animal was continually staring towards the window, becoming almost frantic as Mrs Blashford-Snell got out of bed and quietly looked out of the window.

At first she saw nothing untoward and then a movement caught her eye and, the dog whimpering with exasperation beside her, she saw standing so close to the house that at first she had not seen it, the figure of a man. As she watched the form, a tall, bare-headed man wearing a light-coloured raincoat, walked away from the house towards the pheasant pens. Now Mrs Blashford-Snell had no doubt that a poacher was in the garden. She watched the figure cross the lawn and disappear into the trees; then, quick as a flash, she raced downstairs, followed by the excited dog. She snatched up a torch and opened the outer door as quietly as she could manage it. She let the three excited dogs out of the house and they raced away in the direction of the pheasant pens.

Next morning Mr Blashford-Snell asked his wife what on earth the dogs were making all the noise about in the middle of the night and his wife told him what she had seen. 'Walking across the lawn towards the pens, you say?' her husband queried. 'Yes, as I've said I saw him quite clearly,' Mrs Blashford-Snell replied. 'Well, that's odd, you must admit,' said her husband. 'It would have meant walking straight through the tennis court!'

Mrs Blashford-Snell put down her cup of tea. She walked over to the window and looked out, gazing at the high wire surrounding the grass tennis court and for the first time realised there was something odd about the figure she had seen. 'Well,' she said. 'That's exactly what he did. I saw him, as plain as I see you. He walked straight across the lawn and I didn't see any tennis court...'

A few days later an elderly lady who had lived in the rectory as a child came to tea and without any prompting or even a mention of what had happened, she suddenly inquired: 'Have you see Freddie yet, Rector?' 'Freddie who?' she was asked. 'Oh, we all saw Freddie, as we called him. An awfully nice ghost. Often at night he walked from the house across the lawn and disappeared. I've no idea who he was or why he came back but we saw him lots of times and the dogs always told us when he was about.'

The Blashford-Snell dogs never did get used to 'Freddie' but I have always considered dogs to be good witnesses and I thought it might be an idea to see whether I could find out a little more about the Blashford-Snell Rectory and its haunted garden. I discovered that the property, originally a manor house but long a vicarage was now a guest house run by Norman and Joy Cooke. Mrs Joy Cooke was enthusiastic about my suggestion that a small party of Ghost Club members spend a weekend at Bromfield Manor, for Mrs Cooke informed me of other ghosts at Bromfield. From time to time I had been in the habit of organising interesting weekends for members at interesting places and I proceeded to make the necessary arrangements.

I do emphasise that our visit to Bromfield Manor was planned as an informal and relaxing weekend in an allegedly haunted area but it proved to be much more interesting! The confidential notification distributed to those members attending read: 'We shall be staying at Bromfield Manor near Ludlow. The Manor, long a vicarage, is now a guest house and the home of Mr and Mrs Norman Cooke. It has a ghost monk who haunts the top floor, "a gentle, happy type of spirit who chuckles with delight when noticed" and "a shadowy figure" who haunts the cobbled courtyard where a beggar lad was found dead in 1898. The parents of John Blashford-Snell, the explorer, lived for some years at Bromfield Manor and experienced ghostly happenings.'

Later a provisional itinerary for the weekend outlined the plans for our visit. We were to meet at Bromfield Manor on the Friday evening of 16 May for a general introduction and a lecture by local historian David Lloyd MA of the Ludlow Historical Society on the ghosts of Ludlow. Saturday's activities were to include a visit to Ludlow Castle; coffee at the haunted De Grey's Restaurant; afternoon tea at Ludlow Craft Centre, Dinham House – also reputedly haunted; a look around the ghost-ridden churchyard and finally a talk by Christine McCarthy on Shropshire ghosts. After two nights at

Bromfield Manor, we would leave after breakfast on the Sunday morning.

Before and during the visit, Mrs Joy Cooke was extremely helpful and co-operative with information and help in every possible way which made the event so enjoyable for everyone concerned. Regarding Bromfield Manor itself, Mrs Cooke informed us that it was used as a vicarage until some twenty years previously and it was the top (second) floor that was the especially haunted area. 'During the eight years we have lived here,' Mrs Cooke informed us, 'five separate lots of people have told us that they have seen a "monk" walking on the top floor. He seems to be a very gentle, happy type of spirit, and apparently he chuckles with delight when he is noticed. We did have a medium here, a stranger to the district, and we told her that a "presence" had been reported here and said we would be very interested if she could identify it. We did not even tell her whether the presence was a man or a woman but subsequently she told us many things about the monk – for she said there were two presences – it is quite an interesting story . . .

'Also, at one time, the large downstairs kitchen and rooms were used by a cook/housekeeper and every night, at around 9 p.m. her dog used to "go mad" with his hair standing on end, howling and whining and scratching frantically at the back door leading to the cobbled courtyard and stables . . . and several times the occupants of the upstairs flat saw a stranger, a shadowy figure, pass across in front of the stables and disappear . . . Quite recently we read in one of the very old volumes of "Vicar's Letters" (found in the church and dated 1898): "This month the main thing of note was the very sad business of the poor little beggar lad found dead in the Rectory stables ... we will continue to send a prayer for his peace, and the ladies of the village will put flowers on his grave..."'

About two miles from Bromfield is Stanton Lucy Church (St Peters) dating back to 1103. This was one of the four churches the Rev. Prebendary Leland John Blashford-Snell MBE looked after at the time and there was something distinctly odd about this otherwise attractive Norman construction. 'We made a point of avoiding it,' John Blashford-Snell told me. 'I can't say it was frightening exactly, but it did seem to have a strange feeling about it; I noticed it wherever I went there.'

'Perhaps the most famous, if notorious, incumbent of Stanton Lucy,' Mrs Cooke told us, 'was poor Robert Faulkes who has the distinction of being one of the very few clergymen ever to have been executed for murder. After some eighteen years of respected service in the parish he had a scandalous affair with a young woman placed in his care and, after murdering the resulting child, was eventually hanged in London in January 1679.'

One evening in the 1960s the rector and his son (John Blashford-Snell) went to Stanton Lucy church after the police reported that they had caught someone trying to steal something from the church – the church that the rector and his wife and son had always felt had something distinctly odd about it; something not felt in any of the other three churches under the rector's spiritual care.

When father and son arrived on this particular occasion,

65

they found the church warden with an ashen-faced, middle-aged little man in a blue suit. He was smoking and his hands were shaking. This man had been seen running out of the church with a bag of things. The church warden had called the police and they had caught up with the man by the river. 'We'd like you to look round and see if anything is missing,' the policeman explained. The rector had a look round, everything seemed to be in order and then he opened the bag found in the man's possession and discovered that it contained brass-rubbing tools!

'I'm sorry I didn't ask permission before taking the rubbings,' apologised the little man. 'But I didn't know a new vicar had been appointed ... I ran because there's something evil in the church. I've been in lots of old churches in lots of strange places but I've never met anything so evil in all my life.' After a lot of persuasion the man led them back into the church and showed them where he had been working. He pointed to a carved screen. 'I was looking at that screen,' he said. 'Just standing on those steps there – but I can't stay here ...' and he retreated to the church door and the protection of the policeman who stood there.

The rector, followed by his son, walked slowly up the nave and stopped at the chancel steps. He looked to his right towards the vicar's pew – the usual seat for the minister during a service – and the church suddenly became very cold. In a low but firm voice the rector began to recite the Lord's Prayer. All the time he was gazing at the pew which lay in deep shadow in the fading sunlight. As he finished the prayer the rector walked slowly up to the altar, knelt and prayed for a moment, and then returned to his son. 'Do you feel the difference?' he asked. Whatever had emanated from the vicar's pew, it was evil, but now it had gone and the church was no longer deathly cold. 'It came from the vicar's pew, without a doubt,' John Blashford-Snell has always asserted. 'And there must be some reason, some explanation, but I don't know what it is.'

Months later, when John was home on leave again, his father said, 'Oh, by the way, John, you'll be interested to know that it's said the vicar of that haunted church, a hundred years or so ago, was hanged for murder and his ghost has been seen in the church. That was his pew that gave us that strange experience!'

Among the haunted places we visited in Ludlow were the castle, still harbouring the ghost of sad Marion who threw herself over the battlements of the Hanging Tower. She had an admirer among the enemy and during the absence of the castle custodian, Marion foolishly lowered a rope and helped the knight to visit her. Unbeknown to her he did not come alone and soon the castle defenders were outnumbered and overrun. In her anguish at what she had done she seized a sword and ran the knight through and then jumped to her death. A ghostly White Lady has been seen in the vicinity of the Hanging Tower on numerous occasions and her screams are said to have been heard countless times.

Then there was the ghost of Edward Dobson, a Tudor soldier who died a grisly death at the Globe Inn in Market Street, the oldest part of the town. We saw the churchyard where there is reputed to be the phantom of an unidentified elderly woman with grey hair who shuffles her way among the tombstones, dressed in a long, dark robe. Also we visited the haunted house in Mill Street; the restaurant where the waitresses won't go into one room; the craft centre with its ghost of an eighteenth-century girl and the phantom ticking of a grandfather clock!

The first night at Bromfield Manor was uneventful, as far as I know, but the second night saw a number of curious happenings reported to me and I experienced something of the lure of this haunted house myself.

Among the 'disturbances' reported, one member, allocated a room on the reportedly haunted second floor, said she heard shuffling footsteps throughout most of the night, or at least every time she found herself awake which seemed a lot, and once, quickly getting up and opening the door of her bedroom, she thought she glimpsed a dark shape moving away from her along the corridor but even as she peered hard to make out as much detail as possible, the figure, or shadow, or whatever it was, disappeared. There was no question of the figure going into another room and she heard no sound of footsteps when she saw the figure. Back in bed, she again heard the shuffling footsteps within minutes but this time, when she again looked out of her door, the sounds ceased and she could see nothing.

A member on the first floor, more or less underneath the member on the second floor who was so frequently disturbed, heard no sound of any kind but just once, during the night, she found herself awake and unable to say what had awakened her. She found her attention drawn to the window and when she pulled back the curtain and looked out she thought at first she saw a man in the garden, a man who hurriedly hid himself behind a shrub but when no figure reappeared from behind the shrub and when the moon suddenly shone brilliantly and lit up the shrub revealing no figure or form of any kind anywhere near it, she decided it may have been a trick of the light. Nevertheless she found some difficulty in getting back to sleep and she still wonders what it was that awakened her. The figure she saw briefly could well have been a monk, she said.

I have long been an early riser and on our second night at Bromfield Manor I awoke early and unable to get back to sleep, told my wife I thought I would go for a little walk. Quickly dressing and letting myself out of the room I prepared to descend the stairs – we were on the first floor – when I heard the sound of a door opening, and not wishing to frighten anyone who may have hurried to the nearby bathroom, I stood still, almost hidden in a kind of alcove. To my surprise I saw a figure pass along the corridor opposite, silently; and I do mean that: I heard not the slightest sound as I watched a figure, dressed in white, pass the length of the landing/corridor directly in front of me, no more than a dozen feet from me. It passed swiftly and seemingly smoothly, almost as though without taking steps. So quickly did it pass in front of the wall facing me that I cannot be certain whether it was male or female. The impression was of a figure, solid and life-like, clothed from head to foot in white with its head held high and moving without looking to left or right. Within seconds it had passed out of sight. But it was *not* transparent, that I do remember, and my first thought was that it was a real person. Perhaps it was but I established without doubt, as far as human testimony can establish anything, that no living person had been out of their rooms on that floor at the time I had seen the figure; and nobody it seemed slept in or possessed any full-length white clothing. Even as I watched, trying to establish the objectivity of the figure, I thought to myself, and I still think, how true it is that such experiences invariably take place when they are least expected; they happen when the mind is otherwise occupied – I remember I was wondering to myself whether the outside door downstairs would be open – and they are over almost before one is aware of the experience.

Certainly I was not thinking about ghosts at the time or the fact that the house I was in might be haunted. I was occupied with being quiet and wondering whether I would be able to leave the house and return to it without disturbing any of the occupants. And as I watched the gliding, white and silent figure I remember lots of thoughts rushing through my mind: how long had the figure been visible? Why hadn't I brought my camera with me? Should I go back and fetch it? What would happen if I called out or moved? Alas, they were idle speculations. Before I had time to do anything the figure had vanished from view. It didn't disappear exactly, it simply passed out of my view but there was no sound of a door opening or closing, no sound of any kind I realised, since I had first caught sight of the figure. If no human person had passed that way at that time, just what was it I had seen – and why? Our visit to Bromfield Manor, for me at any rate, had not been a wasted journey.

Also, that second night Ruth Jarvis, one of our younger members, had the idea of leaving a tape recorder running on the top floor. After everyone had retired for the night she did just that and in the morning when she ran it through there was nothing on the tape – except at the very end where there was the unmistakable sound of a heartbeat! A heartbeat that increased in crescendo until the tape ended . . .

The Bull

I have spent many nights at the delightful – and haunted – Bull Hotel, Long Melford, during visits to Borley, during filming and broadcasting, at the height of alleged poltergeist activity there, and under the auspices of the Ghost Club. I first visited The Bull almost fifty years ago and I was there earlier this year (1993).

Following many reports of violent and varied 'poltergeist' activity at the ancient and picturesque hotel, my friend P. I. Thomas Brown joined me in an all-night investigation there. This was quite a few years ago now, and the mellow sixteenth-century hostelry had not at that time been expanded and renovated into the present luxurious Forte premises.

After I had received more than a dozen reports from different people, and most of them first-hand accounts of mysterious happenings at The Bull, I asked a local Ghost Club member, Dr Peter Hilton-Rowe, to carry out a preliminary reconnaissance of the premises and the people involved. His report was distinctly promising and I approached the then manager, a Colonel Dawson, late of the Indian Army, and he promptly invited me to spend a night or two at his establishment.

In the fifteenth-century, Long Melford, now widely known for its antique shops, was already a thriving wool town and there are still half-timbered houses and thatched cottages lining the lengthy High Street that gave the place its name. In 1450, a wealthy wool merchant had a fine, timbered house built here, not far from the village green. By 1580, his substantial house had become The Bull Inn, later a favourite posting house being situated midway between London and Norwich during the busy coaching era.

On my first visit it was not difficult to imagine the quaint old courtyard at the back, surrounded by open weavers' galleries, filled with the clatter of horses' hooves and the rumble of heavy coach wheels. But it was inside the place, as it is today, that the great age of this fine old inn is more evident. In the entrance hall you find yourself between massive oak timbers filled between with plaster and with centuries-old rafters overhead. On the right was the dining room, much of its beauty hidden for centuries behind layer upon layer of wallpaper. Once exposed there could be no doubt that the walls were original fifteenth century. On the far side the great open hearth was, and still is, spanned by an enormous carved beam, probably brought from some other room in the house: the sixteenth-century carving still perfect. In one corner of the room a finely carved upright wall post carried the initials 'A.E.D.' and the figures '49'. Since this carving is of a later date than the rest of the decoration of the post, it is thought to refer to a man named William Drew, landlord of The Bull in 1649, who probably 'modernised' the place here and there.

A century later when The Bull was a coaching inn the Drews were again associated with the property, and in April 1740 one Charles Drew was hanged before a great crowd at Bury St Edmunds for the murder of his father, an attorney, because the old man refused to agree to his son's marriage to one Elizabeth Boyer. The murderer was buried in the chancel of the church nearby in the village of Acton where his brother-in-law was vicar. That village is known for its reputed phantom coach-and-horses but whether there is any connection between the Drews and the coach is unknown.

On the other side of the entrance hall of The Bull is the present lounge, for many years divided into a number of rooms, including the old bar. In here the timber work is even finer than in the dining room for this room contains the most interesting feature of the house: just inside the door, at the top of the upright beams, is carved in bold relief a 'wild man' or 'woodwose'. The significance of this carving is a mystery but 'woodwoses' or wild men of the woods were very popular subjects among medieval sculptors and carvers in this part of England, and they decorate the bases of many fonts in Suffolk churches.

The place is steeped in history: the dull thud of weaving looms must have echoed through this house when America had yet to be discovered and the last battle of the Wars of the Roses yet to be fought. And then the expansive days of the Tudors, when The Bull first hung out its sign – perhaps the paint was hardly dry – when Elizabeth herself came in great state to stay in 1578 with Sir William Cordell, her

Master of the Rolls, in his new moated home, Melford Hall, still standing a short distance away. He entertained the Queen so lavishly that there were those who were embittered by Cordell's hospitality since they were obliged to follow suit to the best of their ability and resources.

On 26 July 1648, a notorious murder was committed at The Bull that may have had repercussions down the centuries. During that troublesome time of the Civil War, one Richard Evered, a well-to-do yeoman of Melford, was attacked and killed as he stood in the entrance hall. No one seems to know the reason for the attack although it has been suggested that Roger Greene, the assailant, felt he had been wronged in some business deal with Evered. At all events Greene was 'taken, tried and convicted' of murder but the unexplained circumstances of the tragedy continued for curiously Evered's body – carried into the area that is the present lounge – had vanished the next day! Local folklore has it that were a certain grave in the churchyard of the nearby church to be investigated, Evered's body which was supposedly buried there would not be found. As to where the body went and why there seems to be no answer, but there is a firm suggestion that the ghost of Richard Evered lingers to this day at The Bull.

His ghost has been regarded as being responsible for many mysterious noises reported from various parts of the inn over the years. Furniture has been moved, doors opened and closed, loud bumps and bangs have sounded at night and disturbed residents, staff and guests and for years it was said that one bedroom, which had gained the reputation of being especially haunted, was sealed up and never used. One room was certainly regarded as 'the haunted room' during our visit years ago with guest after guest reporting crashing sounds and other disturbances and even today there is still one 'haunted bedroom'.

Among the distinguished visitors to The Bull in the eighteenth century were Ann and Jane Taylor who lived at nearby Lavenham. They made frequent excursions to Long Melford and invariably took tea at The Bull. They were the daughters of the Rev. Isaac Taylor and they often contributed to the hymns and poems composed by the family; perhaps their best-known being the nursery rhyme, 'Twinkle, Twinkle, Little Star'.

To return to the twentieth century, Tom Brown and I were welcomed to The Bull by Whayman, the head waiter. We were shown over the mellow old hostelry and then had a long talk with Colonel Dawson. We knew that an adolescent member of a household was often troubled by a poltergeist and that on occasions this young person was found to have been responsible for many of the disturbances, consciously or unconsciously. It seems likely that an unusual combination of psychological tension, sexual awakening, physical energy and intense (but possibly unconscious) concentration may produce a poltergeist which acts independently of the young person concerned. When such an independent entity has been established or has built up, then this 'off-shoot' re-attaches itself to the young girl or boy and noises, the moving of objects and other disturbances have been reported. In recent years we have noticed that something similar occasionally occurs around mature people of either sex and it may be that frustration and unhappiness play a part in the initial stages of so-called poltergeist activity.

At The Bull, Colonel Dawson formerly employed a teenager as a nursemaid to look after his young children. In response to our questions, he told us that when she left nothing of a poltergeist-like nature happened for a time but after a new girl took her place mysterious things again began to occur, which suggested that the 'geist' may be able to attach itself to more than one adolescent. Perhaps the fact that neither girl – nor for that matter the Colonel's children – were at The Bull during our short visit accounted for the dearth of 'poltergeist' activity at that time.

The temperature of a room has long been noticed to fall just before and during psychic happenings, and the thermometer readings, taken every few minutes during the night we spent at The Bull, showed no abnormality. An interesting point is that although objects projected by a poltergeist are frequently seen in flight (as they seem to have been at The Bull) and seen to end their flight, often breaking if the object is fragile, it is very rare indeed for the object to be seen starting its flight. It is almost as though the human eye is a deterrent to movement. Another point is that objects invariably finish at a lower level than that at which they started, thereby using the minimum amount of energy. The great puzzle of poltergeist phenomena is where the poltergeist stores the energy to move things around.

At The Bull, Whayman, the head waiter, told us that he had several times seen objects in flight. There was the occasion when a heavy copper jug hurtled across the dining room in his direction before dropping to the floor. And once a copper urn, which normally stood on a Dutch dresser and was safeguarded by a ledge, flew through the air as Whayman entered the room, landing on the carpet just behind him – he had the impression that this was deliberately thrown *at* him. Another time the same jug was found lying in the middle of the room, having presumably flown through the air when nobody was present in the dining room.

One of the first apparently unaccountable incidents at the pub, Colonel Dawson told us, concerned the movement of some dining-room chairs. One morning, having been left the night before arranged around individual tables as usual, they were found grouped round the enormous fireplace as though people had been sitting there all night! But on each of these occasions and indeed in all occurrences of movement of objects at The Bull, the objects were not seen as they began to move.

Tom Brown and I spent our night in the dining room where the majority of the unexplained happenings had taken place. Only one incident marred (or made!) an otherwise uneventful all-night vigil. Being close to the site of Borley Rectory, 'the most haunted house in England', The Bull has been used by many of the investigators and others concerned with that enigmatic case. We were not far from Acton either, and both Borley and Acton are associated in the annals of psychical research with phantom coaches. Imagine our interest therefore when, at 1.40 a.m., as we were comfortably seated one on either side of the massive fireplace, Brown and I both heard the faint but unmistakable sounds of horses' hooves in the quiet of the night. Slowly but surely the sounds continued, accompanied now and then by the jangle of harness and the grind of wheels as 'something' came nearer and nearer. Unobtrusively we approached the uncurtained windows. The night was dark and although the noises, punctuated every now and again by intervals of silence, seemed to be approaching the ancient inn, no lights were visible. It was only when the perpetrators of the noises were virtually under our noses that we recalled that we were in the heart of the country where the disposal of human waste matter was at that time still carried out in the primitive manner of years gone by!

Colonel Dawson impressed us with his cautious views on the haunting and from him we heard the full story of the disturbances. They began when Dawson had been manager for only six months. After the disarrangement of the chairs in the dining room, a flower vase was found on the floor of the same room. Both these incidents were regarded as being due to a lack of attention on the part of members of the staff. In most cases of poltergeist infestation the initial incidents are the easiest for which to find an explanation, and often it is only in the light of subsequent events that they are regarded as the first curious incidents and the beginning of the disturbances.

After Dawson had been at The Bull for about a year, he and his wife and the maid and nursemaid were having lunch in the dining room when they all heard a loud click and the door leading from the hall into the dining room opened, apparently of its own accord. Colonel Dawson particularly remarked to me that he noticed that the room felt suddenly cold. As we have said, it was in the entrance hall that Richard Evered was murdered and it is the heavy oak door leading from the hall into the dining room (now a comfortable lounge) which was alleged to have opened paranormally on so many occasions. Whayman informed us that he had personally seen the door open by itself at least half a dozen times. He was quite certain that no one was near it on these occasions. We were told that this 'phenomenon' occurred most frequently at meal-times.

It is generally accepted that dogs are usually able to perceive or sense 'ghosts', or perhaps they sense the apprehension of their human companions; at all events cats, dogs and horses have long been regarded as good 'psychic barometers' and further evidence is provided by the behaviour of the Dawson's dogs at The Bull. The Colonel told us he was alone at the inn one night, with the exception of his assistant, when he heard footsteps pass his bedroom door. A moment later he heard them again. Quietly he got up and after ascertaining that the assistant manager was asleep in his room, fetched the two Scottish terriers from downstairs. Immediately they were in the corridor outside his bedroom, the dogs bristled and growled and showed signs of fright, although nothing was visible to Colonel Dawson, nor could he hear footsteps or any other unaccountable noise at that time. The dogs certainly sensed something and absolutely refused to go along the passage. It was some time before they quietened down, but eventually they stopped showing signs of fright and were taken back downstairs.

Some months later, a visitor heard footsteps outside her bedroom door early one morning, in another part of the inn, followed by a knock. Thinking it must be her early morning tea, she called out: 'Come in'. By way of answer, she heard a terrific crash, as though a tray with teapot, jug, cup and saucer, and other crockery had been dropped by someone; and the noise appeared to come from just outside her bedroom door. Quickly she slipped out of bed and threw open the door. No one was in sight but a large Indian gong which normally stood at the head of the stairs, lay on its face. No explanation was ever forthcoming and *no one else at the inn had heard a sound*.

On a shelf in the room then used as a dining room (scene of the majority of the phenomena), a pewter coffee-pot resided on a little shelf six inches deep. On one occasion, we were told, this pot had jumped off the shelf, over six feet from the ground, in the presence of nine people having breakfast. We decided that over a period of time vibration might have caused the pot to have moved and eventually fallen, but it did seem to have jumped. It is not unusual in a building three or four centuries old to find a fine layer of dust almost continually covering surfaces. This shelf at The Bull was no exception. Colonel Dawson told us he carefully examined the shelf immediately after the pot had 'jumped' and found the dust disturbed only in a clear circle where the coffee-pot had stood; there was no displacement of the dust consistent with the pot having slid off the shelf and it could only be deduced, in the circumstances related to us, that the pot had literally jumped.

Two small fires, typical poltergeist phenomena, had also been reported at The Bull since the outbreak of the unexplained incidents, the first occurring in the lounge, just across the entrance hall from the then dining room. A smell of burning heralded the discovery of a small hole burning in the carpet, five feet seven inches from the fireplace – *where no fire was burning at the time*. We examined the hole in the carpet and found it to be one-and-a-half inches in diameter. Colonel Dawson assured us that there was no trace of a cinder or cigarette-end or anything that might have accounted for the fire, which was easily extinguished and did not break out again. The other fire incident, in the same room, consisted of a heavy iron fire-basket being lifted bodily into the middle of the room! A fire *was* burning in it at the time and a very serious fire could have resulted had it not been discovered promptly. The warning was due to a bang or heavy thud (presumably the sound of the fire-basket landing in the middle of the room) and, since it was known that no one was, or should have been, in the room at the time, immediate investigation revealed apparent paranormal movement of the enormously heavy fire-basket, which with some difficulty was put back in its proper position.

There was one other incident that Tom Brown and I experienced during our initial visit. In the morning, Whayman asked how we had fared during the night and when we told him all had been quiet, our instruments showed no abnormality, and we seemed to have been singularly fortunate or unfortunate, whichever way you looked at it, he said: 'Well, never mind sirs, things often happen at meal times . . . now, about your breakfasts . . .'

The 'haunted' dining room, where breakfast was served and where we had spent an undisturbed night, was then served by two doors. There was the heavy, latched oak door leading to the entrance hall and a smaller door with a glass window in it situated in the opposite corner of the room. This smaller door was used by Whayman to bring food from the kitchen; doubtless he used the little window to see when people were ready, and there was a passage alongside the room meeting the entrance hall.

As Brown and I were enjoying our breakfast, Whayman suddenly appeared at the smaller doorway and said: 'Oh look – there sirs!' We turned round and the heavy door on the other side of the room, leading to the entrance hall, was slowly opening. When fully extended the door ceased moving and remained open to our astonishment – and yet? Whayman, with a satisfied smile on his face, disappeared in the direction of the kitchen. Tom Brown and I looked at each other and then together we left our breakfast table and examined the door that we had seen swinging open.

We closed the door, we opened the door, we latched it, we unlatched it; and we discovered several interesting factors. The door was very solid and very heavy and very quiet. When it was shut it stayed shut even without the latch being in position and when it was gently pushed open it stayed wherever it was left except that when opened beyond eight inches of its own weight it slowly swung open! Tom Brown resumed his place at the breakfast table. I went into the entrance hall, pulling the door closed behind me. Then, very gently and quietly, I pushed the door open to just eight inches and as it began to open on its own I walked up the entrance hall, round the corner and, reaching the smaller door into the dining room, I just had time to open it and say: 'There, look at that Tom!' As Tom Brown turned round to face the door, he and I watched it slowly swing wide open as we had done when Whayman drew our attention to it!

Colonel Dawson invited us to pay a return visit to The Bull at a later date in the hope that we might witness some poltergeist activity but soon afterwards the disturbances appeared to cease as unaccountably as they had begun, and as far as I know nothing of a poltergeist nature has happened at The Bull for a long time.

Under the auspices of the Ghost Club, I revisited The Bull once again in 1993 and although I had been back there a good many times over the years, I had not been very recently and it was interesting to see the alterations and improvements that had subsequently been made. The old dining room where we had spent a night was now the delightful Mylde Suite and the old lounge, on the other side of the entrance hall, had been enlarged and improved almost beyond recognition. Melvyn Willin, Ghost Club Society Events Organiser and Investigations Director, occupied the 'haunted bedroom' and slept for two nights undisturbed.

I am sure The Bull has seen some strange happenings over the years and some may well be difficult to explain in rational terms but in all my visits to that lovely old hostelry I don't believe I have experienced anything of a paranormal nature and that includes the first visit; but I have certainly enjoyed all of my visits, all of the time.

Chingle Hall

Tucked away at the end of a Lancashire lane lies perhaps one of the best-authenticated examples of a haunted house, with evidence from over nearly half a century and witnesses who include clergymen, police officers, local house guides, experienced ghost hunters and investigators, the occupants of the house, complete strangers visiting the house for the first time and with no knowledge of allegedly ghostly happenings and scores of ordinary, level-headed men, women and children from all walks of life and from many parts of the world. This property, a sturdy 700 year old small cruciform, fortified manor house, has witnessed much suffering through the ages and it has been the subject of no fewer than four Ghost Club investigations.

Dating from 1260, and with a lot of the thirteenth-century structure remaining intact, Chingle Hall passed to the Wall family in 1585 and the Blessed John Wall, a Franciscan priest who may well have been the last English Roman Catholic martyr, was born there in 1620. Legend has it that after he was hanged, drawn and quartered in

1679, John Wall's head was smuggled abroad and made 'the grand tour' before being brought back to Chingle where it is said to have been buried somewhere in the garden by members of the Wall family, but exactly where has never been established. His ghost is reputed to haunt the house to this day; just one of many ghosts at Chingle it seems, for a writer in 1992 says that, 'at the last count sixteen different ghosts have been seen at the Hall'.

The ownership of the Wall family came to an end in 1794 when the property was purchased by the Farrington family who retained ownership for about a hundred years when the property was bought by the Langton family. Mr and Mrs Howarth rented the house in 1945 and bought it in 1960. After the death of Mr Howarth, his wife's sister Miss Ann Strickland went to live at the Hall. After Mrs Howarth's death, Miss Strickland had many problems and eventually decided to dispose of the place. As it stood empty the house was vandalised and badly damaged by fire. On at least one occasion during this period police arrived at the Hall having been alerted by neighbours who had seen lights inside the empty building. On arrival, the police too reportedly saw some rooms lit up and they heard laughter and music but as they entered the house all was quiet, it was completely deserted and there was no explanation for the sounds and sights they had heard and seen.

After several potential purchasers withdrew their offers, John and Sandra Bruce bought the place in 1986 and they did a wonderful job in restoring Chingle Hall before selling it again a few years later.

Situated on the outskirts of Preston within the small

Viking village of Goosnargh, the small moated hall was built on land which seems to have been given to one Ughtred Singleton in 1067, possibly as a reward for his services to King Harold. After the death of the last Saxon King the land passed through the Singleton line for two centuries until a knight named Adam de Singleton built this interesting house and called it Singleton Hall. The de Singletons and their kinsfolk the Wall family were all devout Roman Catholics and a chapel was built into the property on the ground floor. On our first visit we explored every room in the house and every part of the property. Over the stone bridge that has replaced the original drawbridge is the massive thirteenth-century oak door with its medieval sanctuary knocker and other ironwork. Through the main porch with its 'witches' window' of Tudor glass (where ghost monks appear from the knees upwards for the original flooring was half-a-metre below the present Victorian tiles), the chapel is on the left, containing two hides, one in the floor and the other above an oak ceiling beam. A number of ghost monks and priests have been reportedly seen here, apparently praying in front of the ancient wooden cross; they invariably vanish almost as soon as they are seen.

In the adjoining Great Hall, to the left of the Tudor fireplace, traces of a door lintel can be seen and, through this long disused and blocked-up doorway, silent and ghostly forms have been seen to appear and disappear. The only other rooms on the ground floor are a private lounge (where paranormal movement of objects has been reported) and the kitchen. Several photographs of the centre window pane in the lounge here have seemed to show figures, some resembling a priest and thought to be John Wall himself.

Upstairs, apart from private bedrooms, there is the John Wall Room and the Priest Room, perhaps the most haunted rooms in this haunted house, and a corridor between them is also haunted. John Wall was reputedly born in the room named after him and baptised by the Jesuit Edmund Arrowsmith who was himself martyred in 1628: one of his hands is preserved at St Oswald's Church, Ashton-in-Makerfield near Wigan and is alleged to possess miraculous healing properties. This room at Chingle in particular has ghostly sounds and ghostly lights. The sounds predominantly resemble the movement of chains and it is interesting to remember that 700 years ago the chain mechanism for raising and lowering the drawbridge was operated from this room over the main porch; in fact the two small wall cupboards almost certainly once contained the necessary apparatus for this function.

The unexplained lights here are mainly blue flashes that seem to strike the walls and disappear; on occasions 'white lightning' has been reported. Once this mysterious 'spirit lightning' struck the wall within an inch or two of a group looking over the house. They all saw it but no one could explain it. Here too ghost monks and priests have reportedly been seen kneeling in prayer.

The passage leading from the John Wall Room to the Priest Room is known as the Haunted Corridor and many visitors to the house have reported feeling suddenly 'a strange sensation', especially in the immediate vicinity of a concealed fireplace and a hidden door entrance where ghosts have reportedly been seen. The Priest Room, situated over the chapel, is probably the most haunted room in the house: even the room itself has been known to change its appearance! An unidentified apparition has been seen here, hurrying through the chamber as though being pursued and there is also the ghost known as Lady Eleanor who brings with her, often completely out of season, the overwhelming smell of lavender. Lady Eleanor is thought to have been one of the last of the Singletons, perhaps even the last, and she may have been mad. Yet although only fourteen years old she seems to have somehow managed to persuade three different people that they had bought the Hall and after her death four years later the courts had to settle the matter, with the Hall passing to the Wall family. Lady Eleanor is believed to have died in the room now known as the Priest Room aged about eighteen. One recent writer states categorically: 'She is now often seen within the room and is one of Chingle's better-known ghosts.'

Sometimes a heavy chandelier is reportedly seen in the Priest Room, although such a hanging light support no longer exists at Chingle. One afternoon a party of four visitors all ducked their heads to avoid the 'ghost chandelier' and remarked on its beauty. They could hardly believe their eyes when they returned to the room to find no chandelier.

At Chingle Hall there are many fascinating items to be seen: the 'signal' window used to indicate to the outlawed adherents of the Catholic faith that a secret mass was being celebrated; the piece of charred beam that was found burning from the inside outwards – a possible example of spontaneous combustion or ghostly activity;

a pre-Reformation 'praying-cross' and no fewer than three secret hiding places and a secret well-tunnel in the moat.

I first visited Chingle Hall in the 1970s when my wife and I took tea with the then owners Mrs Margaret Howarth and her sister Miss Ann Strickland. From them we heard of the wealth of curious happenings reported over the years, for example, a rural dean witnessed the sudden and violent rattling of two pictures in the Priest Room, 'as though invisible hands had grasped them and banged them against the wall', a phenomenon also witnessed by Mrs Howarth. A police Chief Superintendent and his wife, shortly after dinner at the Hall in 1967, heard heavy thumps from the 'haunted corridor' above, then a single 'thump', followed by a distinct and sickening 'thud' and then heavy footsteps: these sounds were heard by everyone present. But no one was upstairs and, leaving everyone together in the private lounge, under the eye of his wife, the police officer satisfied himself that no human person was anywhere in the house and that there was no normal explanation for the sounds they had heard. Returning to his wife and hosts and other guests, they were all astonished, about half an hour later, to hear the sound of footsteps again from above their heads and of something heavy being dragged across the room and a rattling noise, as of a chair, followed by more footsteps. Immediate investigation again proved unsuccessful. Two hours later yet another series of similar noises were heard by everyone present and again an immediate search revealed no explanation.

Mrs Proctor, when she was a guide at Chingle, twice saw the cowled head of a monk peering at her through a window in the John Wall Room; a pale face, hardly human she thought, surrounded by a dark cowl. On each occasion it vanished as suddenly as it had appeared but some weeks later Mrs Proctor thought she saw the same figure in the grounds when a pageant was being held there.

Mr and Mrs Jepson were friends of the owners of the Hall and known to them for years although they had never previously experienced anything inexplicable there. On one visit they were spending a few quiet moments in the chapel, looking at the old wooden cross that had almost certainly been used in clandestine and forbidden services in the days of religious persecution when they both became aware, at the same time, of two kneeling figures wearing monks' habits, seemingly praying although no sounds were heard by the watchers; in fact it seemed oddly and unnaturally quiet and still at the time. A little later, in the Priest Room, situated immediately above the chapel, Mrs Jepson distinctly saw the figure of a man with shoulder-length hair walk past the window – a window that is twelve feet above ground level!

Another visitor, Mrs Evans, encountered a ghost monk as she was walking through the main porch towards the Great Hall. She described it as 'a green, diffuse figure' that walked towards her and they met in the doorway of the porch. As Mrs Evans stopped the figure turned and walked back into the Great Hall – and vanished.

On that first visit I learned of many guests reporting the presence of invisible beings: Mrs Walmesley received a violent push in the back while she was alone in the private lounge; Mrs Moorby, a sceptic as far as psychic matters are concerned, had a distinct and very unpleasant impression while in a bathroom that she was being watched. The feeling became so strong that, although she saw nothing, she felt quite terrified and the room became 'frightfully cold'. At last she managed to make her way to the door which she threw open and then she ran down the stairs. She has always remembered that her only thought was to get away from whatever was in that room and she certainly left the door wide open in her flight but halfway down the stairs she heard the door quietly click shut. She immediately took Mrs Howarth back upstairs with her and the door was indeed securely closed. When they opened the door, the room seemed quite normal, and Mrs Moorby had difficulty in explaining what had frightened her.

The same stairway, where a number of people have reported odd impressions, sounds and feelings, is haunted by the sound of heavy footsteps ascending them and Mrs Robinson was one visitor who heard footsteps that seemed to be immediately behind her. Once in the Priest Room she idly tapped once on the wall above the large priest hole (constructed by that master architect and builder of secret hiding places, Nicholas Owen) and was astonished to hear *three* distinct raps emanate from the recesses of the empty priest hole. Then she heard more footsteps echoing through the house and there was a sudden and loud knock on the front door, but no one was there.

Another witness of apparently paranormal activity in the Priest Room was Mrs McKay who was alone in the room, admiring the view from the window, when she suddenly felt a wave of cold air sweep over her and she saw some flowers in the room move as though someone was twisting their stems; then a table lamp shook and then a picture moved –

and then Mrs McKay hurriedly left the haunted apartment!

Mrs McKay, incidentally, also saw a ghost at Chingle Hall from outside, looking in. She and her son were leaving the Hall after a visit one evening when they chanced to look up at the window of the Priest Room and they both saw a human form at the window, a white or light-grey robed figure. When Andrew McKay switched on his car head-lights and lit up the front of the Hall and the window of the Priest Room they were astonished to see that the room behind the figure appeared to be dense and black, quite unlike how it really was.

Another visitor to Chingle was the Rev. Peter Travis and he and a friend spent a night in the Priest Room. During the night they experienced door-opening, a loud groaning sound, interference with a light switch and the sound of a very heavy crash. And another friend of Mrs Howarth, Mrs Rigby, was having a cup of tea with Mrs Howarth in the lounge when an old wooden plaque, which I examined, shot off the fireplace and landed in the centre of the room.

Not that it was only visitors and friends of the occupants who experienced apparently paranormal activity at Chingle. Mrs Howarth's brother, William Strickland, saw a figure resembling a priest walk through the gate and into the field opposite and Miss Ann Strickland told me she had heard knockings, tappings and footsteps that had no explanation, not once but many times. Miss Janet Makinson was another visitor who heard footsteps from an empty room; on gingerly entering the room she found it deserted but freezing cold. Miss Makinson also witnessed doors opening and closing by themselves in various parts of haunted Chingle Hall.

Mrs Howarth told us she had herself seen the figure of a woman in the Priest Room; she had heard footsteps she could not explain on many occasions; and tappings on the walls and furniture; and more than once the dogs had seemed to follow something invisible about the place. In the John Wall Room, Mrs Howarth saw, as distinctly as she saw us, she said, the figure of a Franciscan monk. An Italian, who had been a prisoner of war in the area in 1945, had returned and told her he had seen the same figure in the same room and he had run screaming from the room. He had never forgotten the experience.

When she and her husband were sleeping in the John Wall Room, Mrs Howarth told us they had experienced all sorts of odd happenings. One night the heavy latch of the door lifted by itself and the door opened, although no one came in and in fact no one was there. Mrs Howarth got out of bed and made sure the door was securely latched. No sooner was she back in bed than it happened again – and again. That night it happened six times and on the last occasion she and her husband saw a cloaked figure standing in the doorway; they watched it for several seconds or minutes – they didn't know how long it was but it seemed a long time, and then the figure became dimmer and dimmer and then faded away completely.

On that first visit my wife and I examined the hide in the Priest Room, which had been left open for our inspection, and we met Michael Bingham, a young New Zealander who was staying at the Hall. He told us that on one occasion, in the presence of another witness, he had heard noises like bricks being moved from the hide we were looking at, and when he looked he had seen part of a human hand that appeared to be moving one of the bricks! As he watched the hand froze and then suddenly and completely disappeared.

During his stay at Chingle, Michael Bingham not only succeeded in recording the sounds of footsteps and other apparently paranormal activity but he also used something like 350 yards of film trying to obtain a photographic record of the ghost that, he told us, walked practically every night, and on the last few feet, which he had taken by remote control, there is a short section showing a small hooded figure moving past the camera and then returning before it disappears.

On previous visits to Chingle similar attempts failed, either the tape proving to be inexplicably blank or the sounds scrambled. This time everything seemed to work perfectly. Likewise previous attempts to photograph the visual manifestations met with little success, until this time. An 8mm cine camera was set up in a passage leading to the John Wall Room, the door of which was left open. One 100 watt light bulb was fixed beneath the camera tripod and Michael stationed himself in the adjoining Priest Room, with a remote control switch with which he operated the camera and light when he heard the sound of ghostly footsteps.

On development much of the footage was blank but a short section did show a whitish light in the form of a hooded figure moving past the camera into the John Wall Room; there is a flash of light seemingly from within the room and the figure then returns towards the camera – at which point the film runs out.

Michael told us that one night he was sitting in the dining room when he became aware that hands were lightly but firmly around his throat. He saw nothing but for a few seconds he was all too aware of an invisible someone standing behind him and firmly gripping his throat. Michael, an old hand at ghost hunting after several months at Chingle Hall, was not even frightened.

Mrs Howarth told us that on 17 January 1977, a friend from Hull was staying at the Hall. She was reading a book by the fire when she heard the door leading to the staircase open, and when she looked up she saw a monk in a brown habit and she heard him sigh twice, then he disappeared. At 3.30 p.m. on 24 January 1977, the same ghost was heard by two visitors and this time the footsteps were very loud and appeared to walk from the haunted Priest Room along the 'haunted corridor'. Sometimes the sounds were so loud, Mrs Howarth told us, that she thought someone must have broken in and she got up and searched the house from top to bottom – but no trace of any human intruder was ever found. At other times the smell of burning and even actual smoke has caused Mrs Howarth to call the fire brigade; not only have they found no fire but their thermocouples have established that there was no heat source.

In January 1993, Michael Bingham was good enough to tell me that at Chingle Hall he witnessed, 'the bottom of the priest hide being moved up and down (a light is directed onto the hide); intense bursts of light near the priest hide and moving away. Patches of bright light, limited in area and not throwing shadows from objects nearby. Bursts of green, blue and white lights and reflected in a mirror; what appeared to be blue-grey smoke; there was also a triangle-shaped white light and flickering lights.'

Regarding the film he obtained, also on 24 January 1993, he comments, 'most interesting of all, on one frame only the figure of a cowled Franciscan priest is clearly visible; the film is in colour and the lighting and detail are excellent. This is in the John Wall Room and the light in the room is on, situated on the wall and only about two feet away from the figure which is in front of a portrait which is visible through the figure. It is side profile and no features are visible. The camera, as you know, was operated by remote control and no one was in the room at the time.'

It seems that Sally Wallbank, who has spent a lot of time at Chingle Hall in recent years, has the gift of psychic awareness and she has carried out many all-night visits which have resulted in numerous reports of sightings and encounters with ghosts and ghostly happenings. Oddly enough it has been noticed at Chingle, as at other haunted houses, that the greater the volume of people visiting the house during the day, the more strange experiences are reported at night – it is almost like a battery being recharged.

In 1992, Sally Wallbank published a short book entitled *Chingle: Britain's Most Haunted House* (Owl Books) where she details recent experiences. During alterations in 1987 and 1988, workmen reportedly encountered ghosts at Chingle and there were stories of unexplained figures appearing and disappearing, objects moving by themselves, and inexplicable coldness. One workman in the chapel said the whole room suddenly became icy cold and unnaturally dark although outside it was bright sunshine. Similar experiences were reported in the Great Hall by a chimney sweep. Puzzled by the sudden and considerable drop in temperature as the room became dark, he became aware of a man standing close beside him; when he spoke the 'man' disappeared and a house guide asked him who he was talking to. The chimney sweep was the only human being in the Great Hall at the time. Glaziers have had trouble repairing broken windows and on one occasion first one pane of glass broke, followed by another four!

One afternoon, after the Hall had been open to visitors, two elderly ladies were among a group being shown round the Hall. One of them, resting for a moment halfway up the main staircase, became aware of a young man at her side, dressed in period costume. Thinking it must be a guide, dressed up to look the part, the visitor was astonished when the 'young man' suddenly and completely disappeared and she then discovered that no one else had seen him.

On several occasions visitors have seen a handrail on the left-hand side of the stairway and apparently used it to help them up or down the stairs – but today there is a handrail only on the right-hand side! More than one visitor has been shocked and surprised to realise that they have visualised and seemingly used an invisible handrail! Once upon a time there had indeed been a handrail on the left-hand side of the stairway but not any more.

The Great Hall seems to have a phantom cat on occasions. True, there are real cats belonging to the Hall but sometimes, especially at night, a cat has been plainly heard crying in the Great Hall when no real cat is there. Sally Wallbank says, 'It appears at first with four, then three eyes, until it looks like a normal cat. This is due to the magnetic energy field it comes through.'

Sally Wallbank spent her first all-night visit to Chingle on 29–30 April 1989, in the company of three friends whom she names as Anne, John and Jimmy. It was the first time any of them had attempted such an undertaking and they were not disappointed for they were to report a variety of apparent phenomena. On their arrival they encountered a strong smell of incense which did not seem to have any rational explanation, especially as it seemed to follow them about the house and then disappear as suddenly and as inexplicably as it had arrived. However, in the John Wall Room Sally felt her shoulder touched and her handbag pulled.

It was nearly midnight when the next incident occurred in the Priest Room, where they had decided to spend the night. John was asleep on the floor and Jimmy was resting in a chair when suddenly he awoke in pain from the screaming sound emitted by his hearing aid. He and Sally decided to go down to the Great Hall and warm themselves beside the fire still burning there. They were sitting comfortably and Jimmy had almost recovered from the painful ear sound and laughingly said he wondered what would happen next when they both became aware of footsteps approaching the Great Hall. They counted eight distinct and solid footfalls that came towards them from the direction of the chapel. The footsteps seemed to walk right up to the chair Sally was occupying and then retreated back in the direction from which they had come. Both watchers felt it was almost as though someone wanted them to be quiet. They were decidedly quiet after that and as they enjoyed a cigarette they both felt drawn towards the chapel. Hastily extinguishing their cigarettes they quietly

101

made their way to the chapel and as they entered Sally heard 'boom . . . boom . . . boom' a noise so loud it seemed to hurt her ears – but Jimmy heard nothing! Then he did hear something: the sound of a baby crying.

Back in the Priest Room they encountered blue and white lights, suddenly bright and then as suddenly dim, many times during the rest of the night. Once they heard three knocks that seemed to originate from the priest hide. Photographs taken during the night depicted forms that they could not explain.

On 9–10 June 1989, Sally Wallbank spent another night at Chingle, this time in the company of a journalist friend named Graham and two Chingle Hall guides. After a spell sitting around the fire in the Great Hall, the guides prepared to retire for the night and the ghost watchers decided to spend the hours of darkness in the John Wall Room. As the guides were leaving the room Sally's bag which had been resting undisturbed on a chair suddenly 'jumped' off the chair!

Having experienced some apparent phenomena in the Great Hall the watchers decided to spend a little more time there and they settled themselves comfortably in front of the warm fire. Just before 2 a.m. they were startled out of their complacency by a 'terrible' scream! It came from outside the house but neither of them felt brave enough to investigate. They settled back and waited for anything further to happen.

They didn't have to wait long. Within a few minutes of the scream they heard a curious sound that seemed to come from upstairs; almost as though something was being rolled around in one of the upper rooms. As often seems to happen at Chingle the electric lights malfunctioned throughout the night, sometimes getting remarkably bright and at other times curiously dim, although the electrical system at Chingle has, to my knowledge, been checked on several occasions and found to be safe and satisfactory.

Once in the John Wall Room they heard the door latch lift and the door opened by itself but nothing of great moment happened for the rest of the night. In the morning, however, as they were taking breakfast, the main staircase door opened, slowly and hesitantly, in three distinct stages. Once open they saw the sleeve of a brown monk's habit 'pushing the door – but there was no hand attached...'

Sally's third night at Chingle was 24–25 November 1989 when she was one of a party of eight who stayed in the house on a particularly cold night. During their vigil several cameras malfunctioned although they had all been looked at and checked before arrival. Camera shutters refused to open and, odd as it may seem, some 'cameras only seemed to work when you took one step forward, took a step back and then they would work again'. Those present decided this must be due to 'an all-pervading powerful and magnetic field'.

Later the main hall door jammed and refused to open for about five minutes; a single footstep was heard from the far end of the Great Hall where there were no human beings at the time; two outlines, one of a Cavalier and the other of a tulip, were found in the frost of the window of the John Wall Room; and there was the usual interference with the lights.

Sally's fourth night was 7–8 April 1990 when she was one of a party of five, spending the night in a haunted house on behalf of a children's charity. That night two cameras refused to work; a 'black shape' was seen by two members of the party near the main porch; a peculiar hissing and buzzing noise sounded in the Great Hall; a 'woeful moan' was heard in the Priest Room; three loud knocks sounded on the front door; the lights flickered and dimmed; objects were moved; the sound of dripping water was heard in the Great Hall, quite inexplicably; and Sally saw a 'monk' as she left the John Wall Room – a monk who passed through her! She says she felt sick and dizzy and thought she was going to faint, but one of her friends took a firm hold of her arm, and she revived.

During her fifth night at Chingle on 23–24 June 1990, Sally's camera started to unwind by itself and during her next visit on 11–12 August 1990, with three other people, cameras again malfunctioned; they experienced icy draughts in the Great Hall; a single knock sounded; a latch lifted; a few footsteps were reported and a 'gruff voice' was recorded – a voice that later disappeared from the tape.

In April 1992, Sally accompanied a paranormal research group from Southampton for an overnight stay and among their experiences were: faint tapping sounds; an 'icy paranormal breeze'; sounds of a pendulum; two sighs; three groans; lights dimming; a voice was heard calling and three taps were recorded. Also there were clicking sounds; floorboards in the John Wall Room vibrated; there were odd temperature variations; loud banging noises; heavy footsteps; tapping sounds and malfunction of electrical equipment.

Over the last few years Sally Wallbank has certainly been

fortunate in experiencing odd happenings at Chingle Hall, describing her many experiences in her book and to list 'just a few of the things', there were blue and white lightning; orange circular glowing ball shapes; white clouds; movement of objects; doors opening and closing by themselves and locking and unlocking by themselves; the smell of lavender and of incense; and a clock striking the hour of three although 'no such clock exists at Chingle'.

Four Ghost Club investigative visits were made to Chingle Hall within fifteen months, the first taking place in May 1979. At that time a local man, Fred Knowles, who lived a few hundred yards from the Hall and acted as guide at the house, seemed to have a strange rapport with the ghost of John Wall; and certainly heavy and distinct raps were heard in response to a sincere verbal request from this man.

The first preliminary visit involved Steuart Kiernander and Michael Brett, two valued and experienced Ghost Club members. They arrived at the house at 7.30 p.m. as arranged and met Fred Knowles, at that time a kind of general help, guide and friend to the owners. They were shown round the house and finally left alone in the haunted Priest Room. After a couple of hours both investigators began to feel very bored and frustrated. By the time the light had faded outside it was very dark in the Priest Room where no light was used. Suddenly, without any warning whatever, loud bangs and thuds sounded from the direction of the priest hide and then seemed to move across the floor towards one of the investigators and when the sounds were virtually under his feet and the floor actually vibrated, he moved across the room towards the other investigator. The bangs continued until they reached the window facing the chimney on the opposite side of the room and there they ceased.

Both investigators were very surprised; after a long period of complete inactivity and the continuing noise of the owners' television downstairs, they had been lulled into thinking that nothing unusual would happen. The noise was very loud, so loud that it completely drowned all other noises. Shortly afterwards the noises began again, this time in a different part of the room. Scratching sounds and loud bangs seemed to come from the region of the priest hole beside the chimney and to proceed out into the room. They moved towards and seemingly into a cabinet, then out again and across the floor with such power and force that a chair on which one of the investigators sat literally shook. The bangs travelled across the floor in front of the fireplace and then seemed to move outside the room, in the region of the doorway. After a short pause the bangs sounded yet again: this time they seemed to travel from the floor to the ceiling, by way of one wall, and then across the ceiling where they ceased. The total duration of this happening was about two minutes.

Soon afterwards, at 10.30 p.m., Knowles came into the room and asked whether anything had happened. When he was told about the very loud raps, he said nothing but called on the name of Jesus Christ and banged loudly three times on the cabinet with his hand, asking the 'spirit' to answer him. Immediately three loud knocks came in reply, seemingly from within the room itself. A few more bangs were heard and then the investigators left the house at 11.30 p.m.

The second investigation by the same two Ghost Club investigators was on 28 July 1979. They arrived at the house at 7 p.m., as arranged, to find that a party of nurses and ambulance men from Preston were already in the house carrying out a sponsored ghost hunt! Since they were there they decided to join the party. This time they had brought full recording apparatus and extension leads and were able to obtain a record of the whole proceedings. At 10 p.m. the bangs started and again they seemed to move across the room. Various members of the party present were sitting on the floor and they said they could feel the floor vibrate with the banging noises and one member became very cold. But the bangs were in no way as loud or as powerful as on the previous occasion. Later Knowles came into the room and a few more knocks were heard.

The third investigating party consisted of the two previous Ghost Club members, a guest medium and his assistant and three additional Ghost Club members, myself included. This was in September 1979 and lasted from 7 p.m. until 11.30 p.m. One member felt something invisible brush against her leg as she sat with her back to the wall and facing the centre of the room. A few knocks were heard but of no real strength or duration and only when Fred Knowles joined the party. This was easily the least eventful investigation.

The fourth visit took place on 15 August 1980 and lasted all night from 7 p.m. until 5.30 a.m. the following day. The entire session was recorded. The party consisted of nine Ghost Club members: Steuart and Freda Kiernander, Michael Brett, Dr and Mrs Vernon Harrison, Ken Lazenby, Godfrey Goolden, my wife and myself. We were joined by

Lisa and Bernadette, two mediums from the Northern Society for Psychical Research. The mediums did not seem at all comfortable and reported nothing of a psychic nature and no impressions or sensations, but to be fair to them the recent death of Mrs Margaret Howarth seemed to affect them and one of them claimed to feel various pains and feelings that she associated with Mrs Howarth. The mediums spent part of the night resting in an adjoining room.

A few light raps were heard but nothing of great interest until Knowles joined the party, just after midnight and then, in direct answer to his request, as before, loud and distinct knocks were heard on no fewer than six occasions. A recording machine inside the room recorded everything while another, placed just outside the room, recorded no sounds whatever, so it seems that the really loud knocks heard by everyone present and recorded were confined to the Priest Room and were not heard outside the room. After Knowles left, one of the recordings obtained inside the Priest Room where he asked for raps to be answered was played back – and a single rap responded to this recorded request!

Since the sounds and especially the loud raps and knocks appeared to be associated with Fred Knowles – or at least they were then – it might be instructive to consider one or two aspects of this case. Although the most widely witnessed and spectacular incidents of noises in the Priest Room had occurred in response to verbal requests from Knowles, violent banging noises had occurred when Knowles was not in the room or even in the building. The 'spirit' or whatever it is either knows the man or knows his voice and reacts accordingly. Fred Knowles is a distinctive individual and he really does seem to be able to 'call up' this particular haunting entity far better than any medium who has visited the house under Club auspices. Knowles does not like anyone to refer to the entity as 'it'; this is a person, he says.

Is it possible, we inevitably ask ourselves, that some of the sounds, the bangs and the knockings at Chingle Hall stem unknowingly from Knowles himself? Is it not strange that the only person whom the spirit will answer is Knowles? During the fourth investigation we had with us two acknowledged mediums, sensitive to haunting entities, and both tried to make contact with the ghost at Chingle Hall or any entities available but without success.

A Ghost Club Society member, Andrew Usher, has also quietly investigated the mysteries of Chingle; in fact he spent over 300 nights there and took many photographs, one of which seems to show the right profile of a man with his hand up to his mouth. Nothing was visible in the Priest Room when he took the photographs, one with flash and one without; both taken because he heard a lot of noise coming from inside the priest hide. The photograph taken without flashlight shows up the profile better, the flash seeming to make the image react to the light. It was dark in the Priest Room at the time and no light was entering the room through the window which could have caused a reflection. He never found an explanation either for the figure captured on the photograph or for the noise emitted from the hide.

Three years after the last official Ghost Club visit in

1980, Fred Knowles told me: 'There is still plenty of noise phenomena here ... BBC Radio Lancashire recorded many bumps, bangs and footsteps; and an apparition has briefly been seen entering the haunted bedroom ... there have been numerous instances of cameras malfunctioning inside the house and ghostly monks have appeared on instant snapshots taken on the south lawn ...'

Andrew Usher has told me:

The first night I went to Chingle I was wondering what was going to happen. Fred Knowles introduced me to Michael Bingham at 7.30 p.m. and we all went upstairs. We sat in the corridor so that we could see down towards the stairs and also towards the John Wall Room; we had the light on in the Priest Room and in the John Wall Room but there was no light in the corridor. We put orange bulbs in the sockets of the lights we were using to counteract the harsh white light.

About 8 p.m. I heard footsteps coming towards us from the stairs sounding like shoes on a wooden floor, although the floor was in fact carpeted, and I put my hand down towards the floor, holding the microphone there. The footsteps stopped just in front of my hand and I seemed to feel icy fingers grasp my hand! I pulled myself free and the footsteps then continued towards the John Wall Room; then they turned left and disappeared into an airing cupboard which, I later learned, is thought to have once been an old doorway into the Priest Room. The footsteps were now in the Priest Room and then, for the best part of half an hour, banging could be heard coming from the hide in that room, very loud banging I may say; then suddenly all was quiet and nothing more happened that night.

Two days later I was in the porch when I heard footsteps coming across the stone bridge over the old moat and as they reached the door and stepped into the porch, I prepared myself to say 'Good afternoon' to a visitor – but there was nobody there. This happened several times and once when I heard the footsteps I saw a faint dark figure pass through the porch and into the house; I followed immediately but it quickly vanished.

One night, about 6.45 p.m., I was looking through the window in the chapel and saw a monk dressed in brown walking towards the drive and I ran outside to meet whoever or whatever it was, but it had disappeared. Various visitors to the Hall have also seen this ghost monk: he is always dressed in brown and he is always seen approaching the house.

The barn across from the house feels evil and depressing to me, a sensation that was shared by Fred Knowles; and I think something horrible must have happened there in the past which has left its mark . . . When Michael Bingham saw bricks being moved in the hide in the Priest Room, I was a witness. I distinctly saw four black fingers pulling at a brick. I was filming with a sound cine camera at the time and on the film you can hear the sounds but the image is rather dark because I had to put the camera into the hide . . . We both ran downstairs to the chapel and found several bricks scattered over the floor there . . . I heard and saw things that I didn't believe were possible . . . I have seen and felt some strange things in other places, but never as much as at Chingle Hall... I would like to see the house scientifically investigated from top to bottom as I feel sure there is much to be found there.

Sadly, for one reason or another, such an investigation has as yet proved impracticable.

The house and the apparent haunting seemed to be Fred Knowles' whole life at that time; later during upheaval and alterations at Chingle and changes in ownership Knowles left and now lives elsewhere and has nothing to do with the Hall. But is it possible that such concentration and love and dedication as Knowles showed towards Chingle can be in some way transferred to the place and the objects that he knew best of all? Can this be, in part at least, the solution to the noises heard when he requested them and when he was in the room – putting the phenomena almost on a par with poltergeist activity? There may be another explanation for the sounds heard when he was not present when they were usually much less powerful; perhaps his thoughts were sufficient in the right atmosphere? His calling to the entity and the immediate answering knocks – could they be related and is it possible that some sort of energy was being used, about which we know nothing?

Andrew Usher visited Chingle Hall in July 1993 and was good enough to send me a note of recent reported happenings there. He starts by saying: 'The apparitions don't seem to be as active as they used to be... A man working on the roof of the barn saw a lady walking from the house across the lawn; he shouted down to ask the lady about getting some water which he required, but she seemed to ignore him. Shortly afterwards he saw her return and as she walked towards the house, again he made his presence known, calling for the water which he required, and again she apparently ignored him. On coming down from the roof to fetch the water himself, he inquired about the unhelpful lady he had seen and was told there was no one else in the house; when he showed his disbelief he was invited to look for himself and he looked in every room in the house and indeed it was empty.

'Another workman, this time working inside the house, sand-blasting the fireplace in the Great Hall, suddenly ran outside screaming that the room went very cold and dark and he thought he saw someone watching him. He couldn't be persuaded to return to the Great Hall on his own.

'Other recent reported phenomena include the scent of lavender and odour of incense; small lights hovering in various rooms; temperature drops for no apparent reason; the feeling of being pushed; bangings and crashing sounds, and the eternal footsteps.

'Other news is that one of the priest hides, the one in the Priest Room, has been blocked up; the drawing room is no longer open to the public and the present owners and occupants, John and Sandra Bruce, welcome responsible visitors who wish to spend a night at Chingle Hall, on a commercial basis. It's all changed now and there is something missing, I don't know what, but I can sense it . . .'

I still get reports of odd happenings at Chingle: water appearing from nowhere that returns, however often it is mopped up; visitors experiencing mysterious bouts of profuse sweating and even blackouts; a headless Cavalier seen on the stairs; a Roman soldier seen inside the house; a 'cold spot' in the Great Hall where some people claim to have seen through the floor and to have seen a body lying below ... but I remember the old days when, under controlled conditions and in the presence of scientists and experienced investigators, loud sounds were heard and recorded – sounds that appeared to occur on request when that request came from Fred Knowles, and as one correspondent put it to me: 'Chingle isn't Chingle without his presence.'

Curry Mallet Manor House

In April 1988, I wrote a personal note to Mrs Dita Mallet, then in her nineties, and asked about the possibility of a Ghost Club all-night investigative visit to her historic home, a manor house that had been in her family for some 900 years! Mrs Mallet can prove direct descent from a Norman knight who fought at the Battle of Hastings in 1066.

In her charming reply from Mallet Court, Mrs Mallet said she would have been pleased to accommodate us for she was deeply attached to the house and gardens and felt she had an affinity with the ghosts that walked there but she had recently sold the property. However, she felt sure we would find the new owners sympathetic and she added her own invitation for us to visit her in her new home so that she could tell us all she knew. I lost no time in approaching the new owner, Mr Daniel O'Sullivan. He was rather anxious that any investigation might re-awaken any past phenomena and I was quick to reassure him that this was most unlikely. We have carried out so many investigations throughout the country over the years and have never heard of any re-awakenings as a result; on the contrary, we are often informed that our visits have resulted in a calming influence. I went on to explain what was involved in our investigative procedures: to ascertain scientifically any changes in temperature, photographic abnormalities, unexplained sounds, and generally explore the possibility of superphysical elements that may be subject to physical examination.

Happily, Mr O'Sullivan was reassured enough to invite us to visit his new home. Having settled on a mutually convenient date I advised Mrs Dita Mallet accordingly, requesting we might visit her, accompanied by Daniel O'Sullivan, about five o'clock on the afternoon of our arrival as 'we might be feeling rather ragged after being up all night so I hope we might come before the vigil; in any case it would be nice to know the possibly most haunted parts of your old home'.

The next Ghost Club programme contained details of the proposed visit to Curry Mallet. As a result, fourteen members volunteered for the visit and a provisional schedule was prepared. For this visit I recommended that each member bring the usual supplies and equipment, such as refreshments, a torch, notebook, pen or pencil, watch, soft-soled shoes, a whistle and if convenient a camera, thermometer, tape recorder and any other equipment that might be useful or interesting. I also reminded the investigators, in the event of anything unusual being seen or heard or suspected at any time, to stand completely still, observe as much as possible and then quietly follow if the manifestation appeared to move. As soon as practicable, they should draw the attention of another member to the apparent manifestation by flashing a torch briefly three times or by blowing three brief blasts on a whistle. Members not on rota duty or any other fixed duty should quietly make their way to the area, keeping special note of anything untoward as they went. Immediately after any such event, detailed notes should be made including time, exact locale, description, other members present, etc.

We arranged to arrive at the Manor House between 4 and 4.30 p.m. on Friday 23 September, and were met by Mr and Mrs O'Sullivan before going on to meet Mrs Dita Mallet and her daughter to take tea with them. From Mrs Mallet, whose family lived at the Manor for so many years, we learned something of the history and ghostly associations of the historic Manor where three kings, William the Conqueror, Henry II and King John have dined in the Great Hall. It is believed that there has been a dwelling on the site of Curry Mallet Manor House for over 1,000 years, indeed Roman coins have been found in the immediate vicinity as well as a Roman well and pottery. A Saxon castle built probably of wood by Prince Bitric stood originally on the site.

In 1068 the Mallet family first established their connection with the place when Gilbert, son of William Mallet Sir de Graville, built a castle on the site of the original Saxon building. The Mallet family is one of the few families that can claim direct descent from a knight or baron who fought at Hastings with the Conqueror – and can prove such a claim, according to Leslie Pine, the acknowledged authority on the period.

Gilbert Mallet was sent to Somerset in 1068 by William the Conqueror to build 'a strong castle' to hold the country against the marauding Welsh and there are many legends associated with the area; among them one concerning the three streams running under the property which, it is said, contribute one of the sources of the Holy Well at Glastonbury. One of the daughters of Henry II, Princess Maud, married Gilbert's son. William the Conqueror is said to have stayed at the castle when he visited Exeter and the West Country; Henry II also stayed here and King John stayed at the castle on many occasions whilst hunting in the nearby forest, and he actually signed state papers during his stay that are now preserved in the State Archives.

Lord William Mallet was one of the barons who rebelled against King John and he stood surety for Magna Carta. In revenge King John had the Pope excommunicate Mallet and all his lands were confiscated, some now being incorporated into those owned by the Duchy of Cornwall.

Between the reign of King John (1199–1216) and the reign of Henry VIII (1509–1547) the castle seems to have been destroyed and what remained was incorporated into the present Manor House. It seems that the castle and about 120 acres were left with the family for King John himself was godfather to a son of William Mallet and by church law it was not possible to completely dispossess a godson. Curry Mallet was restored by Henry III to William Mallet's daughter Helewise Mallet who married Hugh Poyntz. During the Civil War there was considerable damage to the property by Parliamentary forces who tethered their horses in the Great Hall. During the Monmouth Rebellion Judge Jeffries hanged one of the Mallets and transported another to America.

The original water supply, a well, is still situated under the floor of the old keep, the present Panelled Drawing Room, which we used as our Base Room. The Great Hall, incidentally, is remarkable for its eleventh-century 'cruck' roof, the oldest existing one of its kind in England. The present house consists of the Norman Keep, the Great Hall, the Norman spiral staircase and later buildings – the present entrance hall for example being erected just before the last war (c.1938) and eliminating an original carriageway that led to the stables, now converted into flats.

Mrs Dita Mallet, over tea and biscuits in her beautifully appointed sitting room, told us that a number of bodies had been dug up in the garden over the years. Tom Corbett, the clairvoyant well known to Ghost Club Society members, spent a couple of days at Curry Mallet and said afterwards that while the house had several ghosts, the garden was crowded with them! Nearby Crimson Hill had once been known as Bloody Hill and was said to have run with blood after the battle at nearby Sedgemore. There is no doubt that there were many deadly skirmishes during the Monmouth Rebellion in the area resulting in bodies being hastily buried. Among the ghostly episodes long talked about in the locality is the spectral clashing of swords and duellists fighting in the courtyard – especially on one (sadly unspecified!) night of each year.

There have long been stories of a phantom lady at Curry Mallet, roaming the corridors and seen by many people, residents and visitors, over the years. She seems to date from Elizabethan times, judging from descriptions of her attire, and she carries keys at her waist and seems houseproud; possibly she is a housekeeper from long ago.

Mrs Mallet told us that once she had glimpsed a dapper, slim Elizabethan man with a ruff around his neck in the Great Hall on the anniversary of the battle of the Armada and she had later discovered that at the time of the Armada the owner of Curry Mallet had repeatedly paced the Great Hall, worried over the outcome of the momentous battle. Indeed a letter exists from this one-time owner of the Manor saying he had heard that the Armada was coming up the Channel and declaring: 'I spent last night walking up and down the house praying for England.' Something of the trauma of that time seems to have lingered here for this phantom was seen by Mrs Mallet around 1965, and although there are no definite reports of sightings in recent times there are a number of unconfirmed reports. Mr O'Sullivan told us that the Great Hall is sometimes used for weddings and other family gatherings and quite recently a band had been engaged to play at a wedding and they were positioned in the Minstrel Gallery overlooking the Great Hall but they soon decamped and came down to the Great Hall and performed there; he never could discover exactly why.

There have long been stories of a brutal owner of the Manor who at one time imprisoned and ill-treated his wife in the end bedroom overlooking the rose garden and there, just once when attending to some climbing roses from the bedroom window, Mrs Mallet found herself completely and inexplicably but quite overwhelmingly sad, almost broken-hearted, so much so that she has never forgotten it. Researcher and photographer Simon Marsden talked to Mrs Mallet about ghosts a few years before we saw her and said afterwards, 'All her stories were recounted in a calm and dignified voice as if they were quite normal occurrences and it left me with an uneasy feeling that I was part of a "ghostly tapestry" that at any moment might come alive.'

Having walked back through the haunted garden to the Manor, we were taken on a tour of the older parts of Curry Mallet Manor House – the allegedly haunted parts. Mr and Mrs O'Sullivan and their family (none of whom had experienced any 'unusual' happenings during their four years at the Manor) were introduced to the members and after hearing about our plans for the visit they left us to ourselves for the night. Having discussed all we had learned about the stories associated with the Manor we decided to eliminate from the night's vigil one corridor near bedrooms occupied by the youngest of the three children for fear of disturbing any of them during the night.

As refreshments were being prepared before getting down to business, Ghost Club Society member Bob Cato prepared plans of the two floors detailing the ten rooms we planned to keep under surveillance. We decided to position tape recorders in the end bedroom (which we named 'the prison room'); on the Norman spiral staircase and in the Great Hall. While setting up his sound recorder in the Panelled Room, council member Philip Moore had the distinct impression that there was some movement in the adjoining entrance hall but no one was visible there. He stayed where he was for fifteen minutes and all the while he felt certain that 'someone' or 'something' was just outside the room and he had the definite impression of an elderly lady wearing a loose, swinging dress. Several odd sounds were recorded at the beginning of his tape that he was unable to explain. We decided to keep a fourth machine, belonging to myself, for mobile use.

Ten thermometers were placed in strategic positions throughout the area and these were checked by a rota of members every twenty minutes throughout the period of watchfulness; none showed any abnormality. We also distributed ten 'control' or 'trigger' objects throughout the rooms and these too were checked regularly by a rota every twenty minutes, timed between the thermometer readings so that there was a check in all the rooms every ten minutes. There was some unexplained activity during the night among the trigger objects. Beside each thermometer and beside each control object we placed a card which described the object and which was marked with a number allocated to each thermometer or object for checking purposes. Some of these cards were found displaced during the night between patrols – in addition to the thermometer and controls checking, there was also a rota of members who carried out patrols every half-hour when members were expected to patrol the whole area quietly and observe and report *anything* unusual, however trivial. We also instituted three quarter-hour periods of total darkness and total silence, at midnight to 12.15, 2.30 to 2.45 and 4 to 4.15 a.m.

Among the puzzling incidents reported during the night were: slight movement of a 'dagger', a trigger object situated in the courtyard at 10.45 p.m.; the movements in a clockwise direction of approximately 5° of a photograph trigger object situated in the Minstrel Gallery at 11.42 p.m.; the slight but definite movement from the chalk line surrounding it of a crucifix trigger object on the window sill, overlooking the rose garden, in the 'prison room' at 2.24 a.m.; and slight movement of a paperweight trigger object situated in the shower room off one bedroom at 10.15 p.m. There was also an unexplained mark made on a piece of paper left in the entrance hall. All these objects, after verification, were returned to their chalked outlines. At 10.20 p.m., parts of the garden near an ancient wall were found to be unusually cold. This fact was reported by two members and verified by another. A curious clicking sound was heard by one member and the same sound, loud and distinct, was reported by the same member forty-five minutes later. At 12.15 a.m. two members reported a 'cold area' in the middle of the lawn near a hedge.

During the midnight to 12.15 'silence' period a 'creaking or squeaking' sound was heard intermittently in the back garden for the whole period and in fact over almost half an hour. The sound seemed to originate behind a yew tree and it seemed to be localised although no material cause could be found. It was heard by two members and subsequently established that it was not caused by birds or the trees. During the 2.30 to 2.45 'silence' period, there was complete silence in the area although, in fact, the wind was higher than two hours previously. A single word that sounded like a drawn-out 'Ju-lee' was heard by two members in the courtyard, seeming to originate from the back garden. However, two members situated there heard nothing. The same word at the same time was heard by one member from the Base Room, which overlooked the back garden. A faint sound of whispering was heard twice in the vicinity of the entrance hall by one member. Also during this period a curious 'creaking' sound was reported: it was loud enough to cause two members to turn round simultaneously while on duty in the courtyard – which several members felt to be one of the most 'interesting' parts of the whole house. At 2.40 a.m. a 'very strong odour' of fresh earth was reported by one member at the top of the Norman spiral staircase, in an area of five feet in diameter; it lasted about one minute. A very similar smell was reported from the same place at 3 a.m. by a different member, who had no knowledge of the previous report. Between 3 and 3.05 a.m. the card indicating thermometer no. 5 (both of which were situated on the window sill of the Prison Room) was discovered to have moved *three feet*! It had remained unmoved and in position from 11 p.m. until 3 a.m. It was discovered by one member and verified by two others. At 4.30 a.m., a button was discovered on a table in the Base Room. It was unclaimed and did not appear to have belonged to any member present, and it was certainly not there a few minutes earlier. It was of comparatively recent design.

At 4.15 a.m. and later a light in the Minstrel Gallery went on and off intermittently for the rest of our sojourn: council member Trevor Kenward subsequently discovered that it was part of the security set-up and was triggered by sound – this was later confirmed by Mr O'Sullivan who had forgotten to turn it off the night before. Interestingly enough, on the first occasion the light seemed to be triggered by a pencil falling from the deep window recess in the Minstrel Gallery although it seemed to be established afterwards that the sound caused by a pencil falling was *not* sufficient to trigger the light. A piece of paper, as well as the pencil, was discovered to have been moved in this immediate area but it was felt that a draught from the window could have caused these movements. Mr O'Sullivan did not tell us about the band moving from the Minstrel Gallery until the morning after our night's vigil, although several members had remarked upon the curious atmosphere in the Gallery that was not noticed elsewhere. It was reported that several members felt very cold in the Gallery and during the night two raps, a rattling noise, an occasional 'click' and a heavy, regulated rustling sound – almost like footsteps – were recorded when the area was deserted: the recording being played back at 4.40 a.m.

During the course of an impromptu seance at 3 a.m., various sounds were heard and 'messages' received. Opening the attempted communication the organiser asked, 'Can I help you?' and immediately there was a loud rushing of wind down the nearby chimney and exactly the same thing happened at 3.16 a.m. when the question was asked: 'Can we help you?' One minute earlier a single ringing sound was heard. 'Messages' seemed to suggest that the communicating entity was a former inhabitant who lived in the 1600s, possibly the figure seen by Mrs Mallet in the Great Hall, but 'he' said he preferred the garden. This entity gave his initials as FR and said he died in the garden and his remains were disturbed. He went on to say he was murdered and that he was a Mallet. The entity repeated that he was murdered in the garden and buried in the garden, adding that there were other 'spirits' in the garden and also in the house, but most were in the garden. Asked to manifest in some way, such as moving a ringed object, the entity agreed to try and this was prior to the movement of the thermometer card in the 'prison room'. Further 'messages' suggested that the murdered person was a lover of the mistress of the house and when the couple were discovered together they were both murdered by a Mallet, in the garden. The initials FR were verified several times and it was stated that there was something in the house bearing those initials.

At the end of the first seance, immediately the lights were turned on again, one member saw a black cloud about a foot in diameter. It appeared in front of a picture hanging on the wall to the right of the door leading to the entrance hall and remained visible for several seconds before suddenly clearing.

During a second seance at 4 a.m., FR seemed reluctant to communicate and the seance was abandoned for a few minutes. At 4.10 a.m., the third attempted seance began with an entity who accepted FR as his initials but nothing of great moment transpired. A fourth attempt at 4.30 a.m. had FR claiming to have left a message, to have been responsible for moving the thermometer card, and to have produced the button. The entity said he would speak into a tape recorder but he does not appear to have done so. Eventually this entity caused violent movement of a wine glass that was then being used as a communication method and 'he' then seemed to agree with everything that was put to 'him'. The seance was halted. The fifth and final seance began at 4.50 a.m. and again there was a great rushing of wind when the opening question, 'Can we help you?' was asked; but the communicating entity seemed tired and when asked 'Shall we stop?', the answer came 'Yes' so the attempted seance was closed – and again there was a rushing wind down the chimney! All the seances were held in the Base Room (the Panelled Drawing Room) in front of an enormous fireplace.

After the investigative visit had come to an end it was discovered by one member that a recorder positioned in the room leading from the Panelled Room and the stone staircase had had its cassette turned over. Side one which had been inserted to play was found to have nothing on it but side two had been inserted ready to play.

The night at Curry Mallet Manor House was very interesting both from a historical and from a psychic point of view. Objects *were* moved; odd sounds *were* heard; an apparently disembodied voice *was* heard at the same time from three positions and *not* heard from other, apparently nearer, positions. There *was* 'an atmosphere' in parts of the house throughout most of the night and this was reflected in the fact that no member of the party felt in the least tired throughout the whole night (except for one member who developed a heavy cold); there was an unmistakable air of expectancy, a feeling that something might happen at any moment and we were all greatly indebted to the owners for their kindness, their thoughtfulness and their co-operation in allowing us to spend a night in that beautiful, historic, alive and utterly charming Manor House. Mr O'Sullivan kindly presented me with eleven pages of 'Notes on the History of The Manor House, Curry Mallet' for my collection.

I asked Ghost Club Society member Michael Williams, who took part, for his feelings and impressions of the visit to Curry Mallet Manor House and he replied:

The night of Friday 23 September 1988 was one I shall never forget: my first experience of an investigative all-night visit by the Ghost Club. The highlight of the night for me was my first ever participation in a seance, expertly conducted by Ruth Jarvis. This was a fascinating experience – I am sure Ruth has it within her to do outstandingly well in this field – and I was astonished to learn she had only taken charge on a few previous occasions. Earlier in the evening she had given me a private 'reading' which proved very accurate at the time and in the light of later experiences. Ruth is clearly a gifted lady.

Getting back to the operation as a whole, though no ghosts were seen, a number of interesting things did happen, nothing dramatic, but collectively they add up to *something*.

I am very responsive to atmosphere and found the Manor House strong in atmosphere. In certain parts there was a strong sense of the past – this was especially so in the garden. Outside, during the night, one felt right on the frontier of the unknown. You had the feeling that something of a supernatural nature could happen at any moment – and this was not mere wishful thinking.

I am sure spirits from the past do come to that garden. There may be some unfinished business or they may have loved the place – or someone there – very deeply. And who can blame them coming back to that lovely corner of Somerset?

Eton Vicarage

One December day, a few years ago, I spotted two newspaper reports concerning a church and vicarage at Eton, Berkshire. The *Daily Mirror* stated:

A congregation has been forced to abandon its church – because they say it is haunted by evil spirits. The parishioners are so scared that they are moving out at the end of the year. They believe that their 130 year old parish church beside the Thames at Eton, Berkshire, was built on a spot where devil worship and pagan rites, including human sacrifice, were performed centuries ago.

Vicar's wife Mrs Annie Johnson, said: 'I have never felt happy here, nor has my husband.' Several years ago church authorities called in an exorcist to banish the ghosts. He failed. Mrs Johnson added: 'He heard young girls screaming and shrieking. He told us the forces were very powerful.' Since then strange things have continued to happen. Fires have been lit in the altar. Pews and mats have been moved.

The vicar, the Rev. Christopher Johnson, believes that the church was recently used for pagan rituals. His wife explained: 'He found a window smashed, his vestments stolen and candles had been placed round the church and lit as if for some awful purpose...'

The other newspaper report, by Robert McGowan in the *Daily Express*, was dated two days later and read:

The parishioners walked slowly, their faces pinched by the bitter cold of the morning. Just eleven people answering the summons of a single ring from the bell of a church some say has been taken over by the devil.

The vicar's wife, speaking softly, not too keen to speak at all, said: 'The devil has won this time, but it's not over yet.' Sunday service at St John the Evangelist at Eton, Berkshire, came and went yesterday with an alleged shadow of evil cast across the joy of Christmas. St John's will close down in the New Year because not enough people pray there any more and because there is not enough cash to keep it going. And, says the vicar and his wife, because of the atmosphere created by the presence of dark forces.

The Rev. Christopher Johnson, vicar of the 130 year old St John's nestling on the edge of the playing fields of Eton College said: 'There is much I would like to say about the evil here, but I have been forbidden to do so.' He added: 'The Archdeacon has told me not to comment.'

His wife Anne was, however, free to speak of the evil

spirits some say have given the devil a victory. She said: 'There is evil here. It has driven people from the church. It is real and it is frightening.' The Johnsons have been at St John's for thirteen years. Nine years ago an exorcism was performed. Mrs Johnson reckoned the prince of evil took a few knocks, but then returned. She added: 'We have not imagined any of this. The then bishop called for the exorcism, not us. It was a subtle force, certainly evil. The exorcist found that the church had probably been built on a pagan burial ground. Windows have been broken, vestments taken, candles unaccountably lit. I agree, it sounds like vandalism, but it is more than that. I have felt physical pain. I have been frightened. It may sound irrational but there are forces here to be reckoned with. After the exorcism, the forces seemed less powerful, but they are still here. The congregation used to be large. This was a fine family church. Once we had a thousand people here. The devil has won this time. But it's not the end of the story. We will not give up. The evil that is here will be driven out.'

But parishioner Mrs Elizabeth Hazell, a grandmother whose husband is a house master at Eton, said: 'Ghosts? I have never seen any and I've been coming here for thirty years. It's all cock and bull. There are no evil spirits.'

I wrote to the Rev. Christopher Johnson expressing my interest and he wrote back suggesting I might like to come over for a chat; adding, to my considerable interest, that in fact the vicarage was more haunted than the church! 'There is much I can tell you about the evil here,' he said. A few days later my wife and I called at the vicarage.

The vicar told us that the church, dedicated to St John the Evangelist, had in fact been closed for financial reasons but odd things certainly had taken place there, especially some fifteen years earlier, shortly before he was inducted to the parish. Soon after being inducted in 1967, he discussed the matter with his bishop and a spiritualist medium visited Eton and 'cleansed' both the church and the vicarage. This man said the spirits of a number of virgins had remained on the site after they had been sacrificed there many, many years before.

Subsequently the Rev. Anthony Duncan, who carried out the exorcism, said: 'There certainly was an evil presence there when I did the cleansing ceremony. Actually it was one of the most unpleasant I've ever done ... there were many very disturbed spirits there.'

The Archdeacon of Buckingham, the Venerable John Bone, also visited the Rev. Christopher and Mrs Johnson and he looked in at the apparently afflicted church. 'The Johnsons had said that there were evil spirits in the church,' he said afterwards. 'I have not experienced any manifestations there.'

My wife and I found the Rev. Christopher and Mrs Johnson to be a charming couple who were genuinely worried by all the odd and strange and frightening things that had happened while they had been at Eton. They always seemed to look for a rational explanation first for their own experiences and those of other people. They talked about what had happened in an open and sensible way and were only too willing to explore all possible explanations for what they, their family, their ecclesiastical

The cottage at Borley, Essex, at the time of the disturbances

ovey House, Branscombe, Devon,
here shadows of the past linger on
e brightest day

Peter Underwood at Bovey House

Bramshill House, long known as Hampshire's most haunted house

Bromfield Manor, Shropshire, where ghostly happenings have been reported both inside the house and in the garden

The Bull, Long Melford, Suffolk, at the time of the alleged poltergeist disturbances

The Bull. Colonel Dawson and the head waiter with one of the 'poltergeist projected' objects

Chingle Hall, Lancashire, the scene of innumerable ghostly happenings

Historic and haunted Curry Mallet Manor House, Somerset

The vicar and his wife outside the haunted church and vicarage at Eton, Berkshire (*Downing/Daily Express*)

The interior of haunted Glamis Castle, Scotland (*The British Tourist Authority*)

The haunted Fox Tower at Farnham Castle, Surrey

The Great Hall at Farnham Castle, where several ghosts and a wealth of ghostly activity has been reported

Gosling Hall, Suffolk, during the Ghost Club investigation. Note the 'trigger' object on the stairs and the thermometer on the wall of the stairway

Berry Pomeroy Castle, Devon, at the time of the Ghost Club visit

Harlaxton Manor, Lincolnshire, a Victorian dream palace (*University of Evansville*)

The atmospheric Great Hall at Harlaxton Manor (*University of Evansville*)

colleagues, their friends and neighbours, and their congregation and strangers reportedly experienced at various times of daylight and darkness.

We spent some time in the nearby church with the Johnsons and also alone there, and although I do not consider myself especially sensitive to what is called 'atmosphere' I must confess that there was something about that place that made me feel certain that the whole environment was indeed conducive to psychic activity. I have visited literally hundreds of places that are said to be haunted, including scores of churches, the commonest of all uninhabited buildings reported to be haunted, and I have to say I have never experienced anything quite like the feeling I had in that church at Eton. I can remember it now and it is not a pleasant feeling. My wife felt it too; in fact, we both experienced this, to us, unique atmosphere immediately on entering the church. It was a feeling neither of us had had in a church before, nor have we had it since. I see from my notes I described it at the time as 'an aura of evil' and I still think that an apt description.

Back at the vicarage, in the comfortable lounge and over coffee and biscuits, the vicar and his wife said they were more than happy for us to bring down a party of Ghost Club members to spend the night with time divided between the empty church and the occupied vicarage. I set about enlisting the help and co-operation of some of our experienced members, including Dr Vernon Harrison, his wife Elsie, council member Ken Lazenby, life member Steuart Kiernander and Mrs Frances Jones, a member for over thirty years. A few days later, armed with various apparatus and an objective outlook, eight of us arrived, met the vicar and his wife, heard the full story of the case from their point of view and carried out an investigation that was as interesting as it was long and varied.

Among the unexplained happenings, we learned, were the deliberate and potentially dangerous tripwires across the path that had caused Mrs Johnson to have a nasty fall and also one of their daughters who came home with a badly cut leg. On a very different level there were unexplained footsteps that sounded in the house and the rattling of the heavy Victorian letterbox on the front door, followed by the sound of running footsteps; this pattern of sounds had been heard many, many times yet immediate investigation never solved the mystery, there were never any letters or messages or any physical explanation for the distinct sound of footsteps, heard by all members of the family, sometimes individually and sometimes collectively. The result was always the same: nothing.

Years later, and it really was *years* after these curious footsteps and apparent rattling of the letterbox had been heard scores of times by all the occupants of the vicarage, the vicar learned that the first incumbent of the parish, who had occupied the then new vicarage more than a century earlier, had been a typical Victorian tyrant of a father. He had, so the story goes, five daughters and he was very strict with them, never allowing any of them to have gentlemen callers when they were quite old enough to be married. Always he actively discouraged in every way he could any association of his daughters with young men.

However, some of the young men were persistence itself, as young men tend to be, and at quiet moments they would write notes to the girls concerned and slip the notes through the noisy letterbox and hurriedly run off for fear of alerting the girls' strict father. He was in the habit of using the front room nearest to the front door of the house as his office and he invariably heard the click of the letterbox, and even if he had not heard the stealthy footsteps approaching the house, he would then hear the running footsteps as the young man made his getaway. This happened on numerous occasions and, immediately on the alert, the anxious father would be out of his room and intercepting any messages before the girls could get there. As we listened to this plausible story of days gone by it occurred to us that something of the tension and frustration and anger associated with this oft-repeated incident may possibly have somehow become locked into the atmosphere of the house, to be repeated, in sound, years later; possibly under special and particular conditions, either climatic, atmospheric or in the vicinity of certain people who unconsciously aided the manifestation.

Interestingly enough, one exorcist who had spent a lot of time exploring the house, said afterwards that he was certain that there were three bedrooms where the spirits of three girls were individually 'impressed', and he said he thought he had succeeded in 'releasing those chained souls'. We were told that each of the occupants' three children had, over a number of years, reported seeing unexplained phantom forms in the bedrooms indicated by the exorcist. Unexplained forms were also reported, by occupants of the house and by visitors, on a turning of one of the stairways – stairs and stairways being usually one of the most haunted parts of a haunted house.

Among other distressing happenings that affected more

than one member of the then household, we heard that there had been several instances of apparent spontaneous possession – some affecting the vicar himself. Mrs Johnson told us that on one occasion she was awakened in the middle of the night by the sound of her husband talking loudly in his sleep. When she carefully awakened him she was astonished to hear him speaking in a strange tongue. On several other occasions he seems to have been completely 'taken over' by some malevolent entity or influence and he then acted completely out of character. Once, to her horror, Mrs Johnson woke up to find herself almost strangled by something invisible, something that had her by the throat, and only with the greatest difficulty did she escape from the frighteningly tangible but completely invisible presence.

Over the years all the various occupants of the house had come to believe that the room at the front of the house, near the front door, once the office of the tyrannical Victorian father, was the most haunted part of the property and frequently, we were told, it had 'a terrible atmosphere'. There were parts of the garden, too, that were 'very haunted'.

Later in the night it was decided that attempts would be made to 'contact' any entity that might be present in the house, with the 'very' haunted front room being the favourite for various attempts at such contact by the means of seances. The Johnsons kindly agreed to our using an antique circular table with 'birdcage' fitment (a small, square, columnal support under the centre of the table) for the seances and this was carefully moved from the lounge into the front room. Everyone present, including the vicar and his wife, took part in the first seance attempt, in dim light. There was little response and after a while the seance was abandoned and the vicar, who had a heavy day in front of him, retired for the night.

Some hours later at midnight, hoping to obtain some result in the haunted room, in the company of psychic and sympathetic sitters, four members of the visiting party tried again, using the same table. Mrs Frances Jones, a sensitive, sympathetic and experienced psychic investigator, took control. Once again nothing happened. After a short rest requests were made for raps or table-tilting or something to indicate to us the possible presence of an invisible entity. Still no result. Those participating in the seance changed places and a glass and letters were introduced as a possible means of communication, but all to no avail; although the glass did seem to show some signs of independent movement at one stage.

After a rest we tried yet again, Mrs Jones reminding us that we must all try to concentrate; we must open ourselves to the possibility of communication; and we must think positively: there could well be an entity present, an entity that only needed the right atmosphere to communicate. Personally she felt sure that some entity was indeed present and she repeatedly encouraged 'it' to manifest.

Eventually a few raps sounded and then there was silence. In retrospect it sounds little and nothing of a supernatural character but I can assure you that having been in that haunted room for hours in near darkness, everyone trying hard to will something to happen, and all to the background of the earnest voice of Frances Jones repeatedly appealing and cajoling and imploring whatever entities might be present, and then suddenly, and from a position in the room yards from anyone, distinct raps – quite loud, quite definite, and certainly not originating from anyone present and seemingly in answer to a specific request – it was quite a moment. We waited, but nothing more was heard.

We all rested again and then returned to the table, sat round it and with our fingers lightly resting on an upturned wine glass, we requested some manifestation – and this time we were rewarded! Some force seemed to be trying to move not only the glass but the table itself which seemed to heave and move and tip at one side, and then the other. Quickly and quietly experienced Frances Jones verbally requested some sign of a presence, either by table-tipping or turning. After a few seconds the complete table seemed to shudder and we all expected it to tilt, but instead the whole top of the table slid round to the right! And, as the legs and lower part of the table remained stationary, we discovered something that none of us had previously known and something that is most unusual for this kind of table: the top revolved on the base. Before we could become accustomed to what was really happening, the table top proceeded to move, first to the right, then to the left, backwards and forwards, backwards and forwards, faster and faster. Most, if not all, the sitters round the table lifted their hands away from the table but still it moved exactly as before: forwards and then backwards, forwards and back again.

Once again the value of Frances Jones' presence was felt and she quickly established a code whereby movement of the table to the right meant 'yes' and movement to the left meant 'no'. She then began asking questions and we seemed to receive sensible answers! Other sitters joined in asking questions and they all seemed to be answered, sometimes with sitters' hands resting lightly on the table, sometimes without anyone touching it. By this means it soon became apparent that the communicating entity was or believed he was responsible for the death of someone who had once resided in the house; a child, it transpired, whose body had been buried in the garden, beside a bush (although a body has never been discovered). The communicating entity appeared to be unhappy, frustrated, lonely, undecided what to do for the best and 'he' requested prayer. The Lord's Prayer was recited by all the sitters and by the time we reached the end the table had become still and did not move afterwards.

Eventually the sitters adjourned to the next room, the lounge, where the rest of the party, including the vicar's wife, were quietly chatting about this and that. As we began to relate something of what had happened during the series of seances, before we had really said anything, Mrs Johnson quickly interjected to say she had always thought there was something very odd about one part of the garden, near a bush. She had always had a feeling of sadness there and to everyone's astonishment she said she had often wondered whether a child could have been buried there!

Little further happened at the haunted vicarage that night but Mrs Frances Jones, who was hardly in her first flush of youth and had driven from her Chelsea home that evening, was invited to rest and spend the next day and night at the vicarage. She told me afterwards that she had not the slightest doubt that the house was haunted by several female phantoms and by a domineering male ghost. She said she had seen 'him' on the stairs and felt she had been able to converse with him and persuade him to depart from the house and leave its present occupants in peace.

After our visit we felt able to write to Mr and Mrs Johnson saying that we thought the atmosphere in the 'haunted room' was much improved after the seances held there and that the whole house was probably now clear of any malevolent influence. We did ask to be advised of any subsequent disturbance of any kind and since we heard nothing we assumed all was indeed well following our visit; a visit that would never be forgotten by all those taking part.

In September 1993, the Rev. Christopher Johnson informed me that St John's church at Eton was made redundant as there were three churches in the parish and that it suffered from persistent vandalism. Eventually a college took it over and it has now been converted into four flats. Perhaps the boundless enthusiasm and practicality of youth has, at last, driven out whatever evil there may once have been there?

Farnham Castle

After I published the first comprehensive gazetteer of British ghosts, *The A–Z of British Ghosts*, more than twenty years ago a correspondent from Hove, Sussex, Mrs Elizabeth Cox, took me to task for not including the hauntings associated with Farnham Castle, where she told me she had once resided and where she had distinctly and unmistakably seen a ghost in the Great Hall, not to mention other witnesses and other ghostly phenomena . . .

Following some correspondence and a personal interview with Mrs Cox, I learned that she had been a lady's maid fifty years earlier when the castle was a private residence. She had, in fact, arrived at Farnham Castle in 1919, when she was just fourteen years old. On arrival at the 'huge, cold and grim' castle – which was how she remembered it – there was an enormous log fire burning in the fireplace of the Great Hall which she was hurried through on the way to the top floor of Fox Tower where she was to share a room with four other young housemaids. Having donned the black ankle-length uniform provided, she hurried to the servants' hall for high tea, and there she was joined by the rest of the staff, sitting on long wooden forms on either side of a long white-wood table.

She learned that a single bell was rung in the tower to call staff for meals, a bell that could be heard for miles ... and in later years various inhabitants of the castle and many local people reported hearing the echoing 'clang' of a bell from the direction of the castle, although in fact the bell, if it still exists in the tower, has not been rung for many years now.

It was quite fascinating to hear Elizabeth Cox talk of those bygone days when she and the other servants were all kept busy, for there were always guests, family and friends coming from far and near, especially at Christmas and other holiday times. She was able to describe in considerable detail the famous people, the great events, and the enormous banquets that used to be held in the Great Hall. Often, on such occasions, the young Elizabeth Cox would join the other servants and steal into the Long Gallery and surreptitiously peep over or through the railings to gape at the fine uniforms and evening dress of the gentlemen and the wonderful gowns and dresses and jewellery of the beautiful ladies. Often there would be thirty or more seated at the long refectory table made, along with other castle furniture, from oak trees that grew in the adjoining park. Even the deer-skin seats of chairs were made from animals that roamed the parkland where there were always at least 365 deer, one for every day of the year. Everyone would be much too occupied to notice the wide-eyed girls hiding in the gallery overlooking the Great Hall.

Beautiful rich tapestries hung from the walls (brought

back from the Holy Land during the thirteenth-century Crusades) between huge portraits of past and present owners and occupants of the castle in a room where Kings and Queens of England have feasted many times over the centuries. In Elizabeth Cox's day, the whole enormous room would be illuminated by hundreds of candles, their light flickering on antique silver, grotesque candlesticks and elaborate floral arrangements. The plain oak floorboards and the doors and panelling would be polished to perfection by the men servants and strictly inspected by the liveried footmen whose word was law. In the winter a roaring log fire would burn in the massive fireplace with its stags' heads over the mantelpiece and the axes and spears and swords brought back from long-forgotten wars; the hand-burnished metal seeming to glow with a life of its own. It was on such an occasion as happy young Elizabeth Cox looked down on the merry scene from the Long Gallery overlooking the Great Hall that she suddenly saw the ghost of a priest or monk.

He stood with his back to the Hall, seemingly looking out of the window at the far end of the Gallery, a window that overlooked the former moat. There were stories of phantom monks walking in procession hereabouts towards the site of a well where several bodies had been hidden for years before being eventually recovered. Could the monk, thought Elizabeth Cox later, have been looking down on such a procession or even on his brethren; or was he worried at what might be found there one day?

At all events Elizabeth Cox watched the figure for several minutes, or so it seemed to her. He was a tall man and he wore a brown habit and a round cap-like hat, putting her in mind of a skull-cap, on his head. He appeared to be absolutely solid and real although she knew at the time that she was looking at a ghost. Having explored the still and silent figure with her eyes, Elizabeth Cox turned away for a moment when a companion whispered something to her. When she looked again the figure had completely disappeared.

At no time did she feel frightened but she was puzzled and interested and, leaving her companions, she pressed herself against the wall where she could not be seen by the guests below and hurried along the length of the Gallery to where she had seen the figure. There was no sign of anything to account for the figure she had seen and she felt sure it would not have been possible for a real person to have completely disappeared so quickly. Examining the place where Elizabeth Cox told me she saw the figure I found it difficult to appreciate how this was possible until she explained that since those days a wall had been built and today the window is no longer visible from the end of the Gallery. Elizabeth Cox often wondered whether repeated reports of the phantom monk were one of the reasons that staff were not really allowed in the Long Gallery. She never forgot that sighting and fifty years later it was still a vivid recollection.

Elizabeth Cox told me that she and others at the castle in those days often had the feeling that they were being watched; that many eyes were watching them, in fact, and the impression conveyed was that the watchers were not happy spirits. In a way the old castle with its many shadowy corridors and dark rooms seemed to be full of intrigue, pulsating with memories of happenings past and present that never reached the outside world. She never doubted that the castle had seen many violent deaths and deeds of wickedness, events that had left behind unexplained sounds and occasionally sights that seemed to be instilled in the atmosphere of the place.

Soon she learned that there were other ghosts at Farnham Castle. Fox Tower, where she slept, was, and perhaps still is, haunted by the ghost of Bishop Morley (1626–84) who lived for years in a small room there. On the one hand he spent thousands of pounds renovating the castle after the restoration of Charles II, while on the other he slept in a coffin in that cell-like apartment, perhaps as a self-imposed penance for some long-forgotten misdeed, and there he eventually died. His ghost was often seen and heard fifty years ago, walking the corridors and in particular one of the landings leading to the tower that he must have known well during his lifetime. Significantly there have been recent sightings and reports of dis-embodied footsteps in the same area.

Other reported ghosts at Farnham Castle included a little dancing girl who may date from about the fourteenth century. Since Roman times it had been an occasional practice to produce tiny but perfectly formed dancing girls – midgets really – for the amusement and entertainment of the upper classes. Some were certainly brought to England at the time of the early Crusades and presented to some of the great houses. This dancing girl seems to have displeased her lord in some way and he punished her by forcing her to dance up and down the massively long table in the Great Hall, time and time again, to entertain and amuse his guests. In the end she fell exhausted off the end of the table

147

and, like some wounded animal seeking a quiet place to die, she crawled away from the mocking laughter and out of the Great Hall and up the stairs – but then maybe she fell again, at all events she expired halfway up the stairway. Elizabeth Cox and other witnesses, including some of the occupants of the castle at the time of our visit, have felt the sad presence of the expiring dancing girl or heard her dying gasps, and there have also been those, completely unaware of the story, who have seen a pathetic little figure dancing for her life in the frantic exhibition that was to lead to her death in this castle of ghosts and memories.

Another ancient stairway in this ancient castle is apparently haunted by a grey-robed, monk-like figure that glides down the stairs on sunny afternoons. Nor is the figure wispy or transparent, as so many people think of ghosts, but it appears to be solid and real although it moves in an odd, disjointed fashion and is seen to be there one moment and gone the next.

Farnham Castle is now occupied by the Centre for International Briefing and the then Director, Wilfred E. Grenville-Grey, agreed to my bringing a half-dozen members of the Ghost Club – and Mrs Elizabeth Cox – to spend a night at the castle, using as our Base Room the Great Hall with its memories of royal feastings and happy and sad associations.

Overlooking the Great Hall, opposite the Gallery where Elizabeth Cox was hiding when she saw the ghost monk, there is a short gallery, now known as the Minstrels' Gallery, although Elizabeth Cox informed us that no music was ever played there to her knowledge. But at the eastern end of that little gallery, Mr Grenville-Grey and various members of his staff repeatedly experienced an almost overwhelming feeling of oppression; a crushing feeling, very frightening, almost as though the very walls would contract with terrifying results. Elizabeth Cox understood exactly, as she had had precisely the same feeling in other parts of the castle; not all the time and not always in the same parts of the castle but various apartments, various silent, deserted rooms, various dark passages and great stairways – all of them seemed to her to emit dark thought waves on occasions.

We met, during our visit, a resident bursar, who had several times heard the sound of footsteps in the older part of the castle, footsteps that certainly had no normal explanation. Others too, residents and visitors alike, have heard unexplained footsteps and other noises which have never been satisfactorily explained. We also met a resident who had encountered one of the castle ghosts on the staircase outside the Great Hall one sunny afternoon in 1973. She suddenly became aware of a silent grey-robed, monk-like figure that seemed to glide towards a window and there it disappeared. Again the figure was not transparent or indistinct but rather it seemed quite solid and the witness at first took it for a real person. But then she noticed that it moved rather oddly, it made no sound and, when it almost reached the window, was there one second and the next second there was nothing to be seen.

We also met a lady who lived almost opposite the castle, in Castle Street, and she told us that one night in 1960 she had stayed in the older part of the castle. It had always been one of her ambitions to sleep in Farnham Castle but she never wished to repeat the experiment. During the night she had found herself awake with the feeling that the bedclothes were being pulled off her bed. She was sleeping, as she always does, on her side, and when she was fully awake she was startled to find that the bedclothes were indeed being slowly but steadily pulled towards the foot of the bed. She took a firm hold of the top of the bedclothes and found that she had to exert considerable strength to keep the sheet and blankets on the bed. There was no doubt about the matter whatever, she told us, and it was extremely frightening; the bedclothes were pulled from the bed by something invisible that had great strength.

As she turned over to ascertain whether she could see exactly what was happening and who or what was pulling the bedclothes, she realised that there was 'something' in the corner of the room. She could see nothing whatever to account for the pulling of the bedclothes but in the far corner of the room something crouched – something that had no definite shape or form but seemed to be huddled, shrinking into the blackness, pulsating and exuding a sense of evil. Our informant told us that after a while the dark form disappeared and the tugging on the bedclothes did not recur. It was the only experience of its kind that she had ever had and she rarely talked about it, but it was quite terrifying and nothing would induce her to spend another night at Farnham Castle. One wonders whether this was the 'haunted room' referred to by the Victorian author Edna Lyall, who stayed at the castle as a child and talks of such a room and the 'eerie terror' therein.

Even the surrounds of the castle are haunted, it seems. There have been many reports of a shadowy and unidentified female form half-glimpsed in the old castle gateway that is frequently open to the public, and on the steep tarmacked hill leading from the town to the castle there have been numerous reports of the sound of boots crunching on gravel, especially on cold winter nights; sounds that must once have echoed here many times in the long distant past but now there seems no possible physical reason for the sounds of shifting gravel that seem to emanate from the centre of the narrow road, and nothing is ever seen.

Sitting in the echoing Great Hall at dead of night we talked of ghosts and we tried impromptu seances. We received a number of odd responses to leading questions but nothing very convincing or evidential. Several of the party reported seeing a dark shape at the bottom of the stairs outside the Great Hall and this occurred not once but several times during the night and to different members of the investigating team, but we never found anything to explain what had been seen. These 'sightings' were accompanied by an indisputable but inexplicable lowering of temperature but within minutes the temperature was normal again and any possible ghost had passed us by.

There were also several incidents when individual investigators became almost overwhelmed with feelings of unhappiness and sadness at one end of the Minstrel Gallery. As soon as they left a particular spot, the feeling disappeared but I see from my notes that this happened on no fewer than five different occasions through the night, to five different people, none of whom was aware that other members of the party had reported exactly the same sensation of extreme emotion at precisely the same place!

I always remember that my wife left us and went home in

the early hours. She had arranged to prepare a hot snack breakfast for us all as we lived nearby. But after she left a 'sensitive' who was present said there was little point in holding any more seances since the person with all the power was no longer there! Be that as it may, Farnham Castle holds many secrets and there is no denying the distinct and very strange atmosphere that is to be found in parts of the castle at midnight and in the early hours.

Glamis Castle

It is a good many years ago now that I first visited Glamis Castle but in common with many visitors the first sight of Glamis is unforgettable. That haunted pile: keep, tower, turrets and battlements, solid and silent and splendid in the sunshine but with a memorable air of mystery about it even in the brightest conditions. I have good reason never to forget the first time I approached that splendid seat of the earls of Strathmore, along the tree-lined drive on a shimmering summer day.

What a place Glamis is for those who love mysteries! Here I saw the Haunted Chamber where unexplained noises and strange nocturnal visitors have been heard and seen; the strange rooms that seem to have no doors; the everlasting blood-stain in King Malcolm's room where Malcolm II was murdered in the eleventh century (no amount of scrubbing and cleaning would remove it so in the end the whole floor was boarded over!); the Queen Mother's haunted sitting room; the tower room where 'Earl Beardie' Crawford is reputed to have played dice with the devil; the 'Mad Earl's Walk', a roof-top walkway where the famous monster of Glamis used to take his exercise; the ghostly crypt with its secret chamber; and the little chapel with its ghostly Grey Lady. For this is the most famous of all haunted castles in Scotland, perhaps the most haunted property in Britain – possibly in the whole world.

Here an unidentified 'tall dark figure' has been glimpsed on numerous occasions; a ghostly black boy haunts the Queen Mother's sitting room in broad daylight; 'Earl Beardie' walks at night time while both the White Lady, who haunts the Clock Tower, and the Grey Lady, at her devotions in the chapel, are likely to appear at any time of the day or night, according to witnesses' reports.

Ghost Clubber James Wentworth Day spent a week at Glamis with its ninety rooms. It was a week he never forgot, and it was the nights he dreaded. He told me that if ever a place was haunted, it was Glamis. He believed it had at least nine ghosts and, under the auspices of the Ghost Club, he sat alone in its haunted rooms, its dark corridors and passages, its vaulted hall, quiet chapel and cold stone dungeons – and he saw and heard some of the ghosts of Glamis.

The ghost most often seen these days is the silent Grey Lady who is usually seen in the vicinity of the delightful, deserted and ornate chapel. When I was there on one occasion, the then Earl of Strathmore told me he had seen the apparition on three occasions and she had also been seen by many of his family and by the occasional visitor. During his stay, Jimmy Wentworth Day decided to take a rest from examining the family papers in the Charter Room and one afternoon he strolled about the castle and found himself in the vicinity of the chapel, off the Great Hall.

His footsteps echoed strangely in the Great Hall and several times he thought he almost glimpsed a shadowy form but if a ghost it was, then it was a shy one for each time as he turned to look directly at it, the 'shadow' had disappeared. He tried to put it down to imagination or a trick of the uncertain light but he had seen the shadow move into deeper shadow as he peered and he was not sorry to leave that part of what may well be the oldest inhabited castle in Scotland.

As he entered the tiny chapel he recalled the stories he had been told and the people he had spoken to about the mysterious Grey Lady. The Dowager Lady Granville, the Queen Mother's sister, was actually inside the chapel one sunny afternoon playing some music, when she suddenly had the feeling that she was not alone, that there was someone in the chapel with her. She looked round and was astonished to see a little lady in grey, kneeling in one of the pews, seemingly praying. As usual with genuine ghost sightings, Jimmy learned that the figure appeared to be completely solid and natural and Lady Granville particularly noticed the dress in detail including the unusually large buttons and the overall neat appearance of the phantom form – for she realised what she was seeing when she saw that the sun shining through the chapel window behind the Grey Lady actually shone *through* the figure and made a pattern on the floor. In spite of everything Lady Granville didn't feel at all frightened or even perturbed and she turned back to her music and continued playing quietly. When she had finished the Grey Lady had vanished as silently and mysteriously as she had appeared. Jimmy knew the Queen Mother herself had also witnessed this gentle apparition.

He recalled too the experience of Timothy, the sixteenth Earl of Strathmore and Kinghorne who went to the chapel one afternoon to check some detail in one of the de Wint pictures that hang there. After looking at the picture in question for some minutes he turned round to leave the chapel when he saw the Grey Lady, kneeling and apparently praying in one of the pews, exactly as his aunt had seen her. Lord Strathmore too felt no sense of fear or even surprise; he had heard too many first-hand and reliable reports of the ghost being seen to doubt that she did indeed appear. He had no wish to disturb her, seemingly at her devotions, so he quietly tiptoed out of the chapel and left the Grey Lady to her own devices.

He told Jimmy that other people had seen the same ghost at different times of the day but usually when the sun was shining, odd as it may sound. He added that he had no idea who she might be or why she should haunt the chapel although Jimmy subsequently spoke to several witnesses and other interested parties who thought she might be Janet, Lady Glamis, wife of the sixth Lord Glamis, who was burned alive as a witch at Edinburgh more than 400 years ago.

Jimmy recalled a personal experience that a visitor had related to him. He too had spent several nights at Glamis and once he was awakened in the middle of the night by the sound of frantic knocking at his bedroom door. Thinking that a fire or some other emergency must be the cause for the urgent-sounding knocks, he hurriedly rose from his bed and opened the door; but outside all was quiet and no one was anywhere in sight. As he prepared to return to bed the knocking sounded again and now it appeared to originate from the spot where he stood, the doorway itself, although no human being was producing the persistent knocking which gradually grew fainter and finally ceased. Then a frightful shriek sounded at his elbow and the visitor rushed back to the comparative safety of his bed and he left the castle early next morning.

That afternoon in the quiet chapel, Jimmy Wentworth Day looked carefully around him and stood for a moment in the shadow of the doorway before he entered the chapel. He saw no movement of any kind now and he heard no sound of any kind; nothing to suggest that anyone or anything was in the chapel or anywhere near. As quickly as he could he opened the door of the chapel and entered. Inside, too, all was quiet and a hurried glance all round satisfied him that he was the only person present.

He walked quickly towards the altar, glancing at the empty pews, the works of art adorning the walls about him and the painted ceiling overhead. When he had almost reached the altar, he thought he heard a sound and he turned, peering into every part of the chapel; every inch seemed clearly visible and there were no odd shadows to alarm him. Having ascertained that the chapel was deserted, he was about to resume his stroll round the oratory when he became aware that, over to his left, a figure was kneeling in one of the pews. At first he thought she (for it was unmistakably a she) must have been there all the time, yet he was certain he had made sure the chapel was empty when he had entered and he felt sure the form had not been there seconds before when he had turned and surveyed the whole place ... odd.

He looked more closely at the form. The veiled head was bowed but he could distinguish some of the features; she wore a ring on one hand and there were large buttons down the front of the grey gown. The figure made not the slightest movement as he watched and he gingerly stepped towards it, slowly and quietly, a few inches at a time. As he drew nearer the form somehow seemed to become less distinct. He stopped and studied it again. It was still motionless, still silent, and it was still there with head bowed and hands clasped but now, he realised, and his heart missed a beat at the realisation, he could see the pew *through* the figure! He took another step forward – and the form completely vanished. A second earlier it had all seemed so real, so convincing and so definite ... Later Jimmy tended to feel that perhaps his imagination was playing tricks on that occasion – but he was careful not to visit the chapel at Glamis alone ever again.

Soon after Jimmy arrived at Glamis Castle, the Earl of Strathmore had led the way and bounded up the dark stone circular stairway of the castle ahead of his guest, showing Jimmy round. When the visitor remarked on the great size of the stone newel they were circling as they made their way up the wide and easy gradient, he learned that the newel was in fact hollow and down its centre passed unseen the long cords and chains and weights of the enormous clock seen outside at the head of the stair turret. The Earl said he always wondered whether the rumbling of the weights in their confined space, especially when the clock struck at dead of night, might perhaps account for some of the 'ghostly' sounds associated with that area of the castle. Jimmy said he thought that an excellent suggestion and one that could, to a great extent, be easily put to the test and established one way or the other. But the Earl was not really listening and instead he flung open a door, high up in the uninhabited part of the castle, and announced, 'This is where the ghost of Earl Beardie gambles with the devil. There's the trap-door through which the devil vanished – or so they say!'

The long, bare, white-walled room seemed quiet enough and free from any psychic atmosphere – and yet? Jimmy told me he found the room intriguing. The so-called Earl Beardie was a Lord Crawford long ago, explained Lord Strathmore. 'A master of all the vices, it seems. He is said to have been gambling here one Sunday with one of my ancestors and they quarrelled. Lord Glamis threw Beardie – a huge man with a straggling beard – out of the room!'

Old Beardie, according to legend, stamped up to his room – the room in which Jimmy Wentworth Day and the Earl of Strathmore were then standing. He roared for someone, anyone, to come and gamble with him but no one dared, not even the servants, for the Chaplain expressly forbade gambling on Sundays.

'The devil take you all,' roared Beardie. 'I call on the devil himself to come and play with me if no one else will . . .' The door of the chamber suddenly opened and a tall, dark man strode in and without a word they started to play. The stakes rose higher and higher as Beardie lost game after game and at last he signed a bond saying that should he lose a succession of games the stranger could command any payment. Soon curses and shouts sounded from the chamber and it was obvious that Earl Beardie was losing. Deep into the night the door of the chamber was flung open and the Earl staggered out to upbraid the servants for listening at the door and to call for more drink – but when he returned to the room the dark stranger had disappeared, taking with him the bond for Beardie's soul.

Five years later Earl Beardie died, but shortly afterwards and it is said ever since his ghost has returned from time to time, stamping and swearing in the narrow room at dead of night . . . Surely, thought Jimmy Wentworth Day, all this was legend and fantasy – and yet he told me he talked to three people at Glamis who swore they had independently heard such sounds emanating from the empty room, especially on November nights. And they were solid Scots whose word Jimmy for one accepted. One said she had lain in bed and shaken with fright at the sounds on occasions, while the Hon. Mrs Wingfield, daughter of the late Lord Castletown, woke one night when she was staying at Glamis and saw, seated in front of the fire, a huge old man with a long, flowing beard – a 'man' who was suddenly no longer there. Intrigued by all this Jimmy asked to be allowed to spend a night in the room but the then Earl of Strathmore would not hear of it. 'Nothing good comes of meddling in such matters,' he said in a tone that tolerated no argument.

However, the intrepid Ghost Club member, who had once witnessed a phantom horde, was not to be dissuaded. The experience, which he had had in the latter days of the First World War in broad daylight on the frontier between France and Belgium, never really left Jimmy. Suddenly, as he and Corporal Jock Barr slashed their way along a deserted, potted road, German cavalry swept out of a nearby wood, their riders crouching low, a score or more, their lance-tips gleaming in the sun, red pennants flying in the breeze and the riders all wore the odd-shaped, high-topped helmets that the German Uhlans had worn at the beginning of the war. Both men stopped in their tracks and each saw clearly the horses and the men, the lances and the flickering pennants, as they swept by – without making a sound! Then, up the slope to meet them galloped a company of French Dragoons, long plumes dancing from their brass helmets. Determined and fierce-looking they swept on to meet the Germans in what looked like being a bloody skirmish – and then the whole vision vanished. It had all happened without a single sound. Jimmy always said he was no spiritualist but the vision had been crystal clear and Corporal Barr, a down-to-earth baker in civilian life, had seen it too. Much later Jimmy learned that the locality was known as a haunted area and had been the scene of several bloody skirmishes in 1914. As he said many times at various gatherings when doubters questioned him: 'You do not forget the sight of thirty ghosts charging towards you...' Now he determined to use scientific methods in an effort to explore some of the mysteries of Glamis while he had the chance.

His opportunity came when there was a power cut and the whole castle was plunged into darkness. As a result, the Charter Room, where he was working, was invaded by frantic servants and Jimmy's papers were disarranged. Talking to the Earl afterwards, Jimmy pointed out that his work on the records had been interrupted and he thought it might be useful if he could have access to one of the many uninhabited rooms where perhaps he could lay out some of his papers and know they would not be disturbed. The Earl agreed and showed him into a medium-sized room nearby, completely unfurnished and lit by a single high window. As he came out of the room and handed the key to Jimmy he said, 'Don't lose this; it seems to be the only key . . . and it won't worry you that the room is supposed to be haunted, will it . . . ?'

Jimmy Wentworth Day spent the best part of the night in that haunted room and he said afterwards: 'The place is undoubtedly haunted . . . I sat alone in that room all night and I knew, as never before in any haunted house, that this was a castle of ghosts.' Before he locked himself in he sealed the door with adhesive tape (the only window was too high to reach), spread powdered chalk around the only entrance to the room, placed an automatic temperature recorder in one corner of the room, portable battery-operated sound recording apparatus in another corner and here and there about the room he placed a number of 'trigger' objects: articles he hoped would tempt or trigger psychic activity and each one he carefully ringed with chalk. Satisfied that he had done what he could in the circumstances and with apparatus available to him, he prepared to sit out the night with whatever might visit him or be already in the room with him.

In fact that night was, he felt, particularly uneventful and although he admitted that he may have dozed off for a few minutes on one or two occasions, he was adamant that he was awake and alert for most of the night. As dawn began to seep in through the high window, Jimmy prepared to pick up his things, tidy up the chalk marks, and return to the Charter Room; but there were a few surprises still in store for him. He had heard not a sound during the night and had noticed no unusual temperature variations; the room seeming to grow gradually colder and colder until the early hours and then very gradually a little warmer with the arrival of the dawn.

When he collected up the thermometer he was astonished to see two sudden and dramatic drops in temperature automatically recorded on the chart inside the machine: these showed a drop of no less than 10° just after 2 o'clock in the morning, lasting for about a quarter of an hour, and a similar drop soon after 3 o'clock, for roughly the same period of time. He was completely unaware of these dramatic drops in temperature, but that was not all. When he rewound and ran the tape recorder he found recorded, around 2 o'clock for about a quarter of an hour, heavy stamping footsteps that paced back and forth, back and forth, and then ceased; while between about 3 o'clock and a quarter-past three, the most horrific screams were recorded! Yet Jimmy had been within feet of the recording apparatus and had not heard a sound. I have listened to the screams many times and I still find them blood-curdling; they sound as though they emanate from a female in the most extreme agony of pain and despair; and the heavy echoing footsteps, back and forth, back and forth, have an ominous and frightening intensity.

The Earl of Strathmore was not amused and Jimmy was told, as my wife and I were politely told when we were there: 'The ghostly associations are a feature that is not stressed.' Jimmy Wentworth Day was not invited back to Glamis and he told me, not very long before he died,

'There is a great deal about Glamis that has never been published.' His widow Marion told me, a year or so later, 'There were things at Glamis that he was asked not to talk about and he had experiences there that he never wanted to talk about.' The mystery continues!

Gosling Hall

One day in 1990, I received an interesting letter from a friend and Club member: the kind of letter I continually hope for but rarely receive. Kevin Hore and his wife Dr Angela Hore had long been valued members, and at a Ghost Club dinner they mentioned a friend who lived in a reputedly haunted house and it was agreed that they would make inquiries as to the possibility of a Ghost Club visit.

The Hores subsequently wrote to me to confirm that the owners of the house in question would be prepared to allow a Ghost Club investigation. They went on to include some details of Gosling Hall. Apparently there had been, on an irregular basis, occasions when objects had been moved at random, particularly an oven door (since removed) that would never stay shut, as well as sightings of a young woman. There were many other stories, including Kevin's own experience of being unable to sleep when staying at the house after a party there. He recalls, 'Even though I was quite intoxicated, I could not sleep at all although very tired; that in itself would probably require little explanation ... until I discovered that the experience has been repeated many times by other people staying at the house.' Kevin also describes being 'very surprised by the "feelings" one gets when walking about the house at times.'

After preparing the ground, the Hores left it to me to approach the owners of the house, Stephen Bowen and Daphne Caruthers, about the detailed arrangements, and I was delighted to receive a charming reply from Stephen and Daphne inviting a dozen or so Ghost Club members to the house on 27 July.

As usual, I prepared a provisional timetable for the visit. Because this particular house, it has been claimed, seems to breathe, sigh or even gasp, I suggested that participants in the investigation – when they were not on fixed rota or otherwise engaged – should wander around or spend time in a particular area of the house just breathing in the atmosphere. I encouraged them to open themselves to the way the house affected their feelings and emotions, and to note whatever came into their minds, however trivial it seemed. Fleeting thoughts, sudden fantasies, a snippet of a song, the hint of a scene, a whiff of perfume may all be clues to the history of the house and its entities.

So, on a beautiful summer evening, a dozen Ghost Club members assembled at isolated Gosling Hall, on the outskirts of Occold near Eye in Suffolk. One of our party, John Bellars, noted that his overall impression when arriving at the hall was that it had 'a stillness, and in the afternoon sun appeared very friendly. The grounds were surrounded by trees which sheltered the garden, and they created great stillness.' We were greeted by Stephen and Daphne to whom we are indebted for their generous hospitality and co-operation during the fourteen hours of our investigative visit.

Gosling Hall in parts goes back to the fifteenth century but there have been many changes over the years and a disastrous fire many years ago that totally destroyed most of the house. The present occupants had been in residence for eight years and during that time they have wrought enormous and tasteful changes including panelling in the living room and elaborate carving over the fireplace and round the ceiling which was in the process of being converted into a 'Tudor' ceiling.

We were escorted round the house, which includes a big modern kitchen, a large and comfortable lounge (which we decided to use as our Base Room), a narrow stairway leading to a landing, and leading off the landing, a small bedroom (no. 1) with an entrance to the bathroom; another small bedroom (no. 2) and a more spacious bedroom (no. 3). Downstairs, almost opposite the stairway another doorway led upstairs to another large bedroom and it was agreed that this whole area would be out of bounds to us for the night.

John Bellars described in his subsequent report that the interior of the Hall was 'on many levels, with narrow entrances to various rooms and the main staircase. As expected in a building of this type the floorboards creaked, adding to the haunted house atmosphere.' He went on, 'Upstairs, the main guest bedroom was eerily impressive as the walls sloped in with the eaves of the roof, and the timbers were ancient and warped.' It was this room where Kevin and Angela Hore had stayed and where they had found difficulty in sleeping. According to John Bellars, 'Of the upstairs rooms, the main guest bedroom had the most strange atmosphere, however nothing definite, and of course we had been conditioned to expect something by the previous occupants' experiences. Even discounting that, the feeling was not over-ridingly friendly.'

The lounge, our Base Room, had windows on the east side and on the west side and a large window facing in a northerly direction. This northern part of the house had once extended further outwards and it was interesting to learn that no 'manifestations' had been reportedly seen through this window although a fleeting figure had passed too quickly for it to be recognised or even described or identified in any way passing the east-facing and west-facing windows, i.e. the older, original fixtures. Such a figure had been glimpsed on several occasions.

Upstairs two apparitional figures had reportedly been seen: a young female and an old man. The old man was reported by Doris Stokes who tells the story in her book, *Voices in my Ear*:

On one occasion I was visiting a journalist friend, Kay Hunter [who was living in the house for eight years before Stephen and Daphne], in her beautiful seventeenth-century cottage in Suffolk. It was a lovely place deep in the country with oak beams and ingle-nooks ... during the visit I popped upstairs to the bathroom.

Like the rest of the house it had a low ceiling and oak beams but the sink, bath and towels were completely modern. I stood there washing my hands and staring at my hair in the mirror . . . suddenly my eyes seemed to go peculiar and my reflection slid out of the glass. Shaking my head to clear it I turned round in time to see the bathroom fade and another room take its place. In front of me was a low truckle-bed covered with a patchwork quilt and sitting on the bed was an old man. 'My name is George Baker,' he told me. 'You'll find my name in the deeds of the house.' And then, before my eyes, George and the bedroom turned paler and paler until they became transparent and I was back in the bathroom again. . . . I mentioned the matter to Kay who said she had long suspected that the bathroom had been converted from a former bedroom. 'It's far too big for a bathroom,' she said. And sure enough when she checked the deeds she found a George Baker.

The female figure was seen by Daphne Caruthers at a time when five children were staying in the house and one of them was ill and fretful during the night-time. About 2 a.m. Daphne was awakened by the child crying and she got up to go to the child; in doing so she had to pass through the landing at the top of the stairs. For a moment she thought the child she saw there was Claudia, one of the guest children, but the figure she saw did not move or seem to be aware of Daphne's presence, even when she spoke. Then she saw that the figure, which seemed to be that of a girl of about fifteen years of age, had long blonde hair and was wearing a long white dress. The figure seemed to be looking in the direction of the sick child and it appeared to be solid – in fact the normal figure of a girl. Daphne told us that she saw the figure for what seemed like three or four minutes and she spoke to it three times, without obtaining any response. She did not really feel frightened until afterwards when she felt somewhat uneasy, and she did not mention the matter to Stephen until some time later when she learned that he too had seen the same figure, in the same place. He too thought the girl to be aged about fifteen. Apparently, poltergeist activity had also been experienced by Stephen and Daphne, with keys and money disappearing regularly only to be found later. They attributed this activity to the girl at the top of the stairs.

Although nothing has been seen by human witnesses in the vicinity of the north-facing window in the lounge, dogs visiting the house for the first time often seem to be aware of 'something' at the back of that northern part of the ground floor of the house, the oldest part of the property.

We learned that it was the door that led from the living room to the stairs that would open and close by itself, and not an oven door, and this stairway door had eventually been removed.

During the course of our vigil between 11 p.m. on 27 July and 4 a.m. on 28 July 1990, we distributed thermometers on the landing (1) where the female figure had been seen; at the entrance to the bathroom (2) where Doris Stokes saw the 'old man'; outside the east window of the lounge (Base Room) (3) where a fleeting figure has been seen; at the doorway to the stairs (4) where the door used to open and close by itself; and on the stone or brick path outside the back door (5) as these stones were recovered from the lounge (Base Room) during renovations. A few other objects were also found during reconstruction work in the same area including a piece of old glass, a very ancient spoon, an early eyepatch and a small and old green glass bottle; these objects were placed as trigger objects on the mantelpiece of the living room.

Other trigger objects that I thought were applicable on this occasion were a miniature doll (placed on the landing at the top of the stairs); a ball (in the small bedroom); a coin bangle (at the entrance to the bathroom); an old penny (in the fireplace in the Base Room); a mirror (on the first step of the stairs); a crucifix (outside the east window of the Base Room); a ring (on the banister at the top of the stairs); a key (in the position of the original doorway in the Base Room – now blocked up); and a glass prism (on the brick path outside the back door towards the garden shed).

Thermometers were checked every twenty minutes with no abnormal readings throughout the night. The trigger objects were also checked every twenty minutes and there were only two reported movements. At 1.10 a.m. the glass prism was clearly moved – one and a half inches from its chalked ring in a south-east direction – and at 1.20 a.m. the mirror on the stairs was slightly out of its marked surround but it was felt that both objects could have been accidentally moved when some of the investigators went about checking instruments on the stairs and the garden path, both used by members of the team.

During the course of various seances in both the Base

Room and the living room and involving, at different times, most of the members of the investigating team and the two occupants of the Hall, a number of odd 'messages' came through amid a great deal of nonsense. John Bellars recalls:

Carole [his wife] and I took part in the second seance with Kevin Hore and his wife Dr Angela Hore, the two members who had arranged for the investigation. Being slightly sceptical about seances, I had decided to attempt to be open minded and allow things to happen. Upon making 'contact' with the 'spirit world', it was made clear that there was a message for Kevin. During this period I had been careful not to physically influence the direction of the glass, but had attempted on a number of occasions to 'will' the glass to another letter once the direction of the movement became obvious. However, all of these attempts proved unsuccessful. Kevin had immediately removed his finger from the glass in order not to influence the movement in any way. The questions from Kevin and the 'answers' from the glass continued and, as the questioning became more and more specific, it became apparent that this was a message about a member of a club, called the 'Bee's Knees' that Kevin had belonged to some while ago whilst serving in the Navy as a submariner. Not only could Carole and I know nothing about his past experiences, having met him only on one previous occasion, but his wife Angela had also never been told of this club. Most of the messages were unintelligible, but there were a number of direct answers that surprised Kevin, and the message that one of his old colleagues was 'dodo', left him quiet and pensive. Soon after that the seance ended. It was suggested that 'dodo' was meant as 'dead as a dodo'. There was a coffee break following and all members moved to the Base Room. After a few minutes I noticed Kevin was not present and wandered through into the dining room to find him poring over the transcript of the seance. Whether the message was correct or not, at the time it appeared to have shaken Kevin.

Entities calling themselves 'L.D.', 'Bob', 'Richard', 'David' and 'Zack' also came through at different times. Other 'messages' included a reference to an accident in the garden shed and conflicting messages regarding a ghost currently haunting Gosling Hall; an accident at the top of the stairs; someone unhappy being buried inside the house, possibly killed during the fire; and something to do with witchcraft. At one point it did seem that some kind of contact had been established with a girl who had once lived in the house and had died there. When asked whether she could manifest her presence and an answer in the affirmative was obtained, the entity was asked to blow out one of the candles. There were eight candles burning in the room at the time and they remained steadily alight. Then someone remembered that we had also left a candle burning in the small bedroom at the top of the stairs and on investigation this candle was found to have been extinguished – and very recently for the wax was still warm and melted. It had not burned out by itself for it was a candle that normally burned for some five hours and when relit it burned steadily until blown out at the end of the whole investigation.

Several individual members of the investigating team

visited the garden shed individually and found the atmosphere there 'unusual and rather frightening'. Once two members tried an ouija board there and found it almost 'alive' but somewhat alarming and possibly evil so attempts at communication were abandoned. During the seance there had been a loud bang from the direction of the wheelbarrow, almost as though someone had struck its base with a hammer. Later a group of members visited the garden shed when the atmosphere seemed quite different and there was no activity whatever when various members tried their hands at the ouija board. John Bellars' father was one of the members who sat alone in the shed. John himself 'had looked into the shed but felt its atmosphere owed more to the darkness of the area being surrounded by heavy trees than anything else. It was a very gloomy spot.'

We held one seance session in the Base Room in which I asked everyone to sit quietly and try to make their minds as open and receptive as possible to any information that may be accessible and after a while I asked everyone to relate anything, absolutely anything, that had come into their minds: any scenes, forms, ideas, words, feelings, anything. Most of those present had nothing whatever to relate but such attempts as these to make some sort of contact are always worth trying and on this occasion my wife, who was taking notes of what was happening, said her own impressions sounded so silly that she hardly liked to mention it but she said she had an impression of water and cars and chickens near the water. We thought little of this but made a note of it for future reference and it was fortunate that we had.

Next day, after we left Gosling Hall, my wife and I

booked into a nearby hotel for a couple of days. We had a rest and then thought we would have a look at Diss. We drove into Diss, where neither of us had ever been before, and found ourselves directed to a car park bordering on a lake with lots of chickens wandering about: here were all the ingredients of my wife's impressions, hours before either of us knew such a place existed – the cars, the water and the chickens in one scene!

Photographs taken during the night showed no inexplicable forms or anything unusual. John Bellars, who is also a professional photographer, took a number of photographs with infra-red film during the night. He reported to me afterwards that unfortunately he had had no 'positive' results from the film and that everything was seemingly normal. The scientific apparatus also showed no abnormality and with hindsight a number of different methods of scientific investigation might have been employed including apparatus with specific functions, such as a magnetometer for measuring magnetic fields and highly sensitive sound recording equipment, and various ploys appropriate to the house and its history.

After the visit one of the participating council members, Trevor Kenward, wrote to me and during the course of his letter he referred to the transcripts I had made of the tape recordings of the seance sessions. Although Trevor felt that little of importance had happened when he left Gosling Hall, aspects of the taped seances did indeed seem to be interesting.

Apparently, he had used side one of his tape to record the session that took place towards dawn – but it transpired that nothing was recorded! He realised that he may not

175

have switched the recorder on, but could hardly believe that this was possible. In the session where the letters 'L.D.' came up his tape recorded the following: '. . . girl aged about twelve years . . . burned as a witch' (hanging was normal in this country followed by burning) and when he asked about Matthew Hopkins (the Witch Finder General), the answer was 'Yes'. It seems that Suffolk was indeed Hopkins' hunting ground in 1646 after he had been through Essex in 1645. And he had spent time in Ipswich and Bury St Edmunds where a major trial was held in 1646.

Trevor Kenward's researches also revealed something else of interest about a seance in the dining room. He managed to find meanings for two words that came through – 'snud' and 'squob'. Snud apparently is an Old English slang word meaning 'to lie under' (from circa 1676 and out of use by 1840) and squob or squab is, according to Penguin's *Reference Dictionary of Historical Slang*, 'a fat person, or to squeeze'.

The all-night investigation at Gosling Hall was fairly uneventful on the whole but at times a genuine entity did appear to be contacted and the extinguishing of the candle, the only one alight in the house not in view of any of the investigating team, was somewhat remarkable. As one member put it, there was considerable cause for thought. In the main, the house and grounds seemed very quiet and undisturbed in any psychic sense.

After sending a note to Stephen Bowen and Daphne Caruthers expressing our gratitude, I received a fascinating letter from Stephen Bowen in which he said:

Your visit here the other month prompted me to do some

investigative work on the history of the house on a more temporal plane so I paid a visit or two to the Suffolk Records Office with considerable success; my findings may be of interest to you: hence my writing.

It appears that prior to the early nineteenth century, this house was Occold Hall, rather than the Regency pile that now bears that name. Following Domesday, the Manor of Occold devolved in a way that I have been unable to trace until 1327, when the Lord of the Manor, De Wilmo Joce, paid 'twelf pence of lawful english mony' as tax on his estates in the Subsidy Return (poll tax) for that year. In 1449, the then lord, John Henman, died, and the estate formed the basis of a charitable trust which he devised 'for certain superstitious uses, the payment of tenths and fifteenths, the relief of the poor, and the reparation of the church and highways'.

The Subsidy Return for 1524 gives the lady of the Manor as one Joan Corbald, and notes that she is a widow, having in her custody £20 for the use of her two daughters. Her commemorative brass, together with that of her husband, William, is set in the floor of the local church, and much of that building was paid for by him. It is also interesting to note at this juncture that Henry VIII's wife, Anne of Cleeves, received a grant for life from the Manor.

By 1568, William Hubberd was lord, and paid £8 for tax in the Subsidy Return. In 1674 a hearth tax was levied, and the returns for this tell us that the lord was now Robert Denny, and that the Hall had six chimneys. In 1689, Philip Sancroft held the Manor, and a letter of receipt for one hundred pounds dated that year is still in existence. In 1727, George Gosling took part in the poll for the Knights of the Shire, and in 1730 his daughter Sarah was married to William Bloss, giving birth to a daughter, Elizabeth, the following year.

The year 1768 saw the birth here of the Rev. John Spencer Cobbold, a writer of theological works, who, after leaving Caius College, Cambridge in 1794, became master of a free school in Nuneaton. Later, in 1831, he became vicar of Woolpit. In 1786, H. J. Close became lord of the Manor here, and commissioned Isaac Walton, a cartographer, to map the estate, and it is from this map that I discovered the previous identity of Gosling Hall. Mr Walton also took the trouble to sketch an elevation of the Hall, which was much larger than the fragment which exists today. At the close of the century it seems fair to assume from the layers of ash in the ground surrounding the house, about which I previously told you, that a disastrous fire destroyed much of the Hall, and that rather than rebuild it, whoever was incumbent at that time chose to erect a new hall on a different site.

I also know that this building was about twice the size that it is today as late as the 1880s, from the ordnance maps of the period and from the second distinct layer of ash in the garden it is my conjecture that another fire reduced the house still further. It is certain that after this time the house and land declined into a smallholding lived in by a succession of tenants.

Our night at Gosling Hall will long remain in the memory of those present, perhaps because of the generosity and friendliness of the owners; perhaps on account of the fascinating house and its atmosphere; perhaps because of the curious seances; perhaps especially because of the simple incident of the candle apparently extinguished by means not of this world.

Harlaxton Manor

Never shall I forget the first time I entered the massive front door of Harlaxton Manor and my wife and I found ourselves alone in the sombre, shadowy, echoing, decorative and distracting and disturbing stone entrance hall, heavy with its massive urns, statuary and stairway.

This 'Victorian dream palace', as John Piper called it, is indeed a palace, perhaps the greatest unknown palace in England. Its size takes your breath away – comprising well over 100 rooms and set in 500 acres of ground, it took twenty years to build and a whole hillside was excavated to accommodate it, resulting in frequent confusion for the newcomer as to which floor level he is on! In 1937, when it was up for sale, the property was described as a 'noble ancestral seat set in magnificently timbered parkland on an eminence commanding wide panoramic views across the Vale of Belvoir and ranking as one of the stately homes of England and probably the supreme example of domestic architecture of its period'.

Had it not been bought at that time by the eccentric but wealthy Mrs Van der Elst, this unique mansion would certainly have been demolished. It was built by Gregory Gregory who inherited the estate in 1822 and he decided to build a new and better house to replace the Old Manor that dated from medieval times – somewhere to house his collection of works of art that he had amassed from all parts of the world and a house that incorporated every feature and style of architecture which he had seen and admired on his extensive travels.

This 'labour of an age in piled stones', a magnificent mansion built at a fabulous cost (probably at least £200,000 in those days) was not completed when the wealthy bachelor died in 1854. The house passed to his elderly cousin who died six years later although he lived to see the house completed in 1857. The property then passed to a distant relative John Sherwin-Gregory and his wife and on her death in 1892 to Thomas Sherwin Pearson, who called himself Pearson-Gregory although he was only a godson of the previous owner.

Thomas Sherwin Pearson-Gregory died in 1935 leaving the property to his son, who decided to sell it. Oddly enough the house at no point passed in succession directly to a Gregory heir, except in 1935 and that inheritor promptly decided to sell it.

The enormous and individual house was advertised in superb estate agents' prose but with increasing desperation and steps were in hand for the house to be demolished when Mrs Van der Elst appeared on the scene. This formidable lady bought the house in 1938 and soon wrought great changes, including the installation of electric light – twenty miles of cable being used in the process. The obsolete plumbing was also modernised to almost lavish standards – previously there had been only one bathroom in the whole house! The new owner of Grantham Castle (as she renamed it) was a passionate and vocal opponent of capital punishment and she was frequently to be seen, chauffeured in her white Rolls-Royce, outside prisons on the morning of an execution and not infrequently her demonstrations landed her in trouble with the police.

After the death of her second husband, John Van der Elst, a Belgian artist, in 1934, Violet Van der Elst, who never did anything by halves, embraced the cult of spiritualism and at Grantham Castle she spent many hours and many nights in what is now known as 'Mrs Van der Elst's Room', the Old Library, dressed from head to foot in black. The room itself was full of black furniture and furnishings and is still full of sombre circumjacence with its black twisted pillars from Italy and huge stone windows once covered with black velvet curtains. Here as nowhere else in the house she loved her style and her personality are strongly and strangely evident. Russell Read in his fascinating collection of pictures and photographs, *Harlaxton* (1978), says, 'if any ghosts walk the corridors at night hers will surely be among them, dressed all in black, in the Old Library where she held seances to communicate with her dead husband or in her bedroom, the present Guest Room'.

And walk she did by all accounts. The various supernormal happenings at Harlaxton all date from her occupation. The daughter of a Middlesex coal porter and general labourer and a Quaker washerwoman, she rose to become a social reformer, a respected composer, an indisputable mystic and a businesswoman of rare ability and acknowledgement. Her considerable fortune was made through her manufacture and marketing of the first brushless shaving cream but Harlaxton ate into her considerable resources to such an extent that eventually she was forced to sell the house and she died in 1966, almost penniless; an extraordinary woman whose life and achievements have been eloquently recorded by my friend (and one-time Ghost Club member) Charles Neilson Gettey in *The Incredible Mrs Van der Elst* (1972).

Earl Attlee, who on one occasion presented to Parliament a petition with more than 100,000 signatures on her behalf, always believed that she did more than anyone else to secure the abolition of the death sentence in Britain. An unusually sensitive person who claimed she had never been able to kill even a fly, she said all her life she acted as a magnet for preternatural phenomena. At the house in Belsize Park where she lived with her first husband, Henry Nathan, a variety of strange happenings were witnessed. After twenty-eight years of marriage he died after an operation, and less than four months later, in March 1928, his widow married John Jakin Van der Elst, aged thirty-six of independent means, a bachelor who had been living with the Nathans. The few years that Violet and John had together may have been the happiest of her life but they were all too brief. Six years after they had been married, in August 1934, John Van der Elst had been feeling under the weather for a while and they decided on a short holiday to Ostend, staying at the Hotel Splendide. After only a few days there he became worse and soon died. A gastric ulcer had burst. Violet never really recovered or came to terms with that bereavement. She took her husband's body home where an autopsy was performed on a marble table in the drawing room of their home and afterwards she had the body sealed in a lead coffin which she kept in the basement of the house in Addison Road, London – a house she believed to be evil. She turned to spiritualism and had many sittings with mediums and she became convinced that her husband lived on beyond the world we all know. His earthly body was of no further interest and a year after his death she arranged for the cremation of the remains at Golders Green crematorium. She had the ashes placed in a marble casket which followed her to Harlaxton and was kept on the mantelpiece in the Marble Hall, the maids having instructions to place fresh flowers there each day. The urn in which the ashes once rested stands today in the entrance hall. When the house and its contents were sold the casket was accidentally included in the sale but was later recovered.

Mrs Van der Elst fell in love with Harlaxton, which, thirty years earlier King Edward VII had tried, unsuccessfully, to purchase and he acquired Sandringham House instead. Like most parvenus she longed for an aristocratic background and, her maternal name being Gundry, she decided she was descended from Sir Guy Gundry, an Elizabethan sea-dog, and the pseudo-Tudor Harlaxton seemed an eminently suitable residence. It was, and still is, an 'astonishing ... landmark of nineteenth-century architecture' (*Country Life*) with its noble façade which is especially magnificent when viewed from a distance.

Inside she revelled in the grand staircase, the drawing room and the library – all in the Louis XIV style – and the

Great Hall and the dining room, both baroquely Jacobean. Mrs Van der Elst soon added to the furnishings of the house by purchasing from Buckingham Palace some Gobelin tapestries, given by the last Tsar of Russia to his sister-in-law Queen Alexandra, and a wonderful carved chair on which the ancient Doges of Venice had once sat as they condemned prisoners to death. And then there were the ghosts. One of Mrs Van der Elst's employees, who had worked at the Manor before it changed hands said, 'the Grey Lady used to walk along the Blue Corridor long before Mrs Van der Elst arrived'.

Soon, in this strange house where vases levitated, objects moved by themselves and strange forms were often glimpsed, Mrs Van der Elst began to hold seances. In a dark room with black curtains, black furniture and herself clothed completely in black, knockings would spell out messages; the 'spirits' would impart wisdom. Something of Violet Van der Elst's powerful personality seems to have pervaded the environment for when the property was bought by the Jesuits in 1948 they soon found the vibrant atmosphere disturbing and the ghostly activity not to their liking and they had the place exhaustively exorcised.

As for Mrs Van der Elst, probably the most colourful woman of her time, she lived to see the abolition of capital punishment and died, almost forgotten, at a nursing home in Kent in April 1966. A little earlier, Harlaxton (which had reverted to its old name) passed into the possession of Stanford University, California, for a few years and then in 1971 Harlaxton Manor House passed to the University of Evansville, Indiana, first as Harlaxton Study Centre and later as Harlaxton College, the British campus of that

University, under whose auspices the property remains to this day.

And still the ghosts walk. I was invited to lecture at Harlaxton and I duly addressed several hundred staff, students and visitors and my wife and I spent a night in the haunted Clock Room. But first we were conducted on a tour of this remarkable, dream-like fantasy with its grand staircase, swarming with cherubs soaring into a blue heaven; a plaster Father Time, high up over the cedar staircase, holding a real scythe; the Great Hall with Mrs Van der Elst's enormous chandelier; and the Old Library with its sombre black pillars where so many seances took place and where so many communications with the dead allegedly took place. This room we both found full of atmosphere (I see from my notes made at the time) 'and one can easily imagine it hung with black curtains as it was in Mrs Van der Elst's day'.

We saw too, the ante room where one of the cherubs decorating the wall has a deliberate hole in its chest and we were told this was a silent commemoration or reminder of a sad event. The story, probably apocryphal since there is no record of any baby ever having lived at Harlaxton, tells of a baby being nursed before an open fire. The slumbering child falls from the lap of the dozing nurse into the fire and is burned to death. What is certain is that the room has been the scene of a number of curious and unexplained incidents involving people who had no knowledge of its reputed history, and stories that included visitors suddenly saying they could hear screams and the muffled sounds of a crying baby.

After my talk one of the students told us he had spent

many disturbed nights in one particular bedroom at Harlaxton where he was haunted by terrible dreams and when he awakened he saw, just for a moment, what appeared to be a sub-human face close to his own; and sometimes, during the quiet of the evening, he had glimpsed a dark-robed figure in the room. Subsequently he discovered that another student (whom I also spoke to) had experienced exactly the same things while sleeping in that bedroom. Later, from one of the officials, I learned that some years earlier a girl student had complained of frightening dreams and seeing a black-robed figure in her bedroom; and from time to time there have been many reports of unexplained figures in the large and shadowy rooms and in the long corridors of Harlaxton. But in the main this decorative, distracting and utterly enchanting place keeps its secrets and hides its ghosts.

My wife and I spent a memorable time at Harlaxton and an unforgettable night. We had hardly settled in the Clock Room, high up in the Clock Tower which rises 120 feet from the ground, when we heard the most weird sound of ropes and chains moving and straining and clattering, followed by the boom-boom of a clock! Not without cause was this apartment named the Clock Room! We saw no ghosts at Harlaxton but that ghosts have been seen there I have not the slightest doubt.

A few years ago the curator, Frances Watkins, spoke of 'many' students and teachers over the years, reportedly 'seeing ghosts in the house and several members of staff leaving unexpectedly, saying that they felt uneasy living there . . .' One visitor described the house as 'alive with the spirits of the past' and perhaps it is. A teacher who was resident at Harlaxton for two years has told of having a number of unnerving experiences including encountering the 'hazy outline of a tall man standing in the doorway of the library for some twenty minutes' while she and some of her students watched in turn.

An artist, staying at the house as a guest, confided to us that he had twice seen a ghost at Harlaxton; a black-robed figure, possibly female, and seemingly at home. The audience changes, it seems, but the same endless drama goes on.

Knowle Farm

Some years ago, four Ghost Club members carried out a twenty-four-hour preliminary investigation at this Oxfordshire farmhouse where varied phenomena had been reported by the occupant, the seventy-eight-year-old widow of Lieutenant-General W. H. E. Gott, CB, CBE, DSO, MC, the man selected to take over as Commander of the British Eighth Army in 1942 but he was killed in action and Lieutenant-General Bernard Montgomery took over in his place.

Mrs Pamela Gott informed us briefly on arrival that she had experienced the movement of objects, inexplicable coldness, unexplained noises and in particular one peculiar night-time noise on numerous occasions, and the appearance of a phantom form. It was agreed that she would give us no actual details of the disturbances in the hope that we might discover or encounter or experience some activity that corresponded with previously reported phenomena.

We carefully examined the property which in parts dated back to the sixteenth century and was once occupied by monks; and we settled on a comfortable back lounge as our

Base Room. This was a very old room with a lower floor level than the rest of the house and possessing an enormous and ancient open fireplace. We were allocated two bedrooms for rest, if required, and we had the run of the whole house except for Mrs Gott's bedroom which was situated at the rear of the premises. We set up our various apparatus in the Base Room, the hall, the reception room and in an upstairs hall and bedroom.

We never could get the thermometer we set up in the Base Room to function that night. It simply would not register any variation in temperature whatever, even when we breathed on it and tested it in other parts of the house and in other ways. In the end we decided it must be faulty but once out of the house the next day when it was being packed in the car it functioned normally and there has been no malfunctioning of this instrument since. *Afterwards* Mrs Gott told us that she had recently let the house to some Americans for a period and when they left they told her they could never get warm in that back lounge and after a couple of days they never used the room.

The hall had a strange and almost tangible atmosphere. As soon as we entered the house all four members of the visiting party were aware of 'something' in the hall. *Much later* Mrs Gott told us she and many of her visitors and friends always felt the hall was 'full of psychic atmosphere' and once she had seen the figure of the ghost that haunted the house reflected in a mirror in the hall. The hall was among those parts of the house that had been structurally altered over the years. All four visiting investigators felt the atmosphere in the hall altered for the better several hours after their arrival and when they left next day all of them felt it to be quite normal – in marked contrast to the circumjacence, the feeling, the aura if you like, that had been so apparent when the party arrived.

Soon after our arrival and before we had heard any details whatever about the ghost reputed to haunt the house, my wife Joyce, in the Base Room with the other members of the party, Steuart Kiernander, Michael Brett and myself (now Ghost Club Society members), said she saw a shadowy form resembling a woman standing by the fireplace. At first she thought it was a man as the short hair seemed to be very close to the head but then she realised that the form was wearing an apron and her hair was drawn tightly into a bun at the back of the head.

Much later Mrs Gott told us that the ghost in the house was a woman wearing an apron, presumably a servant, and at first some people who saw the figure thought it was a man because of the short hair but then saw that the hair was drawn off the face into a bun at the back of the head. Mrs Gott and her family had named the phantom 'Alice' and she had been seen and sensed all over the house but especially in the back lounge near the fireplace. It was her form that had been seen reflected in a mirror in the hall. The figure of 'Alice', we were told, had been seen continually by all sorts of people over a period of many years.

During the night several objects were moved in the Base Room, including a heavy plate and a thermometer, which at 10.30 p.m. was moved onto its side; one electric light in the room flicked off and then back on again at 11.20 p.m.; and a cushion was moved from an easy chair onto the floor. In addition, voices were heard but nothing was recorded; a shuffling noise was heard from the direction of the hall and a little later from within the Base Room while we were all there; and extreme coldness was felt, but not recorded scientifically, in the vicinity of a pink-embroidered chair. At one stage, while sitting in that chair, my feet felt frozen and I had to move. A nearby thermometer did not record any drop in temperature. *Next morning* Mrs Gott told us that the ghost of 'Alice' had 'often' been seen 'sitting' in that pink armchair. That back lounge and the small room behind it were supposed to be haunted by a group of monks and Mrs Gott told us she continually felt that the room was full of presences although she saw nothing. They seemed to be looking over her shoulder, interfering . . . the last few years had not been quite as bad but previously the feeling had often been very strong.

The investigator occupying the Base Room during the night could not rest at all; he said the room seemed alive with people although he saw nothing. He also heard what sounded like a man's voice from the direction of the hall and this sound was recorded but no words were distinguishable and it was not the voice of anyone present.

Two members resting in the bedroom known as Alice's Room found the room restful and relaxing except that at 6.20 a.m. a loud pecking noise was heard at the window, followed by very loud beating and banging sounds that suggested an enormous bird or birds were trying to get into the room. Nothing was visible. Ar. investigator in an adjoining room hurried in to report hearing the same sounds although neither the investigator in the Base Room below nor the occupant of the house in her bedroom nearby heard the very loud sounds that morning. However, at breakfast Mrs Gott told us that she usually slept well but was often awakened in the early morning by something that sounded like a large bird pecking at the window followed by the loud flapping and beating of wings. She had frequently hurried to the window and opened it but she never saw any birds or indeed anything that might account for the sounds. There were no physical signs of anything pecking at the windows. These sounds were not heard regularly but perhaps two or three times a week and then not for a month or so and then two or three times a week again. One of Mrs Gott's daughters heard the mysterious sounds when she was spending a night in Alice's Room and would never sleep there again.

Next day we walked in the garden and pasture land bordering Knowle Farm. The land to the west had been the scene of several battles during the Civil War, we were told, and horses pastured there 'frequently showed inexplicable signs of fright'. Unidentified forms and shapes had also been reported from time to time hereabouts but the visiting party did not sense or detect anything unusual in the field.

In the garden of the house, on the other hand, three of the investigators felt distinctly uncomfortable and one 'almost saw' a form: he felt there was something in the garden and he seemed just about to see it when the feeling cleared. Another member of the party glimpsed a 'shadowy form' near the house that was there one moment and gone the next. In that garden on that still summer morning I sensed presences – a most unusual thing for me to do – but I did feel there were people on one side of the garden and when I moved to the other side of the garden I had the impression that someone was saying, 'What are you doing here . . . ?' But I saw nothing, I heard no objective sound in the garden that I could not account for and perhaps it was caused by a combination of the circumstances, the surroundings and the lack of rest: whatever it was it is a very vivid memory.

Beyond the garden there was an overgrown area which was reputedly a burial ground of some kind and we heard that it was exceedingly difficult to get anything to grow there and animals were always unhappy on that patch of ground. We were also told that some of the local people refuse to walk up the main drive to the house, saying they had heard and seen things they could not explain; but the drive was successfully inspected, explored and used during the daytime and night-time while we were there and none of us encountered or sensed anything untoward.

Some sort of explanation for parts of the haunting may be forthcoming when one considers that the whole surrounding area has rich historical associations with the Civil War, and local legends tell of hauntings involving the King's nephew Prince Rupert. One medium, visiting the house, told Mrs Gott that the soil thereabouts suffered from 'psychic interference'. Another medium who visited the house said there were a number of bodies buried underneath the building, all in a foetal position; and beside the fireplace inglenook in the Base Room (where a shadowy form had been seen by one of our party) the medium saw a large hole in the floor, directly beneath the great beam over the fireplace where some curious burn marks are visible; possibly the beam had been used as a testing place for branding irons used in torture in days gone by.

The effects of fighting and bloodshed and violent death in the area may have left some impressions that can be picked up by psychic people or animals; and the fact that monks once lived in the property that later became a manor house may account for the feelings reported by various visitors that monks were still present in the back and older part of the house. 'Alice' was probably a servant and in the psychic atmosphere of the house she was able to manifest after her death. Mrs Gott told us she was often aware of the presence of Alice and she sometimes talked to her, not unkindly but firmly, telling her that while she may once have lived in the house it was now occupied by the living and she must leave the house and not frighten people. But it didn't seem to do a great deal of good although Mrs Gott told us that she felt that whatever was haunting the house was not as persistent as it used to be.

Before leaving the area, we visited Weston Manor Hotel, almost next door. There we were shown over that venerable building, more reminiscent of a stately home than a hotel, and we heard about the ghosts including a phantom coach and horses that travels through the back yard; the ghost of a nun executed some five centuries ago and known as the spectre of Mad Maude; and the ghost of a dairymaid who fell to her death from the tower. Nicholas Price, the proprietor, said he was utterly convinced of the authenticity of the ghosts associated with Weston Manor Hotel and it may well be that the ghosts of that former manor and nearby Knowle Farm are connected in some way, perhaps even superimposed on one another.

Miss Davis, Mrs Gott's housekeeper for fifteen years, informed me in September 1993 that Mrs Gott had died in

1985 and that the house is now occupied by a lively family with three young sons and to her knowledge they have no feelings about 'Alice' one way or the other. The four individual investigators came away with the feeling that in all the circumstances the house probably was haunted but not by any presence that would be likely to be established scientifically, and we did not feel a larger or longer investigation was justified. Perhaps we should have persisted in discovering more about Alice but it really was a fascinating visit to a beautiful house that, in all probability, had been the scene of spontaneous psychic activity.

Langenhoe Church

A lonely and isolated church, standing like a sentinel on its mound overlooking the Essex marshes and the scene of virtually the whole gamut of psychic activity, drew me like a magnet and I well remember when I resolved to spend a night in that haunted place.

It all began when I received a letter from my good friend James Turner, poet and author, then living at Borley and busy restoring the garden of 'the most haunted house in England' to something of its former glory. Part of the letter read: 'I have just returned from a visit to Langenhoe; I think the church there would repay some of your quiet and thorough investigation.' How right he was! I lost little time in visiting the area, never dreaming that it would be the beginning of an investigation that would extend, on and off, for over twelve years!

During the course of my investigation a fascinating story emerged; but first let us meet the Rev. Ernest A. Merryweather, Rector of Langenhoe. Mr Merryweather, author of a limited edition of *Some Notes on the Family of Merryweather of England and America*, lived in a small but comfortable house in West Mersea where he was looked after by his housekeeper Mrs Gertrude Barnes, widow of the Rev. Herbert Barnes, and daughter Irene.

Mr Merryweather, on his return home from Canada in 1918, took charge of two parishes in West Derbyshire; in fact he told me, before coming to Langenhoe in 1937 most of his life had been spent in the north of England and he had never experienced anything of a psychic nature before he arrived in Langenhoe. In fact he had never been interested in the subject nor had he come across anything of that kind until he found himself at the apparent centre of inexplicable happenings.

Ernest Merryweather was a large, easy-going, kindly man; a widower with a son who lived abroad. I found the puzzled rector had a very sensible approach to things he could not understand; he kept his feet firmly on the ground and was blessed with an infectious sense of humour and a natural inclination to optimism. Because he was at the isolated and almost deserted church far more frequently than anyone else, he had personally experienced a wealth of alleged paranormal activity. I was delighted to find that he had kept a diary of his life and events including the curious activities he had encountered at Langenhoe church; everything was entered down with dates, details, names of other witnesses present, his immediate reaction and all sorts of other relevant information. Some years later he presented me with this diary.

I noticed with interest that the first recorded incident, door-slamming and paranormal locking, were typical poltergeist manifestations, and yet nothing more worth recording in the diary seems to have taken place for several years. But these two incidents intrigued the new rector. 'It wasn't long before things happened that suggested to me that there was something odd about the place,' he told me, pointing to that first entry.

On 20 September 1937, a quiet autumn day, he was standing alone inside the church with the big west door open. Suddenly it crashed to with such force that the whole church seemed to shake. 'Doors don't usually slam to as if an express train had hit them, when there is no palpable cause,' wrote the rector. 'My curiosity was aroused.' Accordingly he made every effort to find a natural explanation but there was no wind, he could not make the heavy door swing shut of its own weight, no human being or animal was in the vicinity and he had no rational explanation for this sudden and 'somewhat curious' incident.

As far as the 'paranormal locking' was concerned, this involved both the vestry door and the rector's valise which he always used to take with him to the church since it contained his vestments and books and notes. Twice during the month of November 1937, Mr Merryweather discovered that his valise had unaccountably locked itself when it was left in the vestry and every effort to unlock it proved unsuccessful in the vestry, in the church or in the churchyard; although on both occasions the valise unlocked without difficulty once he was in the lane and away from the church. On the first occasion a friend who was with him witnessed the 'locking'. The diary entry reads: 'after the 11 o'clock service I was about to leave the vestry and placed my robes in the valise. Having forgotten to put something else inside, I tried for some little time, to open the catches, then gave it up as hopeless, they were fixed tight. When I reached the bottom of the lane I tried again. The "influence" had gone and the catches worked perfectly.'

On several occasions in those early days the vestry door locked itself. Sometimes when the rector arrived he could not unlock the door and after a number of attempts, he turned to the churchyard and busied himself for a while, making the place tidy. When he returned to the vestry door he was able to open it immediately. On other occasions, having let himself into the church and completed the purpose of his visit he found, when he went to leave, that the vestry door had locked itself. Sometimes he was able to unlock the door immediately but on other occasions he had great difficulty in doing so and only after he had turned to other things and then went back to the door was he able to unlock it.

It has to be admitted that such activity might possibly be the result of movement of the structure of the church but it is important to bear in mind that this mysterious locking took place twice during one month in 1937, once during the following month, twice the month after that – and *never* afterwards for the twenty-two years that Merryweather remained rector of Langenhoe. The only other locking incident concerning the vestry door occurred in 1949 and was witnessed by James and Cathy Turner, as we shall see.

However, there was an earthquake in 1884 that virtually destroyed the church at Langenhoe, as photographs taken at the time show. The later church was built from the old materials two years after the earthquake. Much of the tower and some parts of the body of the church survived the earthquake and these were embodied in the new building. It is likely that some of the curious incidents reported at Langenhoe church could be the result of the condition of the building following the earthquake and indeed photographs I took there show distinct signs of movement in the walls and flooring: *some* of the incidents probably, but by no means all of them.

Langenhoe church stood on a slight hill above the flat marshlands of Mersea Island and from the top of the tower it was possible to see the village of Langenhoe (comparable in size to Borley), the town of Mersea and the great expanse of water at high tide which floods over the road and holds up traffic at the Causeway, reputedly haunted by a phantom Roman centurion, for Mersea Island was famous for its oyster-beds even before the Romans arrived. Oddly enough both Langenhoe and Borley once belonged to the powerful Waldegrave family.

Sir Edward Waldegrave, whose huge tomb dominates Borley church, had been one of Queen Mary's Privy Councillors but those were turbulent days; times of allegiance to the old faith, of changing to new ones. In 1551, Sir Edward was sent to the Tower for refusing to inform the then Princess Mary that mass must not be celebrated in her household. He ignored the Act of Uniformity, passed at the beginning of Elizabeth I's reign to enforce the use of the Book of Common Prayer, and then, when he was convicted of holding mass at Borley, he was sent to the Tower where he died in 1561.

Frances, his wife, survived him and married again, this time to the third son of the Marquis of Winchester, who may be the unnamed figure on the Waldegrave tomb. In

1589, the Waldegraves became owners of Langenhoe and although Sir Edward and Lady Frances never owned Langenhoe their son, Nicholas, who married Catherine Browne, did own the estate. The Brownes were Roman Catholics and would have helped Frances after the death and disgrace of her husband in 1561. She would probably be trying to get her son Nicholas and her daughter-in-law away to France and where better to steal out of the country than from Langenhoe? It is known that she moved from the village when she remarried and lived elsewhere. Although Nicholas Waldegrave seems to have been back at Borley by 1563 it seems indisputable that Frances Waldegrave was at Langenhoe during a very troubled period of her life, and this is important in view of the apparitions the rector saw in Langenhoe church. But let us make some attempt at presenting the evidence chronologically.

There was little further for the rector to report until 1945. Then, on Easter Sunday, there occurred the first of a number of incidents involving flowers that have never been satisfactorily explained. The rector, Mrs Barnes and Irene were busy decorating the church with flowers before the congregation arrived. Mrs Barnes had placed some flowers in a vase and stood the vase of flowers in a pew for a moment while she attended to something else. A moment later Mrs Barnes turned back to the vase and saw that the flowers had been removed from the vase and laid neatly on the pew beside the vase. Had she *not* put the flowers in the vase at all? No, for the stalks were wet as they lay dampening the pew. Clearly no human being other than the three present in the church at the time could have moved the flowers and, as related to me independently by these three witnesses, this incident must have been the result of something other than human agency.

The Tudor farmhouse hard by the church had once been the manor house. By 1945, it was weatherboarded and almost as isolated as the church. During the course of the long investigation into the apparent haunting of Langenhoe I came upon a persistent legend that was told to me by several totally independent people; sources as far away from Langenhoe as Stratham and Torquay and even New York. The story was always the same: years ago the young rector of the parish fell in love with the daughter of the lord of the manor. The feeling was reciprocated but the respective parents were opposed to the match. The couple met clandestinely in and around the church and soon they made plans to elope. They arranged to meet secretly at the church (there used to be a path leading from the manor to a private church entrance) and then together they would leave for a life together. But things did not work out. They met in the church but then things went wrong and either another admirer of the young lady, or someone else, showed up and in the heated argument and mêlée that followed the young lady from the manor house (and perhaps her would-be lover too) were killed and hastily buried beneath the huge stone step outside the thirteenth-century church door.

There are reports, which I have been unable to confirm, of human bones being found here during excavation. Certainly this area has been the subject of reported psychic activity, including the temporary stench of rotting flesh; the sound of whispering and a man's voice; footsteps and muffled thuds . . .

One day the Rev. Merryweather, thinking he had not seen the occupants of the former manor house near the church for some time, called at the dark and forbidding house and at first thought no one was at home but then his knock was answered by Mrs Cutting. She invited the rector inside and, when she learned that he had not been in the house before, offered to show him round. Little did Rev. Merryweather think that he was literally to walk into a tactual phenomenon almost unique in the annals of psychical research.

After exploring the downstairs rooms, he was shown upstairs where Mrs Cutting led the way into each room until she came to a charming front bedroom which the rector duly admired, whereupon he was surprised to learn that the family did not use that particular room and they all felt 'there was something queer about it'. She herself preferred to sleep in a north-facing bedroom although the view was no comparison; but there at least she was assured of a good night's sleep. As she spoke Mrs Cutting, who had been in the room only a few seconds, left saying, 'Have a look round by all means, I'll wait for you downstairs; I *don't* like this room.'

Alone in the apparently delightful bedroom, the rector walked across to the window and admired the view. After a moment he turned back and as he did so, he told me, he 'turned into the unmistakable embrace of a naked young woman!' The singular tactual phenomenon lasted only seconds . . . 'One frantic embrace and she was gone,' as Mr Merryweather put it. There was no auditory, visual or olfactory accompaniment to this remarkable experience, but the rector was quite emphatic that it was not just his imagination and it was the very last thing that he expected. This unusual experience was a very real and lasting memory for Mr Merryweather for the rest of his life.

Gradually the variety of reported psychic activity at Langenhoe expanded. While celebrating Holy Communion the sound of heavy thuds came from the direction of the vestry door, not once but on a number of different occasions and they were, of course, heard by members of the congregation as well as by the rector. Yet always upon investigation nothing was visible and no explanation or cause or reason for the noise could be found. These thuds were heard on ten occasions, I see from the rector's diary, between July and December – they were not heard before and never again.

During the same period the rector, visiting his lonely church at different hours of the day would frequently have the feeling that he was not alone; that someone or something was near him in the deserted church and churchyard. Sometimes the feeling was so overwhelming that he left and went home and once, on a sudden impulse, he threw a metal rod into a pile of coal near the vestry door and taking off his biretta, he hung it on the end of the protruding iron rod, wondering as he did so whether anything would happen: to his amazement the hat began to revolve slowly as he watched!

As the hat gradually ceased revolving and came to a standstill, the rector removed the biretta and let himself into the deserted church, where, five minutes later, he heard a disembodied voice! And on this occasion the words were distinguishable. For some time past there had been hooliganism in the area, mainly from some boys who lived at a nearby village and, when he heard that people on their own had been threatened and even attacked in the lonely lanes, the rector, visiting his isolated church, had decided to take with him an ornamental dagger which his son had sent him from Cyprus. While inside the church that day Mr Merryweather placed the dagger firmly in a belt around his waist and beneath his cassock. Having just recovered from the biretta incident, he walked into the church and, as he stood quietly in front of the altar for a moment, he suddenly felt the dagger jerked from the belt and as it clattered to the floor, he heard a female voice say, very clearly, 'It was you that killed her. You are a cruel man.' The rector turned round immediately. The church was quite deserted. The voice had seemed to come from behind him, from the tower end of the church. From the feelings he experienced then and on other occasions, and from material that subsequently came through at seances, Mr Merryweather came to believe that a murder had been committed at that spot near the tower.

A fifteenth-century south door to the church once opened to disclose a path across the churchyard and so to the old manor house. It was a door that must have been used by the Waldegraves as their private entrance to the church when they lived at the manor. During the restoration of the church after the earthquake this door had been blocked up, and in front of it on an Elizabethan altar table stood a statue of St George, a beautiful brass credence bell and two altar lights, in memory of the parishioners killed in the 1914–18 war. One December morning the rector heard, 'as clear and distinct' as he had ever heard anything in his life, he told me, 'an old man's cough'. It seemed to come from the St George statue and a moment later the credence bell rang of its own volition. 'I could scarcely bring myself to believe what I had heard,' Mr Merryweather said afterwards. 'A statue cannot cough and the church was deserted so I rushed out into the churchyard to see if anyone was there. No one was anywhere around: the statue had coughed and the bell had rung itself!'

A few days later a loud crack, as of a rifle, was heard in the same place inside the church by the rector and again no other person was in or near the church at the time. Several times the credence bell also rang again, once when the rector, his housekeeper and her daughter were in the church cleaning and polishing on the eve of my spending a night inside the church. I hoped it was a lucky omen!

Two strangers to the parish went to see the rector. They said they were intending to have a look round the church one sunny morning but as they were approaching the church they heard the sound of singing coming from within the church; a woman's voice. As they loitered, wondering what to do, they realised that there was no music and the singing was in French. As they stopped, still undecided what to do, the singing seemed to fade and then ceased so they quietly opened the church door and went inside. The church was deserted. They went outside again and one of them went round the church one way and the other went the other way. They met by the vestry door at the back. They had seen no one and there was no sign of anyone anywhere near the church.

One afternoon when he was visiting the church the rector was surprised to find two workmen with their ears to the closed main door of the church. In response to his inquiries as to what they were doing, they said they were puzzled by the fact that a woman was singing inside the church although all the doors were locked. The rector listened and he too could hear the faint sound of a lovely young female voice singing in what the rector thought sounded like Norman French. After a moment the singing gradually faded and then ceased. Mr Merryweather unlocked the church door and the three of them entered the church. It was completely deserted. The rector hurried to the vestry door but that too was shut and locked from the inside.

The church bell reportedly tolled by itself on several occasions. Mr Merryweather showed me the bell, after we had climbed the old stone steps to the bell tower. The ringing was reported by local people, visitors and parishioners. Once a maid at the farmhouse was sent over by her mistress to see why the bell was ringing. She found the church deserted and no sign anywhere of anyone in the vicinity of the church. The tolling of the bell seemed to stop as she stepped into the church. I asked her whether she had seen the bell still moving but she said she had been too frightened to climb up to the bell tower. While she was inside the church her mistress arrived and she had climbed to the bell tower. The bell was at that time completely still and she wondered whether the bell-ringing was in fact independent of the existing bell.

Odd things happened during services in the church and these were witnessed by members of the congregation as well as by the rector. Once the lamp above the altar of St George suddenly and quite inexplicably went out. During a break in the service the lamp was relit and ten minutes later, when everyone had almost forgotten about it, the lamp suddenly went out again. In fact this happened on three occasions in the space of two months ('once actually on St George's Day!' Mr Merryweather told me) but never before and never afterwards. However, on one subsequent occasion this particular lamp was seen to swing mysteriously to and fro and on yet another occasion, at the conclusion of the service, the lamp suddenly burst into flames – which the rector hurriedly extinguished. The lamp, I was assured in answer to my question, had *not* recently been refilled.

A month after this lamp had burst into flames the rector was celebrating Holy Communion. As he turned round to read the Gospel, he saw near the west side of the church at the tower end, the figure of a young woman of no more than thirty years of age. She walked soundlessly from a position near the window in the north wall, across the chancel, and disappeared at a corner of the south-west wall. When I asked the rector to explain exactly how the figure disappeared, he told me that 'part of the wall seemed to open' and she passed out of view and then the wall 'closed up again'. He particularly noticed that the figure wore some kind of flowing headgear that reached over her shoulders. She was dressed all in white, was about five feet six inches in height, walked with a slight stoop and her expression seemed to suggest sadness and unhappiness. The figure appeared to be solid and substantial and acted entirely as a normal person – 'until she disappeared into a solid wall'.

I was intrigued by Mr Merryweather's insistence that the figure vanished into the tower wall and not through the present doorway, and it was not until I located some photographs of the interior of Langenhoe church, taken after the 1884 earthquake (in Colchester Public Library), that his story made sense for the photographs clearly showed a former doorway in the internal tower that had been several feet away from the position of the later doorway. This means that Mr Merryweather's account of a figure disappearing 'into the tower wall' could be historically correct and it was not until I showed the rector the photographs that he knew about the earlier doorway.

Some time later, when Merryweather was sitting at the organ in the church, he saw again the same woman in white. This time she seemed to stare in his direction for a second and then she was gone. Again she appeared to walk out of the west wall of the church but this time she was there one minute and gone the next.

I kept in touch with the Turners during the whole of the long Langenhoe investigation and one summer morning James and Cathy Turner thought they would pay a surprise visit to Langenhoe church. They arrived to find the main door locked and no one about. They went round to the back and found the vestry door-handle smashed. It was torn off and lay in two pieces on the ground nearby. They tried the door but it was locked fast. Shortly afterwards the rector arrived and when he inserted his key into the lock he found the door was in fact unlocked and they entered the church. The Turners, always the most practical of people, told me that on this occasion they found the atmosphere of the church very frightening. It was quite dark inside the church, they told me, even on that sunny day, and there was something sinister about the place that morning, in spite of Mr Merryweather's cheerful presence and they were both pleased to make excuses and leave the church and its ghosts.

Soon voices were heard on odd occasions inside the church and these were not only heard by the rector. Mr William Ware, a bricklayer and former bell-ringer at Langenhoe, was there to do some repair work and when he had difficulty in opening the vestry door he went to the nearest cottage for help. When Mr Cross returned with him to the church the vestry door opened without difficulty! However, when they were inside the empty church they were both startled to suddenly hear what sounded like a woman's voice say 'Ow!' They could find no explanation and were not exactly comforted to learn that in exactly the same spot (where a murder *may* have been committed) a week earlier the rector had also heard what he described as a woman's voice saying something like 'Ow!'

I personally interviewed Mr Ware and Mr Cross independently and the former told me that although previously he had been sceptical of the alleged haunting of Langenhoe church he had to admit that recent experiences had caused him to change his mind. On one occasion he was climbing to the church roof to replace some tiles when suddenly the church bell chimed twice, loudly and clearly, although no one was inside the church at the time, as he very well knew. Later, having completed his work on the roof he climbed to the bell tower and carefully examined the bell. He told me he found several cobwebs linking the bell to the bell-pull and in no way could the bell have been rung recently without breaking the cobwebs, so Mr Ware too asked me whether it was possible that the bell-ringing he had heard emanating from the church tower could in fact have been independent of the existing bell. A former parish clerk told me there was a long-standing tradition of the bell of Langenhoe church ringing without human agency and he is among those who have heard disembodied heavy footsteps and other unexplained sounds in the church.

Inexplicable smells and paranormal odours now joined the wealth of curious experiences at Langenhoe. One Saturday morning an overwhelming smell of spring violets surprised the rector and Mrs Barnes and a friend – 'completely out of season', as Mr Merryweather put it. But less pleasant smells were reported too; once the rector noticed a 'vile smell', which he compared to that of a rotting corpse, at the west end of the church where the nun-like figure had disappeared and incidentally where a 'sensitive', visiting the church for the first time and knowing nothing of the reported hauntings, immediately suggested to me that the body of a murdered woman had been hidden. Here, on more than one occasion, unexplained sounds as well as odours have been reported, quite spontaneously, by visitors.

It was from the same area, the west end of the church, that a few months later the rector suddenly heard the voice of a young woman singing in the church. He described the music as resembling Gregorian plainsong chanting but much 'sweeter' somehow. As the singing ceased, the rector heard the unmistakable heavy tread of a man's footsteps, walking, as he put it 'with slow and sinister tread' up the nave. The rector hurriedly moved to give himself a better view but as he did so the footsteps abruptly ceased and, search as he would, he could find nothing that might have accounted for either the singing or the footsteps.

Two years later, almost to the day, the rector stepped into the vestry and immediately became aware of the sound of voices coming from the direction of the body of the church. It sounded like two or three people holding an animated conversation but in undertones somewhere in the chancel. In particular, a man's voice seemed to predominate although no actual words were distinguishable. Almost as soon as the rector became aware of the sounds, and stood still to listen, the voices ceased. Then he heard a deep sigh, 'as though the speaker was depressed beyond words at the state of affairs' and then silence reigned. Needless to say, the rector went immediately into the deserted church but found nothing to explain the sounds he had heard.

One January morning the rector arrived at the deserted church and after spending some fifteen minutes inside the church, he chanced to go out into the churchyard to throw away some dead flowers. As he returned to the church he discovered the full and clear imprint of a white hand on the vestry door! The print was so obvious and distinct that he was positive that had it been there fifteen minutes earlier when he had first arrived and unlocked the vestry door, he could not have failed to notice it. The mark suggested a hand dipped in some sort of white substance such as cornflower or powdered chalk; yet no one else was near the church, the rector assured me. Mrs Barnes and Irene, arriving shortly afterwards, found the imprint immediately and they both thought it represented the hand of a young woman. The mark remained for ten days before gradually fading away.

Six months later the figure of a young woman wearing a flowing head-dress was seen again, two years after the last

215

time. The rector, about to conclude the reading of the Gospel, suddenly noticed a figure in the aisle. It was the figure of the young woman he had seen before! She was dressed exactly as before but this time she stood facing the statue of St George, the credence bell, and the old church entrance used years before by occupants of the manor house. As he watched, the figure seemed to float through the table on which the statue stood, and 'she' disappeared from sight through the blocked-up doorway.

A similar figure was seen four years later. This time, as the rector was singing a psalm before the 10.45 a.m. Sunday service, he felt someone was watching him, and looking towards the lectern he was astonished to see the figure of a young woman wearing a cream dress. She appeared to be quite normal and had a sweet oval face and blue eyes. She seemed to give the rector a 'strange, sad look' and as he was about to speak to her, she was no longer there; but, and this I found interesting, the cream dress seemed to linger on for a little while after its wearer had vanished.

Another apparition was seen by the rector on just one occasion. One Christmas Eve morning, alone in the church about 10.45 a.m., the rector was walking up the nave towards the chancel when a 'vague form' appeared in front of him from nowhere. It slowly glided across the nave and disappeared in the vicinity of the pulpit. Although Mr Merryweather found great difficulty in describing this apparitional form, he had the distinct impression that it was a man in fairly modern dress, possibly a tweed suit.

During the following months and years a variety of incidents were reported to me: light footsteps in the churchyard, coming round the north side of the church;

rattling and banging at various church doors; door-opening; a singing girl in the churchyard; voices; music; and various unexplained movements of objects.

I determined to spend a night in the haunted church but meanwhile inquiries in the area itself and miles away proved instructive too. Local people often referred to the church as 'that haunted place' as it had been known for many years; an elderly local lady recalled her aunt warning her about a 'ghost lady' that walked round Langenhoe church: this would be about 1910; a former superintendent of the firing-range at nearby Fingringhoe remembered, years ago, some people telling him they had seen a 'ghostly lady' walking round Langenhoe church, dressed in white; while early in the days of the present century there was a story about Langenhoe church bell ringing by itself.

My friend John Dening, as part of his preparation for the Ministry, took part in various church missions, especially among the hop and fruit pickers not many miles from his home at Fleet in Hampshire. There he chanced to make the acquaintance of an elderly gipsy named Mrs Booth who, to John Dening's considerable surprise, knew all about Langenhoe church and its ghosts.

Many years previously when Mrs Booth was a young girl, she and her sisters and their parents often camped in the lane leading to Langenhoe church. As long as she could remember Mrs Booth recalled hearing stories of the haunted church and the ghost that sometimes walked in the churchyard. One night she and her sister decided to 'sit up for the ghost' Mrs Booth said; she was about fifteen at the time and her sister was a year older. It was probably 1908 or thereabouts. The girls sat up in an open-sided barn that in those days faced the north-west side of the church. Soon after midnight, in bright moonlight, they heard the church bell clang twice, softly yet clearly, and a moment later a figure appeared at the east corner of the church, moved along the path beside the church, and disappeared into the north wall, towards the west end of the church. The grey-white figure, that of a young woman, was quite clear-cut and solid-looking; it seemed to be dressed in old-fashioned, rather 'nun-like' garb with what appeared to be plaits hanging over her shoulders. Both sisters had the impression that she was a young woman. As the figure came clearly into view they heard the sounds of a beautiful feminine voice singing in the clear night air. But there was an interesting difference in the receptivity of the experience by the two sisters. Whereas Mrs Booth said she saw and heard the apparition including the apparent rustling of the long dress against the grass, her sister only heard the bell-ringing, the singing and the rustling – she saw nothing! This curious difference was realised almost immediately when the sisters described their experiences on the spot.

What is extremely interesting is that, when Mr Merryweather saw what would appear to be the same figure inside the church, it appeared out of the north wall of the church near the tower – precisely the place where the figure seen and heard by Mrs Booth and her sister would have appeared had she passed through the wall where she disappeared!

Mr Merryweather was kind enough to say that he had no objection to my spending a night in Langenhoe church; that my vigil would be confidential and undisturbed; that I was free to make such experimentation and investigation with or without scientific instruments as I wished; and I was free to have with me anyone of my choice. John Dening had collaborated with me in this investigation rather more than any other individual and when James Turner, whose integrity and level-headedness I appreciated, said he would rather not spend a night in 'that haunted place', and John Dening suddenly came up with the same idea, I decided that John Dening it should be and so it was arranged.

I took with me that night various instruments for measuring temperature, humidity, magnetic fields and electric fields, both inside and outside the church; and I attempted to 'control' a number of objects both inside the church and in the surrounding churchyard. I sealed all doors and windows, ringed with chalk a number of movable objects that had attracted attention in the past and added a few possibly tempting objects; a crucifix, a Bible, a mirror, etc. I even left pencils and pads of paper here and there about the church in case an entity should feel inclined to leave a message!

Objects that had been moved or disturbed in the past – doors and doorways, lamps, the credence bell, the statue of St George, the path of the 'phantom girl' – were all under special surveillance throughout the night. Powdered chalk was spread along the route taken by alleged apparitions and where footsteps had been heard, and sensitive recording apparatus was placed where voices had been reported. Threads and wires were also strung across the church at strategic places – in fact the whole range of the psychical researcher's investigating paraphernalia and simple commonsense precautions were all brought into play in an effort to prove scientifically the presence of a paranormal entity or being in the vicinity of Langenhoe church that night, should one be present. Unfortunately, there was a tremendous thunderstorm that lasted for hours and the repeated crash of thunder and the steady downpour of rain beating on the roof and running through the guttering and down the drainpipes could well have drowned any paranormal auditory phenomena in the church that night.

However, once or twice, between the sounds of the storm, we were alerted by sounds not of this world, or so it seemed, for we never did find a rational explanation for the loud 'thuds', the vibrating 'bangs', the strange sibilant whispering sounds, the apparent footsteps or the snatches of music. Certainly we had no recorded evidence but those fragmentary and spontaneous flashes of momentary psychic activity, if that is what they were, remained as lasting memories of Langenhoe at night.

In fact none of my instruments showed any abnormality and all my 'controls' were untouched and everything seemed normal. We may have been on the edge of the unknown that night, and it certainly sounded like it on occasions, but nothing manifested its presence and one of the few memorable moments of that visit for me was the magnificent view from the top of Langenhoe church tower, away across the marshes to Mersea Island, as the autumn dawn was breaking.

Subsequently a series of seances, mainly organised by John Dening and held at Langenhoe and elsewhere, appeared to shed some light on some of the strange happenings at Langenhoe. But that is another story, a story that may well see the light of day from the pen of the Rev. John C. Dening.

In 1993, I asked John Dening for his memories of that night and he said he remembered so well all the trouble I went to with instruments and 'controls'. 'In theory,' he said, 'this should have been "bait on a plate" to a poltergeist, since all it would need to do to register its presence would be to move one of the objects a fraction of an inch over the chalk line . . .' But it was not to be.

On one of my last visits to Mr Merryweather when I was accompanied by my wife and daughter and Dr Peter Hilton-Rowe, the rector presented me with his private notes on the case and also a relic from Langenhoe church: the beautiful little credence bell. I am hoping it will ring for me one day without a human being anywhere near it, as it did at haunted Langenhoe.

The church that had defied five centuries and one catastrophic earthquake was finally closed in 1959; it stood for a few years empty and alone with its ghosts and was finally demolished three years later. Today all that remains of what must have been the most haunted church in England during its heyday is a small field ringed with gravestones, eerily overgrown with weeds and brambles, leaning at different angles towards the empty space in the centre where a very haunted church once stood.

Loventor Manor and
Berry Pomeroy Castle

Loventor Manor stands within a stone's throw of the haunted castle ruins of Berry Pomeroy in Devon. A haven of peace, rest and good food, the Manor was an ideal 'get away from it all' place and Anne Weston who ran it as a hotel a few years ago was a mine of information about its history and its ghosts.

Atmospheric Loventor Manor with its haunted cellars and bedrooms is mentioned in Domesday Book (1086) where it is described as a Devon longhouse. According to persistent reports, a ghostly medieval monk still walks the ancient stone floors until he disappears into the solid, thick walls. The years have brought alterations to Loventor and during both the Elizabethan and the Georgian eras wings were added to the main building. It is appropriate therefore that ghosts of an Elizabethan lady and a Georgian dandy haunt this beautiful house – or did at one time. The former appeared most frequently in the large bedroom with an original canopy bed and windows looking out to the rolling Devon countryside – a room where my wife and I spent nights in spring, summer and autumn.

During one visit to the Manor we heard footsteps in the night; nothing very odd about that perhaps, except that the footsteps sounded as though they mounted the stairs and approached our bedroom door and then stopped. After a while the whole performance was repeated – footsteps audible as they climbed the stairs and then distinct and definite as they approached our room where they seemed to stop outside the door. After the whole performance happened yet again I determined to see whether I could forestall whatever was seemingly striving to visit us.

Sure enough, just as I was about to drop off to sleep again, I heard faint footsteps mounting the stairs; the sounds grew louder, more definite and more determined it seemed as they reached the head of the stairs. They were quite loud now and as they steadily approached our bedroom door I was out of bed in one bound and I flung open the door! Only silence and darkness greeted me. The moonlight, filtering through the windows, confirmed that the stairs were devoid of anyone and there was no one in sight who could have caused the footsteps. I stood for a moment in the darkness; listening, but no sound reached my ears, except my own breathing. Quietly I returned to the bedroom, closed the door gently and stood just inside, waiting and listening. But I heard nothing more and I returned to bed and was soon asleep and I slept undisturbed until morning. I never solved the mystery and often wonder whether, in opening the bedroom door, I let someone or something in! At all events we always slept soundly and undisturbed in that room afterwards. Others had not only heard sounds but seen an Elizabethan lady and I was rather disappointed that she did not deign to visit us . . .

The other ghost, the Georgian dandy, reportedly appears in one of the original spacious reception rooms. It was in that room, when I took a party of Ghost Club members to Devon, that we were told by erudite and charming Deryck Seymour (not related to the Pomeroy Seymours, to my knowledge) and his late wife about the story of Berry Pomeroy Castle: its history and its ghosts. Deryck Seymour is the author of two books devoted to the castle and its ghosts and hauntings entitled appropriately, *Berry Pomeroy Castle* (1982) and *The Ghosts of Berry Pomeroy Castle* (1990). He has also written books on Torre Abbey and the ghosts of Torbay.

Few places in Devon, or anywhere else for that matter, have been in the hands of only two families for 900 years. Berry Pomeroy Castle is one such place. The lands at Berry Pomeroy were held by Alric the Saxon before William the Conqueror gave them to one of his chief supporters, Ralf de Pomerae, and of the fifty-five manors in Devon so bestowed, Berry was by far the richest.

Generations of Pomeroys married and remained at Berry and the lands prospered. In 1292, the demesne consisted of a hall, with chambers, kitchen, grange and other buildings; gardens; a dovecote; church; arable and meadow land and a park overpopulated by wild beasts. At the end of the thirteenth century Henry, the ninth generation Pomeroy at Berry, built a great castle on a small promontory of land. The castle was finished before Henry's death in 1305 and here the Pomeroys lived for almost 250 years. The great gateway in the massive surrounding wall still stands with its guardhouse above with Norman pillars.

In 1549, Thomas Pomeroy became one of the leaders of the Prayer Book Rebellion and although captured and marched to London, he escaped with his life and even retained his knighthood but all his property was forfeited to the Crown and Berry Pomeroy castle was purchased by the then Lord Protector, Sir Edward Seymour.

Within the castle walls Sir Edward and his son built two-thirds of a beautiful late-Tudor mansion, making three sides of a square with the Norman building. The walls of the great section to the east still stand, their huge rectangular mullioned windows stark against the sky.

By about 1800, the building was deserted and it stood abandoned for many years, gradually becoming the wreck of a once stately home – a tragedy in broken stones, it has been called. But the Seymour family never parted with Berry Pomeroy and today the castle belongs to the nineteenth Duke of Somerset although under a Deed of Guardianship in 1977 the ancient castle is maintained by English Heritage. Recent renovation and improvements have changed the castle where once scores of men and women lived and worked and loved and schemed and died. Today the ghosts of Berry Pomeroy are many and varied and Deryck Seymour has records of over eighty living people who can testify that strange things have happened to them at Berry Pomeroy Castle.

One of the schemers was Eleanor de Pomeroy who, as mistress of the castle in her day, had a beautiful sister Margaret. Both sisters were enamoured of the same man and Eleanor, jealous of her sister's beauty and effect on the man they both loved, caused Margaret to be imprisoned in the deep, dark dungeons of Berry Pomeroy where she starved to death. Her ghost, sometimes known as the White Lady, rises from the dungeons, according to the time-honoured story, and leaves St Margaret's Tower in flowing white robes and walks the ramparts, beckoning those who see her. In recent years this ghost has reportedly been seen by Craig Rowland in 1982 and by Warren Hunt in 1987 among others.

A ghostly Blue Lady has been reported at Berry Pomeroy for over 200 years. The celebrated writer and ghost hunter Elliott O'Donnell (1872–1965) once told me he had traced back reports of this particular haunting many hundreds of years and it became widely known when a physician to King George IV, who later became Sir Walter Farquhar, from nearby Torquay, was summoned to the castle to attend the wife of the then steward. The castle was in a ruinous state but a few rooms remained habitable. While waiting to see the patient the doctor, in what he described as a large, lofty and oak-panelled room with a flight of stairs in one corner which presumably led to other chambers, encountered something quite unexpected.

Suddenly the door of the room opened and a richly dressed lady appeared wringing her hands, obviously in great distress as she crossed the room, oblivious it seemed to the presence of Dr Farquhar, and mounted the stairs. Before she disappeared from sight the doctor had an excellent view of her features: she was young and beautiful but her face exhibited infinite sadness and the agony of remorse.

Almost immediately afterwards the doctor was called to

see his patient whom he found so ill that he gave her his undivided attention and said he would return next day. When he did so he was pleasantly surprised to find her much better and before leaving the steward on this occasion, he inquired as to the identity of the lady he had seen the day before, describing her appearance and countenance in some detail. The steward became greatly alarmed and said repeatedly, 'My poor wife . . . my poor wife . . .'

When he was calmer he told the doctor that he was now certain that his wife would die and he recounted the story of that castle apparition. It appeared that the ghost was that of the daughter of a former lord of Berry Pomeroy who had borne a child to her own father and had promptly strangled it in that upper room. The steward added that the appearance of the ghost always preceded the death of someone in the castle. He had lived in the castle for thirty years and he had never known the omen fail. On a personal level the ghost had been seen the day his son had met his death by drowning. Now nothing would convince the steward but that his wife would die.

Dr Farquhar consoled the man, assuring him that his wife was much better and he was very surprised when the steward's wife died next day. *The Annals of the Seymours* (1902) quoted by Deryck Seymour, goes on to record that many years later Sir Walter Farquhar was called upon by a lady who wished him to see her sister who seemed to be suffering from shock. Sir Walter learned that while accompanying her brother on a visit to Torquay they had visited the ruins of Berry Pomeroy and there they learned the steward was ill and they had some difficulty in obtaining the keys. While her brother had gone in search of them, he left his sister in a large outer room (from her description the same one the doctor had waited in to see the steward's wife). When he returned he found his sister in a terrible state of alarm and distress and she declared that she had seen an apparition – and its description corresponded with the figure Farquhar had seen years before. The steward had in fact died while they were at the castle. Sir Walter saw the lady in question and she recovered; indeed according to the *Annals* the apparition was never seen again since the old steward who died on that occasion was the last person to inhabit the castle. However, Deryck Seymour challenges this and quotes three further appearances involving an army officer, the daughter of a clergyman, and Mrs Jane Everett of Torquay as recently as 1980. Some versions of the sightings of this apparition suggest that the Blue Lady attempts to lure those who see her to some unsafe spot where they are liable to have a serious accident . . .

In the records of the Pomeroys there is a story that long ago two brothers, when besieged and driven to the point of surrender, chose to save their families and retainers from the horrors of yielding to a ruthless foe by bargaining for the lives of the castle occupants with their capitulation and in fact forfeiting their own lives. The two knights, in armour and all the regalia of medieval warfare, mounted their charges and galloped along the north terrace and spurred their horses over the brink of the precipice on which the castle stands at a spot subsequently known as 'Pomeroy's Leap'; thus riding to a terrible death but saving the honour of the family and earning the respect of their enemies who permitted the burial of the brothers within the precincts of the castle and the castle itself an honourable surrender. Substantiation of this or any similar story is difficult but something of the kind probably took place to give the escarpment its name and to account for the strange sounds and echoes from the past that have been reported hereabouts – including the clash of arms, the thunder of horses' hooves, the clink and clang of armour, and screams and sickening thuds – all of which seem to have no rational explanation.

Still other ghosts at Berry Pomeroy include a black hound; an old man with a scythe; an old lady in old-fashioned garments and a cavalier; while totally unexplained phenomena include incidents of a blue light; freezing air; the sound of doors slamming; footsteps; crashing noises; the sound of a baby crying; touchings; smoke; odd odours; puzzling shadows that have no substance; and interference with photographic apparatus.

In 1967, the author Robert Graves told me of the time he had found Berry Pomeroy castle closed to visitors but having discovered a gap near the main gate he had wriggled through. Once within the castle precincts he became 'overwhelmed by a nameless horror' but he resolutely visited the dungeons and parts of the ruins until he could stand the strain no longer and he fled back to safety. Two days later he and his wife were visited by Mr Beer, the husband of Graves' local typist, and over a cup of tea he casually asked whether Graves knew Berry Pomeroy and then he brought out a photograph and said, 'What do you think of this?'

Robert Graves continued: 'The photograph showed a tall, thin woman in fourteenth-century costume, walking past the gate that I had wriggled under – and leading a small ape on a chain. When Mr Beer had gone, I burned the photograph. It was too horrible. But, fortunately, my wife will testify to the woman and the ape. I recalled the Elizabethan phrase: "To lead apes in hell". Shakespeare used it in *Much Ado About Nothing*, meaning to be a passionate woman cheated of her sex life. And I concluded that Mr Beer, a simple soul, had felt the presence of that unhappy woman in the castle court and somehow impressed the picture on his sensitive camera plate. But if so, who was she? She had nothing to do with me.

'Years later, I read that Isabella of France, Edward II's widow, had spent some years at Berry Pomeroy. As a young woman, after providing the throne with an heir apparent, she had been neglected by her homosexual husband in favour of his lover, Piers Gaveston. Eventually, she deposed him with French help, procured his murder and put her son, Edward III, on the throne. He did not, however, prove grateful and sent her off, under guard, to various castle keeps remote from London until, after many years of "leading apes in hell", she took the veil of the Order of St Clara. I began to think again about my feelings of fear at Berry Pomeroy. I have never forgotten that awful feeling of absolute terror and I never shall. There is something not of this world at Berry Pomeroy.'

On midsummer's eve, 1983, the night of the summer solstice when various psychic activity has been reported at Berry Pomeroy, I took part in a ghost watch with Deryck Seymour, Bob Daulby, Jack Hazzard, a lady 'sensitive' (Eileen) and a few other people interested in the mysteries of the place, as recounted by Deryck Seymour. In view of the unrestrained, uncontrolled and unscientific nature of the proceedings, interesting as they were for a few hours, when nothing of a paranormal nature seemed to have happened by 12.30 a.m., most of us departed leaving Bob Daulby, Eileen and a couple who had arrived and joined the assemblage. It is a decision I have always regretted; at least Deryck Seymour and I should have stuck it out . . .

After a while the latest couple to join the ghost watch decided to spend some time in the dungeon at the base of St Margaret's Tower. Time passed and in his subsequent report Bob Daulby says nothing of great moment happened for a long time and he and Eileen were quite enjoying the seemingly peaceful night. They had not heard a word from the young couple in the dungeon. Then, as Bob bent down to pour himself some hot soup he, as Robert Graves had been, was suddenly gripped by an overwhelming fear such as he had never experienced before in his life. The hair on the back of his neck stood up and he knew what it was to be petrified with fright and yet there was nothing that he could see or feel that might so affect him. He is certainly not the type of person to be so affected and one wonders what it could have been about Berry Pomeroy that caused such feelings.

As the utter terror subsided very slightly, he turned towards Eileen and tried to tell her of his distress when he saw that her face was contorted with horror and she appeared to be trembling with apprehension herself. She was transfixed, her eyes fastened on something at the top of the old stone staircase. He said later that he had never seen such fear on a person's face as she silently pointed towards the object of her terror. She said afterwards that she had the impression of a girl – but she could not say more. At this point Bob became aware that his face literally ached from yearning to release a scream, but no sound would come. Suddenly, however, a harsh and hopeless scream echoed from the depths of the castle. The girl who had been calmly sitting in the dungeon with her friend for over two hours screamed at such a pitch and with such volume that it seemed the very castle itself was screaming. As Bob later put it, 'Suddenly, on a warm summer night in the heart of Devon, madness reigned.'

A feeling of utter terror seemed to fill the air and some awful power seemed to hold Bob and his companions in such a grip that they all felt doomed to an unimaginable fate – the power of that force of horror was so great. At long last and with considerable effort Bob managed to exert some control over his emotions and as soon as he could utter a few rational words it was to suggest that they leave the castle at once. It had exerted its power and he encountered no opposition when he suggested they interfere no longer but leave the castle to its own destiny.

Yet, even as they hurriedly collected their things together and fled it was as if the entity that was aware of their presence, whatever it was, followed them out of the castle, out of the grounds and surroundings and none of them felt completely free of that awful force until they had passed the Lodge, having hurried, subdued and thoughtful, all the way along the winding glen banked high with shrubs and trees. Bob said afterwards, 'It was one of the longest walks of our lives.'

It was a full three days before Eileen could bring herself to describe what she had seen. Apart from the frightening figure of a girl, she had seen what seemed to be a huge black cloud and with her clairvoyant talent she felt that within that cloud there seemed to be embodied everything that was evil. It was an awful experience and she vowed never again to as much as go near the castle of Berry Pomeroy, let alone enter it. But Bob Daulby was made of sterner stuff. Although that night had been an experience he hoped never to repeat, he was curious and in fact he returned and spent hours and hours sitting within the castle walls on no fewer than seventeen further occasions, eleven throughout the night and six in daylight. But, to his enormous relief, there was no repetition of the events or impressions or feelings of that night in June.

Still Bob Daulby was not satisfied. Since nothing further transpired at Berry Pomeroy he decided to see whether contact could be made with whatever was haunting the castle via the ouija board or glass and letters. The board had worked quite well for him on two previous occasions but this time, in the company of some treasured friends and Eileen and Anne, Bob's wife, he was astonished at the immediate 'power' that seemed to run through the glass. Almost immediately the glass moved erratically and speedily round the board as if, whoever or whatever it was, was in a state of panic. After a moment Bob gathered himself together, ordered the communicating entity to stop and give its name. The glass slowed momentarily and then spelt out, with concentrated deliberation, the name 'Isabelle'.

At this Eileen put her free hand to her mouth while the glass moved swiftly, covering the whole board at a tremendous rate and in an uncontrollable manner. Eileen asked whether the communicator was the same person she had seen at Berry Pomeroy. The glass stopped in its tracks and darted round the board to come to a dead stop at the word 'YES'. Then there was more energetic speeding round and round the board and, trying to bring reason to the rising panic that was beginning to envelop them all, Bob asked, 'How old are you?' and the reply came: 'Nine'.

Again the glass seemed alive and tore round and round the board but before Bob could think of another question to calm the proceedings Eileen suddenly screamed. She took her finger off the glass and was obviously very shaken. 'I've just seen her,' she said in a subdued voice. 'She's horrible . . . horrible. I saw just her head poking out of the top of the table. I couldn't see her body, just her head. She was looking at me and grinning. She's really horrible! I can't stay here . . .' Nothing would persuade her to stay and she promptly left the house, slamming the front door behind her.

After Eileen left, the remaining sitters put the board and glass away and Anne decided that she too would call it a day and she retired for the night. Some of their friends left too but a couple of them stayed, saying they could not yet face the night. Suddenly there was a knock at the door. It was Eileen; she said she couldn't face walking down the next street alone – could she stay the night? An hour or so passed in complete peace and quiet when suddenly there was a scream from Anne upstairs in bed. Bob rushed up and found Anne huddled in a ball and buried under the quilt. She was so tightly wrapped up that it took Bob several minutes to get her to release her grip and unravel the quilt.

After a while she was able to recount what had frightened her. First, just as she was dropping off to sleep, she felt the impression of someone sitting against the back of her legs. Thinking it must be her husband, she told him to get off, and when the weight stayed there she became a little annoyed, opened her eyes and turned over. It wasn't Bob – it was Isabelle! 'She was sitting on my legs!' Anne told Bob quietly. 'And when she turned to look at me, our eyes met and she grinned – a really evil grin. Her eyes looked dull and dead – but that grin: there was no humour in it, and I knew for certain that she wanted to harm me. I felt she wanted to harm everyone in the house in any way she could, starting with me. She's really evil!'

They were interrupted by a scream from downstairs! Bob rushed down to be greeted by three startled and pallid faces. Eileen said, 'She's there, Bob, sitting in that chair, laughing at us. Can't you see her? She's evil! Look at her!' Bob looked, and so did the others, but they could see nothing. 'She's there, I tell you,' insisted Eileen. 'She's sitting there, laughing at you now . . .' Bob took his courage in both hands and sat down in the chair he was told was occupied by the ghost. He felt nothing but the three frightened people looking at him said it all: the real fear that Isabelle *might* be there had got to them. Bob was undecided what to do. If Isabelle was indeed there, then she would sense his feelings – he felt angry and wanted to grapple with whatever was there, but there was nothing visible to attack! Before he had time to make a move, however, Eileen called out that Isabelle was running out of the room and going upstairs towards Anne! Bob ran upstairs and tried to call the tune, commanding Isabelle to sit down and not to move.

Ever since Isabelle had, apparently, appeared the house had seemed abnormally cold and nothing they did seemed to warm it. The whole night, it seemed, Isabelle moved from one person to another, frightening them in turn and by now everyone was in a state of exhaustion. Slowly, very slowly it seemed, dawn came and the feeling that Isabelle was present disappeared. It was almost as though daylight and the warmth of the sun chased her away. Everyone felt the change and Bob's friends and Eileen decided they could now leave the house and go home to bed.

Late that afternoon, just when they were beginning to think that it was all over, Isabelle returned. Eileen, who lived not far away, dashed in and said Isabelle had been running about her house all day and touching her. She had stood as much of it as she could and now she was afraid that Isabelle had followed her and that she was back in Bob's house again! This time, to his horror, Bob could feel her presence; there was no denying it, she was in the house and she must be very powerful, thought Bob to himself, to make her presence known to a non-psychic like himself. Then he felt her touch him and he knew what Anne and Eileen had gone through.

For three days and nights the awful infestation continued. The nights were terrifying and the days not much better. At his wits' end Bob telephoned the friends who had been at the house when Isabelle had first 'appeared' but they had not been unduly bothered by the phantom form. Bob and Anne and Eileen wondered when it would all end and how they wished they had never visited Berry

Pomeroy. Finally, on the third night, Bob had a very strange and realistic dream. When he awoke something told him that he had Isabelle beaten. He *knew* she could not bother them again and his conviction eventually won the day and he at length convinced both Anne and Eileen that they had nothing more to fear.

That night Bob brought out the ouija board and glass and letters again. He knew that Isabelle would make contact but he was no longer frightened of her and nor were Anne and Eileen, the other two participants in the seance. At first the glass seemed dead but they tried again and again. At the fourth attempt Isabelle made contact. Bob told her he was not frightened of her and neither was anyone else; she was just a little girl and it wasn't her they disliked, only the silly and alarming things that she did. Over the next few months, via the ouija board, Isabelle told them a great deal about her life, her death and the reason she had chosen to keep close to them in particular, among the many people who visited Berry Pomeroy.

Briefly, Isabelle said she was a bastard Pomeroy and rarely saw her father; in fact she was such an embarrassment that she rarely saw anyone. She had lived her life within the stone walls of Berry Pomeroy but she did not have the freedom of the whole building, only certain parts were open to her and such freedom as she enjoyed was severely curtailed whenever strangers or guests appeared. In spite of numerous attempts the sitters were unable to obtain the names of her father or mother, nor that of a close friend or any guests.

Isabelle said she was a 'Pomeroy pet' inasmuch as she was always well dressed, well looked after and respected to a degree by the servants. 'Pomeroy in part was better than no Pomeroy at all,' she said and this demanded certain privileges. She was seen to her bed each night by a servant and her room was always warm and the bed aired and supplied with fresh linen. She could hardly have been treated better had she been royalty!

One evening, however, she surprised a drunken orgy of the lord and his friends and one of them, when the bewildered little girl tried to interfere, threw her roughly to the floor. Her head hit a stone step and she died instantly. Not aware that she was dead she still tried to help a servant who was being cruelly treated and only realised that something was wrong when she met no resistance in encountering any of the rough men. Whatever she did had no effect; in fact when she tried to grasp someone or protect herself her hands went clean through those around her and no one took any notice of her whatever – they didn't seem to see her and they didn't seem to hear her; and then she saw her own body lying crumpled on the floor and she realised that she was dead!

For the next 500 years the bewildered and troubled child haunted the castle. She saw the last of the Pomeroys leave and the arrival and departure of the Seymours, and in particular the opening of the castle to the general public, bringing to Isabelle as never before the opportunity of mixing with sensitives, mediums and psychics from whom she drew strength and increased her powers of materialisation and mental influence. She discovered that she could gain attention by frightening people with any form of psychic activity or demonstration and she claimed to be the source of many of the mysterious happenings reported at

Berry Pomeroy. However, the love and kindness shown by Bob Daulby and his wife and friends helped Isabelle and they came to believe that she has now progressed beyond Berry Pomeroy castle where her ghost no longer lingers.

Be that as it may, ghosts and ghostly activity continue to be reported from Berry Pomeroy. The figure of a woman of thirty to thirty-five in a long grey dress, and looking white and haggard and desperately unhappy has been seen by the gatehouse around midnight; unexplained lights have been seen pulsating in the dungeons; freezing air has been encountered; voices are heard among the empty ruins and in July 1993, when I was in the middle of writing this book, I received a letter from a stranger, Terry Buttery of Weston Park, Longton, Stoke-on-Trent in which he said:

On Thursday 8 July 1993, I paid a visit to Berry Pomeroy castle with my daughter Rosalind, aged thirteen years. We made our way through the gatehouse into the ruins taking photographs, and proceeded by way of the Margaret Tower and Rampart Walk to the restored chapel above the Gatehouse.

Whilst in the chapel I was admiring the fresco on what I believe is the south wall when Rosalind suddenly exclaimed 'Oh!' I asked her what was the matter and she told me that she had seen the shadow of someone descending the spiral steps to the cellar below. I asked Rosalind to repeat what she had seen and she said someone had gone down to the cellar.

I dashed down the steps followed by Rosalind only to find the cellar empty. At this point Rosalind complained of feeling hot and sweaty and she was actually sweating profusely although it was not a particularly hot day.

We made our way out of the cellar and through the Gatehouse and stopped to speak to the ladies in charge of the admission kiosk and tea-room, and we were informed that others had experienced the same sensations in that area of the chapel.

I must state that I had heard of the Castle being haunted but was of the opinion that the 'haunting' was confined to the Margaret Tower. My daughter had no previous knowledge of any reputed haunting of the Castle. During our visit I never felt any of the Castle's supposed malevolence, in fact quite the opposite, to me all was very quiet and tranquil.

As for me, memories seep up from the heavy darkness of my mind: the long, quiet lane that leads to Berry Pomeroy, and inside the ruins the pulsating atmosphere of events long past, and the approach to brooding Loventor Manor with its entrance porch that seems to lead from this world into the next.

Mermaid Inn
and Lamb House

To walk along the incomparable Mermaid Street, rated by some as one of the seven most famous streets in the world, and into the coolness of the ancient Mermaid Inn, now one of the Hotels of the Cinque Ports, is to step into another world. In fact this wonderful inn was *rebuilt* in 1420! With its secret staircase, priests' hole and the ghosts of a young lady murdered by smugglers, a portly gentleman from a bygone age and a pair of Elizabethan duellists, it seemed an ideal location for a Ghost Club Spring Visit and so it turned out to be, for here the presence of the past is well embedded within the ancient walls.

The young lady, so the story goes, had a lover among the smugglers who certainly used the inn for many years – indeed at one time it was the headquarters of the infamous Hawkhurst Gang. Soon her infatuation and constant yearning to be with her lover was thought to be a liability and she was murdered. Some years ago now the proprietor at this most picturesque of all haunted inns, became irritated by the constant disturbances reported by staff and visitors – not to mention the ghostly appearances – and he invited a medium to sit up with him in one of the haunted areas where in fact, only a week before, a phantom duel had reportedly been witnessed.

The medium was suitably impressed by the building and its atmosphere and said she was certain the old building would provide them with a ghostly appearance. But in the way of such things the medium fell into a deep sleep and the proprietor witnessed more than he expected! Like a motion picture he saw the two ghostly protagonists fight an exciting duel which ended when one of them ran the other through with his rapier. Then, after only a moment's hesitation, he disposed of the corpse beneath the floorboards of the room. Hardly able to believe his eyes the proprietor watched the whole episode acted out, almost like a dream, with the adversaries dressed in Elizabethan costume and each striving to kill the other – but he heard not a single sound!

During the night of 29 October 1913, a Mrs Aldington awoke at the Mermaid to find a duel taking place in her bedroom, the Elizabethan Chamber, with its four-poster bedstead. Two combatants dressed in doublet and hose were earnestly fighting with rapiers. When one disposed of his opponent, the victor opened a secret passage in the panelling and threw the body into the 'oubliette', a secret dungeon hole with a trap-door entrance in the corner of the room. The secret passage and the oubliette (with the entrance blocked) are still there today – we inspected them – and if the ghosts are not often seen these days there are several October anniversaries when they were reported during the 1970s and 1980s.

The unidentified 'portly gentleman' appears in Dr Syn's Bedchamber, the spacious bedroom with its magnificent carved bedheads and secret stairway concealed behind a bookcase. It may seem strange to commemorate the name of 'Dr Syn', a fictitious character created by Russell Thorndike, but the inn was undoubtedly frequented for years by smugglers. Who recognises the names of Gray or Kingsmill as 'Gentlemen'? Yet most people have heard of Dr Syn, immortalised in books, plays and films, for he was the embodiment of all the rascally attributes and artful abilities that distinguish 'the Gentlemen' . . . and perhaps it is one of these 'Gentlemen', corpulent and expansive, whose ghost has been glimpsed many times in this room; a figure that seems to fade into the oak panelling almost as soon as it is seen.

Incredible as it may seem, The Mermaid probably dates from about 1156; certainly in 1300 the inn stood on the present site, built of wattle, daub, lath and plaster. In those days the Mermaid brewed its own ale and charged a penny a night for lodging. Then a busy sea port, the town contributed four ships to the Cinque Ports Fleet in 1336 and maintained and repaired the King's Galleys.

In 1337, the French made one of their frequent raids on the town and this time with considerable success. They destroyed by fire every building that was not built of stone. This included The Mermaid and only the present cellar survives. In fact The Mermaid's cellar is cut from rock and has a barrel-vaulted ceiling. It is the oldest part of the inn and it has always been a wine cellar.

In 1420, The Mermaid was rebuilt, much as it stands today; not only were ship timbers used in the construction but also baulks of Sussex oak. Several of the fine fireplaces were carved from French stone ballast rescued from the harbour.

In 1530, The Mermaid harboured Catholic priests, fleeing to the Continent, and the forbidden letters 'JHS' (*Jesus Homnium Salvator* – Jesus Saviour of Man) may be seen cut into the magnificent linenfold carving in the room to the left of the entrance hall, now known as Dr Syn's Lounge.

In 1573, Queen Elizabeth I visited Rye, dubbed the town 'Rye Royal' and presented it with 100 gold 'angels'. The arms of the Tudor queen above the fireplace in the richly panelled Residents' Lounge commemorate this visit. Another royal visit took place over 400 years later, in 1982, when the Queen Mother as Lord Mayor of the Cinque Ports, dined at The Mermaid.

So the history of Rye and of The Mermaid goes on: in 1680, Rye was the most important cross-Channel port with regular sailing packets connecting with the London stage coach. King George I was shipwrecked in Rye Bay in 1726 and rested for a few days at Lamb House, visiting The Mermaid. In 1751, a gang of smugglers, numbering 600 men and known as the Hawkhurst Gang, used Rye in general and The Mermaid in particular on numerous occasions and doubtless they used the hidden apartments and false panels in several of the rooms to their advantage, including the moving panel in room 18 and an entrance to the priests' hole through the back of the cupboard above the bar fireplace.

But to return to the ghosts at The Mermaid, we saw no ghosts while we were there but it may be that, almost like a battery, the visual aspect or power of the ghosts are running down and only occasional, fleeting 'shadows' and half-registering footsteps and other sounds are all that remain of once full and complete hauntings with visual and aural happenings. Certainly some of the Ghost Club members, spending two springtime nights at The Mermaid, heard sounds they could not readily explain, including harsh whispering, dragging sounds, the clash of metal and footsteps: the latter were reported by a responsible council member of the Ghost Club, on both the nights spent at The Mermaid. On the second occasion he checked 'quickly enough,' he told me, 'to find nothing'. In the cold light of day he decided to rule the 'footsteps' as 'non-proven' – 'which is not to say that I haven't lingering doubts,' he adds.

While we were in Rye we visited Fletcher's House, the birthplace of dramatist John Fletcher (1579–1625), a contemporary of Shakespeare, where a daylight and modern-looking ghost form of a young man dressed in a grey lounge suit has been seen walking up the stairway. Although apparently solid and real-looking, it suddenly and inexplicably disappeared when Mrs Betty Howard addressed the clear and distinct form. Subsequently, 'disembodied footsteps' have been reported on many occasions from the same area.

We visited, too, Turkey Cock Lane where a mad friar used to be heard gobbling like a turkey cock, giving the street its name. We saw Monastery Hall, once a fourteenth-century monastery of the Augustine Friars and long haunted by the ghostly figures of seven friars. When the monastery was sacked, seven men chose to be buried alive and their cowled forms have been seen many times moving slowly in single file and disappearing into a wall. In 1939, a row of seven skeletons was unearthed, in upright and kneeling positions; yet still the ghosts walk. We visited the parish church, which we found full of interest, and the churchyard, haunted by a tall male figure wearing shining leather boots and a long black cloak, a figure that leaves no footprints even in the snow – possibly the ghost of the man executed in error for the murder of George Meyer. After the death penalty had been carried out the real culprit was discovered but the ghost of the man unjustly sent to his death still walks occasionally, especially on snowy nights in Rye churchyard.

Lamb House (famous as the one-time home of novelist Henry James) was opened specially for us, and charming Charles De Salis conducted us on a tour of the house and garden and talked to us at length about the house and its occupants with special emphasis on the ghostly associations.

Lamb House has beautifully proportioned Georgian windows and an elegant front door but it is a curious house with a large and spacious study, a perfect place for writing books (and it was certainly used by Henry James, E. F. Benson, Edith Wharton, who frequently stayed at Lamb House, H. Montgomery Hyde and Rumer Godden); and an entrance hall that is larger than any of the other rooms. There is a panelled parlour situated below the imposingly named but inappropriately small King's Bedroom, so called because George I, returning from one of his frequent visits to his beloved Hanover, was caught in a storm and driven onto Camber Sands. James Lamb of Lamb House, thirteen times Mayor of Rye, immediately rode out that wild and windy night to meet the King and offer him the hospitality of his house. In fact he gave up his own bedroom for his royal guest who stayed four nights and acted as godfather to one of Mrs Martha Lamb's sons (she had nine children) who was born the night the King arrived and was, of course, named George.

Three years later, James Lamb narrowly escaped death when his brother-in-law, Allan Grebell, was murdered in Rye churchyard by a paranoid butcher who thought he was attacking James Lamb who had loaned a cloak to his brother-in-law. The butcher, named Breads, was duly hanged on the Salts outside the Landgate and his body suspended from a gibbet nearby, a place still known as Gibbet's Marsh. The ghost of Allan Grebell is said to have haunted Lamb House ever since.

Henry James, the novelist and author of that poignant ghost story, *The Turn of the Screw*, lived at Lamb House from 1897 until shortly before his death in 1916. Among the unexplained happenings he experienced there was the mysterious fire that occurred within a year of his moving in. It broke out in the middle of the night and was eventually discovered to originate and be still burning *under* and *behind* the hearth and stove and it took firemen more than three hours to extinguish.

Visitors to Lamb House in Henry James' golden days included H. G. Wells, who lived in the neighbourhood at the time, Max Beerbohm, Hilaire Belloc, G. K. Chesterton, Joseph Conrad, Stephen Crane, Ford Madox Brown, George Gissing, Edmund Gosse, Rudyard Kipling, the incomparable Edith Wharton, Compton Mackenzie and Hugh Walpole – many of whom wrote about psychic activity in a sensitive and convincing manner.

Henry James was followed at Lamb House by the Benson brothers, E. F. Benson the novelist and A. C. Benson, Master of Magdalen College, Oxford. The brothers did not get on with each other so E. F. lived at the house in term time and went abroad during the college vacations, leaving it to A. C.

E. F. Benson was interested in psychic phenomena (as H. Montgomery Hyde reveals in his *Story of Lamb House*, 1966) and he recounted several personal experiences while he lived at Lamb House, including witnessing the famed apparition of the murdered Allan Grebell. E. F. Benson used Lamb House as the setting for his Mapp and Lucia novels.

One summer's day E. F. Benson was sitting in the garden with the vicar of Rye, facing the garden wall, when he saw the figure of a man walk past. 'He was dressed in black and wore a cape over his shoulders,' he said afterwards. 'His head was turned away and he vanished after walking a couple of steps.' The vicar saw him too and jumped up, exclaiming, 'Who on earth is that?' They looked all round the garden and in the 'secret' garden beyond the wall but there was no sign of the figure they had both clearly seen. There was no way out of the secret garden which was enclosed with high walls.

On another occasion, during the course of a seance held in the Garden Room (demolished by a direct hit in the Second World War), the medium, just before she went into the trance state, pointed to an empty mahogany and cane armchair and asked, 'Who is the man in a cloak sitting in that chair?' The story goes that it was the actual chair in which the dead body of Allan Grebell had been discovered. After being attacked he had staggered out of the church-yard and had managed the short distance to his own home, opposite Lamb House, and had there collapsed in the chair and bled to death. Subsequently James Lamb was given the chair 'as a souvenir of the tragedy'. According to E. F. Benson the medium had never heard of the Grebell murder.

Rumer Godden, author of more than fifty books and a two-volume autobiography, lived at Lamb House with her husband James for a time in the 1970s and during their first few weeks in the house they experienced poltergeist activity, especially in the dark, airless and old-fashioned kitchen. They raised the flooring, knocked down the back wall and made the room sunny and light but the distur-bances continued. The new boiler burst; new pipes burst almost as soon as they were installed; saucepans flew off shelves; electricity fused. The Goddens asked a priest to come and bless the house. He came and for a while things improved.

During Rumer Godden's time at Lamb House the place was alive with children – her own grandchildren and their friends and this seemed to promote an atmosphere in which Rumer distinctly sensed and perhaps saw the two children so splendidly portrayed in *The Turn of the Screw*, Flora and Miles, although that immortal story was not in fact written while Henry James lived at Lamb House. In fact there had been no children at the house for 200 years. James and Martha Lamb had had nine children and no doubt their descendents had children too but the last Lamb, Augustus, was a celibate clergyman. After his death the house was bought by a Mr Bellingham who had no children; Henry James followed and then the Bensons – all bachelors. An elderly lady, Mrs Fullerton, was next and then an elderly Montgomery Hyde followed by the equally mature Rumer and James Godden.

Yet in some odd way perhaps the essence of the two ghost children, Flora and Miles, so influenced Henry James that they returned when children were actually in the house. Rumer Godden explains it in *A House With Four Walls* (1989) like this:

Now suddenly Lamb House was alive with those shrill, sometimes piercing child voices, scampering of feet – thumping of feet. There was sliding down the banisters, toys left on the stairs, a new untidiness, a quickening of life and, sometimes, in the hurdy-gurdy I had a strange sense of 'presences', two other children, silent, well-behaved. It was as if they were watching. Soon I knew who they were, Miles and Flora. Our own children had brought them out of the Green Study where Henry James had conceived them. After our four had gone I had the feeling that Miles and Flora were still there.

There was also the 'ghostly tale of the missing pages' as Dr Leon Edel, the author of several classic biographies of Henry James, put it. It was something else that happened at Lamb House that was never explained. One day when James and Rumer Godden were alone in the house, Rumer left the book on which she was working, as yet only a few pages, on her table in the Green Study at the end of the morning and took the Pekinese out for a noontime walk.

Afterwards they had lunch and then Rumer returned to the Green Study to continue her book but the pages she had completed had vanished! She and James and the daily help, Peggy, searched high and low: inside the study, outside the study, in cupboards, on shelves, even in the attic bedrooms and in the kitchen. No sign of the missing papers.

Two mornings later when Rumer entered the Green Study, the pages were back on her desk! When she told Dr Edel, an authority on Lamb House, the tale of the missing pages, he said, 'Ah! Things like that do happen in Lamb House.' Another thing that always puzzled Rumer was the odd circumstances surrounding her pen. She had used the one pen all through writing *In This House of Brede*. Finally she wrote 'The End' and laid down the pen – and it split from top to bottom.

For me a lasting memory of that visit to Rye is sitting with Charles De Salis on the seat in the garden, facing the bricked-up doorway to the 'secret garden' where E. F. Benson and the vicar of Rye were sitting when they saw the ghost of a murdered man; and the fascinating disquiet of those nights in the loveliest of all English inns.

Newark Park

One of my investigators headed the notes he passed to me on this case 'A Really Haunted House', and I think that about sums up the opinion of the majority of those of us who were fortunate enough to spend a remarkable night at atmospheric Newark Park. Hardly anyone had heard about the ghosts at Newark Park before we went there; in fact hardly anyone had heard of Newark Park for we spent a night there before it was even open to the public.

It all began when a Ghost Club member, Moira Maxwell-Heron, told me she had just returned from a weekend with a friend who lived in a haunted 'castle' in the Cotswolds. What she told me encouraged me to contact her friend and so set in motion the investigation of one of the most interesting and rewarding cases that has come to my notice in half a century of ghost hunting.

Robert L. Parsons, Moira Maxwell-Heron's friend and the only occupant of Newark Park, responded favourably, if not enthusiastically, to my request that I might bring a dozen or so Ghost Club members to his home for a night, as and when convenient. Bob Parsons had been at Newark Park for seven years when we descended on him. He is a Texan who came to England in the 1960s and obtained a thirty-year lease on the National Trust property described in their Handbook as an 'Elizabethan "standing" or hunting lodge built on the edge of a cliff by the Poyntz family'. In fact the house was built in 1550 by one Sir Nicholas Poyntz whose peculiar likeness can be seen in the National Portrait Gallery in London. His career fluctuated between a debtors' prison and Vice Admiral of the Fleet; he was a noted womaniser and when he completed Newark Park to his satisfaction, one noted chronicler of the day remarked, 'Sir Nicholas Poyntz has built a fine new house to keep his whores in.' Later, in 1790, the property was remodelled into a four-square castellated country house by James Wyatt for the Rev. Lewis Clutterbuck; a house of specialist architectural interest.

The house remained in the Clutterbuck family until 1949 when, in memory of a son killed in the War, it was bequeathed to the National Trust. They rented it out as an old people's home but the company failed and the fine old house, empty for several years, quickly began to deteriorate. Then Bob Parsons found it and decided to take on the mammoth task of restoring the house and grounds to something approaching their former glory; work that is still continuing today.

There is no doubt that the property would have literally fallen to pieces had Bob Parsons not taken it over. He has done a very remarkable job but he is a remarkable man who seems quite prepared to spend the rest of his life restoring Newark Park. The few parts of the existing house that date back to 1550 are composed of stones from nearby Kingswood Abbey which were incorporated into the structure; indeed it has been suggested that the ghost of the one-time Abbot of Kingswood is responsible for some of the happenings at Newark Park, perhaps seeking his lost abbey. Or could it be that something of the monks has remained attached to some of the structure removed from the Abbey? At all events ghosts have long been associated with the panelled stairway at Newark Park and although that stairway is no more – the present one dates from 1790 – the previous one could well have come from Kingswood Abbey. Certainly the main stairway, leading from the entrance hall to the first floor, seemed to be the centre of much psychic activity, as we were to find out.

In his initial letter to me Bob Parsons said, 'Actually nothing much has been *seen* but the first year I was here, from the bedroom I then used, almost every night I would hear footsteps in the hall and stairway outside. Various guests have also heard footsteps, doors opening, drawers opening and things being moved. Also, various people heard bell-ringing in the basement in the daytime; where bells no longer exist. You are welcome to come when (and if) you wish,' ending his letter, 'and as many as you wish but it can be cold here and I can promise nothing in the way of ghosts – when people wish to hear them, they do not, I have found . . .'

I began to make the necessary arrangements and soon told Bob Parsons that the night had been fixed and sixteen members would comprise the party. I said we would bring all necessary refreshments and wrap up warmly. His hospitality was magnificent and practically everyone arrived on time – to be met in the drive by Bob's enormous black Great Dane, Trudi, and by Percy the Peacock. The exception was a member who was with Television Continuity at the BBC and had been working from 6.30 a.m. until midday but she arrived in due course and joined the party as they explored Newark Park.

This fascinating house has been much altered and added to over the years and already the remarkable work of Bob Parsons was evident everywhere. From the impressive entrance hall with its macabre sheep's skull frieze our attention focused on the main stairway leading from the entrance hall to the first and second floors, for in common with many staircases in many haunted houses, it seems to have been the scene of much psychic activity over the years. Especially disturbing was the sound of footsteps heard on the stairway itself and in the passage on the first floor that has three rooms leading off it and a passage leading to the stairs leading to the top floor.

Bob Parsons told us that when he first came to live at Newark Park he heard footsteps on the stairs practically every night and he gave up trying to find an explanation. Various other people have also heard the sound of footsteps walking up and down the stairs. Once, two visitors heard the footsteps from different parts of the house. Odd and unexplained sounds including loud crashing noises and definite voices have been heard in the room above the enormous kitchen, the door of this room being at the head of the first flight of stairs. Other noises have been described by witnesses as dragging sounds, thumping and very loud rustling.

On one occasion Newark Park was used by a company

making a Gothic style film and when one of the producers was upstairs he heard footsteps and thought it was Bob Parsons but then found that at the time he was completely alone in the house.

We carefully picked our way down the stone steps into the vast old cellars and were met by a collection of strange miniature figures, ancient coins and other articles that had been dug up in the grounds or discovered hidden inside the house. Bob Parsons had uncovered several secret hiding places including one under the floorboards in one of the bedrooms. None of our party liked the cold cellars of Newark Park.

It was in the old kitchen that the sound of bell-ringing had been reported most often but not always. Certainly there were bells here once – bells that would be used to summon the servants to attend to the wishes of their master or mistress – but they had long disappeared. The huge fireplace may well have been there for several hundred years . . .

On the stairway in 1910 there are records of an occupant hearing the rustling of skirts pass her; she had no doubt that the sound was that of a woman in a long dress that rustled as it passed. Another visitor was awakened by repeated knockings on his bedroom door. No visible person was there but no sooner was he asleep again than he was awakened once more by the loud knockings – it was a night he never forgot.

Once Bob Parsons felt 'something' touch him in his bedroom located off the middle landing. His dog, Trudi, was at that time in the habit of sleeping in the corner of his bedroom and on this particular night he was awakened by what he thought was Trudi, touching him with a paw. He put out a hand to send her back to her corner and when he found there was nothing there, he turned over to find Trudi fast asleep in her usual place in the corner of the room. Then there was the really frightening experience of great pressure being exerted on his bed in the middle of the night; just when he became frantic to know what to do, the pressure ceased, much to his relief. He said he had never seen anything but most of the people who had stayed at Newark Park over the years had reported similar disturbances to those he had experienced and often they were strangers to the area and he never told them about the odd happenings.

Another time Bob was awakened by the sound of two people arguing. It was so real he lay there and listened for some time, wondering what on earth was going on. He didn't manage to catch any of the words spoken but the voices were raised in anger. He was completely alone in the house at the time. In the room where there is an original William Morris ceiling the sound of whispering has also been reliably reported.

One evening Bob Parsons was entertaining Elsbeth Huxley, the celebrated author who lived in the vicinity, with stories of his various ghostly experiences and everything he could remember about strange happenings in the house but he ended by saying that he didn't really believe in ghosts himself. That night was the most frightening he had ever spent in the house with footsteps walking up and down the stairs, thumps and dragging sounds that seemed to originate within the room he was occupying, and the bumps, bangs and thumping sounds were really loud and heavy 'as though a dozen people were moving things about in the empty house . . .' It was a night that may have altered his scepticism; it was certainly a night he has never forgotten.

One evening heavy thumping sounds seemed to come from the direction of the kitchen where the enormous fireplace takes very large logs. Bob thought that some of the logs must have fallen off the fire but when he reached the kitchen all was quiet and there was no sign of any movement of the logs or anything else that might have caused the loud noises he had heard.

A friend stayed at the house one night and he heard a double rap on his bedroom door about 4 o'clock in the morning. Wondering what on earth could have persuaded Bob Parsons, the only other person in the house, to wake him up at such an hour, the visitor hurriedly opened the door as a second knock sounded – to find no one there. While he was up he went along to the loo and on his way he heard footsteps walking down the deserted stairs ahead of him. When he returned to his room he noticed that the knocker on his bedroom door did not appear to have been disturbed and he had difficulty in using it; he also realised that the door knocking, loud enough to awaken him, had not awakened or even disturbed his dog asleep in the bedroom with him.

This was the first time I had attempted to conduct the serious investigation of a haunted house with such a large number of people and it was not an easy task, but it did enable us to have the whole property under surveillance for a full twelve hours, from 7 o'clock in the evening until 7 o'clock the next morning. During the whole night we took it in turns to take readings from six thermometers situated in different parts of the hall, the main staircase, the landings and bedrooms. None of the readings suggested any abnormal temperature variations.

Various other apparatus – strategically placed 'trigger' objects and trap wires leading to a bulb or a bell, and our sealing of certain rooms, cupboards, etc. – recorded no abnormality and there was no sign of any interference with our attempts at controlling the psychic activity or obtaining some record of it except for one or two notable exceptions.

Several seances were attempted in different rooms and various parts of the house and one in a room on the top floor did seem to produce some intelligent responses but in the main the 'messages', 'replies', 'requests' and 'statements' were garbled and conflicting and even meaningless. Once or twice a table moved with quite considerable force (quite inexplicably) and knocks were produced on command on the floor – and these were also reported by watchers on the floor below.

During a number of set periods of total darkness some interesting sounds were recorded including a very heavy rustling or swishing noise, reported several times and heard by four of the five watchers in the immediate vicinity. An immediate and thorough search failed to reveal any possible physical or rational explanation and these sounds were recorded from two different positions.

Various voices were also recorded and eliminated after exploration and consultation except for one interesting instance in which two voices, a male voice and a female voice, were recorded; voices that were not heard by the investigators.

Lonely and haunted Langenhoe Church, Essex

The interior of Langenhoe Church at the time of the reported disturbances

Loventor Manor, Devon, at the time when ghostly happenings were being reported and investigated

A seance at the haunted house in Nottingham. *Standing, left to right*: Peter Underwood, Steuart Kiernander, Col. Ralph Morris, Alan Roper, David Cuttler. *Seated*: Mrs M.M.T. Overgaard, Dennis Bardens and Sandra Hill

Charles Hill and his daughter
Sandra, who both saw the
ghost of a suicide at their
house in Nottingham

Attempting to attract and
cajole the Nottingham ghost

The haunted stairway at
Newark Park,
Gloucestershire

Newark Park

Prestonfield House, Edinburgh, where ghosts were encountered unexpectedly

Peter Underwood and the haunted bomber at RAF Cosford Aerospace Museum

The puzzling photograph of the Tulip Staircase at the Queen's House, Greenwich, which sparked off a Ghost Club investigation

The Ghost Club hold a seance in the Queen's House. *Clockwise from the left*: Hector McQueen, Margery McQueen, Peter Underwood, Dr Peter Hilton-Rowe, Richard Howard. *Back to camera*: the sound engineer

Rushbrooke Hall, Suffolk, scene of the re-enactment of a murder
(Stewart P. Evans)

Slaybrook Hall, Saltwood, Kent

A seance at Woodfield, Aspley Guise, Bedfordshire. *Clockwise*: Leslie B. Howard, Peter Underwood, Peter Craven, Thomas Brown, Florence Thompson, Councillor H.W. Richards, Dr Donald West, George Kenneth

At the time a camera loaded with infra-red film was trained onto the area of landing on the main stairway where the 'swishing' or 'rustling' noises had been heard. What had happened was that after the 'rustling' or 'swishing' sound was heard (twice) we had a discussion in the area we had designated as our Base Room about what we should do next, and it was decided that we would sit again in exactly the same place with the camera, again loaded with infra-red film, aimed at the place where the unexplained sounds had appeared to come from and if we heard the sounds again the member designated as camera operator would take an exposure. We knew it was unlikely that anything of interest would be recorded on the resulting print but we thought it worth trying. We also set in motion a cassette sound recording instrument with built-in microphone, to record any sounds.

So we sat, quiet and still, the camera aimed at the area agreed among us as being the place where the sounds had originated and then we waited, and we waited, and we waited. We heard no more sounds and so we did not activate the camera but afterwards, back in the Base Room, we thought we had better run the cassette tape just in case something had been recorded that we had not heard – and we were in for a shock. Halfway through the tape, at just after 4 o'clock in the morning, a man's voice was clearly heard saying: 'Yes it's looking, yes' and this was followed almost immediately by a woman's voice which said, 'Yes, it's looking at us'. It was almost as if the possessors of those voices were referring to the lens of the camera pointing at them! Those voices remained to puzzle us and I can offer no possible explanation in the circumstances in which they were recorded and in which I took part. There were other sounds recorded that night in various parts of Newark Park that do not appear to have a natural explanation but the voices – well, they were really something.

Among the other sounds recorded on cassette tape that night were dragging and rustling sounds, a heavy shuffling sound, several loud rustling sounds, a sharp knocking sound (almost like a stone mason working), a heavy metallic sound (as though metal had been dropped), clicks, footsteps, a bang, a very loud metallic sound followed by a softer one, the sound of something being dragged and something heavy being moved and very heavy breathing sounds, seemingly quite close to the microphone. It is important to realise that all those sounds were recorded in scientific and controlled conditions; they were witnessed and verified and confirmed by experienced and hardened research investigators.

Near each thermometer and elsewhere an appropriate article was placed within a carefully chalked circle. Each and every article remained within the confines of the chalked ring except for one: a large key, placed beside a thermometer on the main stairway landing. At 4.30 a.m. this key was found moved two-and-a-half inches so that it was completely outside its chalked ring.

At 5.25 a.m., during a 'silence and darkness' period I was situated with a fellow investigator in a bedroom on the first floor. During these periods whistles are blown to signal the beginning and end of the agreed period and it is understood that no one moves or makes a noise of any kind during that short period – perhaps a quarter of an hour. Within a few minutes of the beginning of this particular 'silence and darkness' period both my companion and I heard heavy footsteps walking down the stairs from the third floor and with a glance of something like annoyance at my companion and more than a little disappointed that one of our investigators would walk about when I had asked everyone to remain still and silent I quietly walked towards the stairs to have a word with the person concerned. As I reached the corridor into which the stairs from the upper floor led, the footsteps ceased and I found the area icy cold. I waited; whoever was responsible had evidently realised what had happened and had stopped in their tracks, but there was no retracing of the footsteps, no sign of anyone on the stairs and when I went upstairs to discover the culprit I found everyone just as puzzled as I was – no one from the upper floor had moved! Certainly no one had passed my companion and me, which would have been necessary for them to get to the stairs from which we both heard the clear footsteps descending.

So often I find that these odd happenings take place at the least expected moment; perhaps when we are *not* engrossed in any particular method of investigation and when we 'switch off' for a while and thereby allow other forces to operate. The memory of those heavy footsteps and the recollection of finding no possible rational explanation will always remain with me.

Unfortunately the stairway and corridor concerned were not under separate surveillance and were not covered by a sound recording instrument at the time. However, other sounds – thumps, light banging noises, chain rattling and dragging sounds – were recorded on different instruments in various rooms and parts of the house but with so many people present it was admittedly difficult to establish in every instance with any degree of certainty that all the noises were of paranormal origin – the heavy footsteps I heard are, of course, an exception for they were heard during a 'silence' period and were checked for possible human origin.

Once, we were told, when a party of six people were spending a night at Newark Park, a series of curious knockings was heard and five of the party felt suddenly cold at the same time. Almost immediately windows in the room they were occupying suddenly vibrated and rattled at an incredibly fast rate although it was a still night and there was no breath of wind. The same thing apparently happened on three separate occasions in three different rooms and those occurrences were verified by everyone present.

Although the night, in all the circumstances, had been extremely interesting and not a little rewarding, I did feel that fewer investigators in more controlled conditions was something that we should strive for. We were, of course, immeasurably indebted to Bob Parsons who was so very co-operative and in a letter following our visit he said, 'So pleased it was not a completely wasted night . . . I did enjoy your visit . . . it would be a pleasure to see any of you any time. Large numbers of people are more pleasant perhaps but, as you say, less conducive to ghostly activity.'

Eight months later he agreed to have two experienced Ghost Club members to stay at Newark Park while he was away in London and our valued members Michael Brett and Steuart Kiernander spent eight days and nights in the house, seven of them when no one else was there *at all*. The one exception was one day and night when they were joined, on invitation, by a local medium.

They decided to share a room so that if anything happened during the night there would be two observers present. During the second night, just before midnight, Steuart heard a tapping sound which seemed to emanate from the corridor which ran outside their room. He described it as like the sound made by a blind person tapping their stick, except that a blind person usually taps in duplicate, not triplicate. Another time a similar sound seemed to originate from *within* the room they were occupying, tap-tap-tap, followed by a moment of silence, then tap-tap-tap again. Steuart woke Michael immediately, but unfortunately the sound had ceased when he did so. However, shortly afterwards, while they were both awake, they heard the sound of something being dragged along the corridor towards the large window at the far end of the passage.

On the fourth day, they decided to go out for the afternoon. Michael was sitting on a garden seat in the courtyard waiting for Steuart who had forgotten his camera. Back in the house, Steuart heard his name being called but when he asked Michael about it Michael replied that he hadn't moved or spoken.

During the week at various times in the daytime, during the evening and at night-time, they took up various positions using blackout conditions. Although nothing worth reporting happened they both sensed that they were being watched and came to the conclusion that it was not simple imagination. The atmosphere at Newark Park used to change dramatically once the daylight had faded. While they were there the medium held several seances in various parts of the house and the most startling piece of information that he imparted happened whilst they were all seated in the corridor, where previously they had heard the dragging sounds. He claimed that a young servant boy in a previous century had been murdered and his body dragged along the corridor and brutally thrown out of the window. He also claimed that the bedroom Steuart and Michael were occupying appeared to be from where most of the psychic activity emanated.

During their last night Michael distinctly heard, while lying in bed, the sounds of two men's voices downstairs. Although their voices were loud, he could not distinguish what they said. Unfortunately, during all this activity Steuart was fast asleep and Michael knew from past experience that if he got out of bed to awaken him the noises would cease. Michael could only describe the sounds that he heard as belonging to a period in time when Newark Park had a large downstairs hall, for the sounds appeared to echo around the room.

Steuart Kiernander's report added: 'Many noises and voices were heard, by both of us, individually and collectively, for which we could find no explanation.' Both investigators noticed that many of the bangs and thumping noises occurred when the watchers were lying down, resting; in a relaxed, receptive and uninvestigative mood.

The same two investigators heard, when they were upstairs, the sound of horses' hooves and the grind of wheels on gravel but immediate investigation revealed nothing whatever to account for the sounds. Numerous bangs and thumps were heard, varying in intensity from something that might have been a garment dropped to the floor outside a closed door to something that could have been a heavy log being dropped.

The recorded voices obtained on our first visit were fascinating; when we first played them over at Newark Park they were quite loud and distinct and definite. At a later play-through those of us present, who had all been at Newark Park and heard the recording previously, thought the voices sounded fainter. I asked our members from Holland, who had come over especially for the visit and whose recorder had picked up the voices, to let me have a full evaluation of the voices and any other sounds that might be on the tape and take an exact copy for our archives.

In a subsequent letter I was told: 'The sounds are still there but the voices have faded. It's more difficult to hear them and there is an awful lot of noise on that tape that we cannot explain. Our recorder is a very sensitive one but at the time, as you know, we were sitting in darkness, close together, and there were *no* sounds at all to be heard with human ears.' Later I learned that the voices had completely disappeared from the tape!

Some of Catherine Duval's thoughts and impressions of Newark Park are interesting:

The impression that Newark Park made on me was one of emptiness, silence and great loneliness. Nothing bad or threatening, until the last half-hour of the investigation. Then the atmosphere changed. That was on the landing, near the haunted room with the two beds. I felt it coming towards me quite clearly. After that I heard those awful loud footsteps, as if someone walked with heavy boots on. My husband heard the heavy footsteps, too ... When I was absolutely alone on the landing with my camera (loaded with infra-red film) and the tape recorder there were absolutely no sounds. Yet on the tape there are; almost as if rocks are rolling around and something I would describe as a slight rustling sound, as if a skirt was sweeping over the floor ... I have always regretted that I was not able to stay there a couple of days longer, without the large party! Not being English, only a foreign guest, I did not want to be pushy. But I am sure that had I stayed there, I would have gotten more. Of that I am sure. There was *nothing threatening* there; until just before the end of the whole session, that last moment when the heavy footsteps were going up the stairs. Then something changed; there was a presence there and it was not a kindly one ...

I am a very down-to-earth person, not easily frightened, but I must confess that at that very moment, when I heard those unusual, loud footsteps, and being alone on the landing, I had a strong feeling of uneasiness. Something not quite friendly was approaching me. At that moment the kitchen door downstairs opened and there was the sound of muffled voices and some lights were turned on ... I cannot explain those heavy footsteps. They were on the tape, but they have gone.

I have studied this subject, ghosts, from several aspects, but what caused the footsteps, I just don't know. Nothing had been seen. Where a 'ghost' is seen, I understood that it was usually heard too, because for a form to be sufficiently substantial to be visible, there must be a modicum at least of ectoplasm in its composition; and ectoplasm is capable of exercising force on the physical plane, in some degree at least. Where a 'ghost' is both seen and heard, it would seem that there is an actual haunting. Where it is seen but not heard, it may possibly be that a person with psychic tendencies is perceiving the images in the reflecting ether, the 'photographic plate of nature' and there may be no actual entity present.

Where the disturbance is *heard*, but not seen, it may be due, I understand, to astral forces set in motion by ritual magic or something of the sort and that may continue for a while after the original impulse is withdrawn. This may be harmless, save that it disturbs sleep. I am not without experience of haunted houses. In fact, I have lived in three! One of them a really notorious one, that had been officially investigated by experts on various aspects. It has never been explained why the truly frightening happenings took place. It was in all the newspapers for quite some time and I can assure you that I was glad to be able to leave the place. It was absolutely impossible to continue living there . . .

During the visit to Bob Parson's I took several pictures with infra-red film. Nothing on them. But . . . one of them is showing a round lightball. I did not pay any attention to it at the beginning, dismissing it as a reflex caused by the mirror on the floor of the room. A friend of ours, an expert on infra-red, tells me, however, that he thinks I may have caught something as he said it is most definitely *no* reflex caused by the mirror or anything else . . . I took the picture in total darkness and the place of the 'lightball' is *not* in front of the mirror . . .

271

suggestion? Maybe . . . but maybe it occurred at the same moment as the voices on the tape . . .

Looking back it was a night to remember. There was the harsh building itself in its bleak surroundings; there was the movement of the seance table; the strange voices on tape; the loud footfalls, bumps and various other unexplained sounds – sometimes recorded from two different positions – and, for me at least, there were the footsteps I certainly heard that could not have been made by any living person.

Bob Parsons has told me that we were unusually lucky and that, especially recently, nothing seems to happen at Newark Park except when he is alone in the house. On such occasions, he said in December 1992, doors open and close by themselves; there are footsteps and other sounds which have no explanation; and he feels that perhaps the monks may have become attached to some of the structure removed from their Abbey.

One visitor to Newark Park said afterwards he felt the house 'had an underlying feeling or presence of evil, of dreadful secrets still hidden within its walls', and those of us who have spent a night there may not entirely agree with him but we know just what he means. There is a strange feeling in that strange house and I am sure it has yet to yield up many secrets.

Nottingham Council House

One day I heard about a young family who had been driven out of their home, a council house, by the appearance of a ghost. My informant was a Ghost Club member who then lived in the Midlands and the little she told me about the case sounded interesting although I confess to have had reservations for all too often I had come across allegedly haunted council houses being nothing more than an excuse to move to another house.

However, as I say, the few details passed to me on this occasion sounded impressive and I soon arranged a meeting with the occupants of the house concerned. Within days my wife and I travelled to Nottingham, met up with Ghost Club members, Freda and Steuart Kiernander, and together we visited Charles Hill and his children, seventeen-year-old Sandra, Margaret aged fifteen and John aged twelve. We met them at the home of Leslie Parker, a friend of Charles Hill, who was giving the Hill family temporary refuge from the haunted house.

In a calm and matter-of-fact tone, bus conductor Charles Hill told us that he had waited a long time to qualify for the council house and he was delighted with it when he was at last able to move in but they had only been there a short time when Sandra had to go into hospital for an appendix operation. One night Charles Hill awoke in his bed around 2 o'clock in the morning and he saw the figure of a young man walking towards the window. He wore a white cricket shirt and trousers and seemed to have a handkerchief over the back of his neck putting Charles Hill in mind of a soldier in the French Foreign Legion. After a few seconds the figure disappeared and Charles Hill decided he must have dreamed the whole thing.

A couple of nights later, however, he saw the same figure again. He had sat up very late, watching a late movie, and he was having a last cigarette in bed when something caught his eye. It was exactly as before and it seemed to hover for a moment and then it disappeared. Again he said nothing to his family but there could be no question of a dream this time; he was still smoking his cigarette. He did not mention the matter to Sandra when she returned from hospital.

A couple of days later Sandra saw the same figure, in daylight, on the stairs and she described the figure exactly as her father had done: a young man, white trousers and shirt and a handkerchief draped over the back of his neck. The family were terrified and they left the house with a few things and refused to return, although it meant abandoning many of their belongings and the home they had waited so long to move into. Nothing like this had ever happened to Charles Hill before; he had never believed in ghosts and he was, quite simply, frightened. His doctor had advised him not to return to the house.

Over lunch at the Strathden Thistle we decided that the

people concerned and the circumstances and confirmatory evidence warranted some sort of investigation. We saw Charles Hill again and asked whether we could spend a night in the house. I remember he said, 'You can do what you like. We shall never live there again but you do whatever you like.'

So I made arrangements to spend a night at the council house on Bilborough Estate to see whether we could discover any cause for the repeated appearance of the apparition and ascertain any facts pertaining to the reported haunting. As a start I contacted Nottingham City Council and asked for a list of previous occupants of the premises. They supplied me with a short list and said their records did not go back any further.

I then selected an appropriate, convenient and available team of investigators including Mrs M. M. T. Overgaard who had brought the case to our attention. When everything had been arranged I contacted Charles Hill again and said I knew they would never contemplate living in the house again but I wondered whether he and Sandra would consider visiting the house on the afternoon of our arrival as I felt members would like to hear their first-hand experiences. In the event, Charles and Sandra Hill spent the night with us.

The house seemed to be a comfortable and typical council house comprising a kitchen, a parlour or sitting room, a bathroom and three bedrooms, the largest of which, overlooking the back garden, was the one occupied by Charles Hill when he had twice seen the ghost of a young man. He also told us that he had several times heard a young man singing although he had never traced the origin of sounds which seemed to increase in volume and then fade away.

We all explored the house and then I explained our plans and rules for the night. Those rooms not under investigation were sealed and the seals checked at the end of each observation period. If footsteps or any other sounds were heard observers were to try and judge the direction of the sounds, note the duration and indicate the type of sound: whether heavy, light, metallic, soft, padding, shuffling, or whatever. Should an apparition of any kind be seen or glimpsed or even suspected, it was not to be approached, rather it was to be observed carefully with the watcher remaining quite still and silent and noting as much detail as possible; and then drawing the attention of the nearest person to the form, without speaking. Similarly any knocks or raps heard during observation periods should be located as carefully and quickly as possible, again noting duration, location, type, etc. A number of 'trigger' objects, including a bell, were distributed and ringed with chalk and each observer in turn checked that there had been no movement.

During one period, when we were all crowded into the 'haunted' bedroom with no lights and keeping as still and silent as possible, a number of knocks were heard. When there was silence again we gave a couple of raps on the door, in case an entity wished to make contact but there was no response. We all heard measured footsteps which seemed to originate from the area of the ceiling; we all heard a dragging sound emanating from a locked and sealed and empty room; and during a period when I sat alone for a while in the 'haunted' bedroom I saw nothing but heard a sharp crack, almost like a pistol shot which seemed to come from a distance and yet from within the room – a sound not heard by anyone else in the house or recorded on a tape recorder running downstairs.

Once, during an observation period in which Sandra and a lady member of the Ghost Club were keeping watch in the bedroom Sandra had occupied when they had lived in the house, the silence of that cold house (the 'haunted' room incidentally was several degrees colder than other parts of the house) was shattered by a piercing scream followed by hysterical sobbing. Sandra claimed to have seen the same figure of a young man, in white shirt and trousers and with a handkerchief over the back of his neck – stepping into a wardrobe! The lady with Sandra had seen nothing but this did not mean that Sandra hadn't; she had obviously had some sort of experience and was very disturbed.

Downstairs, as she was being comforted by a cup of tea and a chat, I was puzzled as to what the figure could have been doing stepping into a wardrobe. I went upstairs, entered the bedroom and examined the wardrobe. I noticed that the varnished surface reflected faint moonlight entering through the uncurtained windows but there did not seem to be any resemblance to a figure and the reflection did not move. I opened the wardrobe door and inside were lots of photographs of Sandra, on the back of the wardrobe and on the back of the door – something I am sure lots of teenage girls do but could the photographs have been the attraction for the mysterious figure?

When I returned downstairs things were getting back to normal and with everyone calm and relaxed we decided on another short session of total silence and darkness.

Everyone in the house gathered in the sitting room and we all sat for a few moments in silence. There was absolute quiet in the stillness of the night. And then, from the empty 'haunted' room, came the sound of measured footsteps. They lasted just less than a minute but everyone heard them. One of the party was detailed to explore quietly but the room in question and indeed the whole of the rest of the house was empty and quiet.

During one seance a man's name came through and he said he was the ghost. The name meant nothing to anyone present and it was not on the list of occupants supplied to me by the local council. Still insisting he was manifesting in the house, 'he' added, 'I love Sandra'. Later, at another seance, when we seemed to be getting nothing but jumbled phrases and nonsense I suddenly asked, 'Did you commit suicide?' – and the reply was an emphatic 'Yes'. Later still we obtained information that was not common knowledge among us; things like the names of people connected with Charles Hill and his family and friends and then, suddenly, the message came through: 'Sandra I like'.

None of the 'trigger' objects was moved; no bell was rung; no footprint or handprint appeared in the powder we had sprinkled here and there; no recorded voice was on the tapes used; and there were no unusual fluctuations of temperature. But once during an impromptu session in the 'haunted' room involving four of us – Dennis Bardens, Colonel Ralph Morris, David Cuttler and myself – there was a sudden physical reaction from David Cuttler. He shook violently, felt he was almost being 'taken over' and experienced a strange tightness in his chest and his head was spinning. A man whom twenty-four parachute jumps had failed to unnerve was shaking with fear! After we hurriedly put the light on, he quickly recovered but something distinctly odd had happened. 'I saw a smoky haze,' David said afterwards, 'and I had this terrible feeling of panic. I heard heavy breathing close to me ... I never want to experience anything like that again.'

So what was the sum total of that strange night in the council house in Nottingham? Well, to be selective: the ghostly figure of a young man had apparently been seen again (this was the fourth time the figure had reportedly been seen in the house); measured footsteps had been heard that could not have had a normal explanation (*all* the occupants and visitors to the house that night were in one room, everyone heard the footsteps, and an immediate search revealed no explanation); Sandra did seem to have been singled out by entities, if entities they were, that manifested at seances; a sound like a shot had been heard; and, also in the 'haunted' room, a hardened member of the team of investigators, a young and fit man, had been strangely and physically affected.

After spending a night at the house we set in motion a number of inquiries especially concerning the name that had come through so emphatically claiming to be the perpetrator of the disturbances. But we had no joy. Questions in the area and elsewhere brought no solution and it was five months after we had spent that night before we had any luck.

Then one of my investigators who had followed the trail to Bristol discovered there an elderly widow with the surname that had come through at the seances, and she had once lived in a council house in Nottingham. I lost no time

279

in going to see her and I learned something of the tragic story that could account for some of the reported happenings in that Nottingham council house.

Some years earlier this lady had indeed lived in the council house on the Bilborough Estate where we had spent the night. She was a widow and had one son who was the joy of her life; 'he was such a happy boy, always singing about the house,' she told me. In his teens her son and a friend had operated a window-cleaning business but one day there had been an accident. The friend had been killed and her son had been paralysed from the waist down. The rest of his life had been virtually spent in the 'haunted' room. He had always been fond of sport, cricket in particular, and during the summer he was always dressed in white cricket trousers and a white shirt and because he could not move out of the sun, a handkerchief had been arranged to shield the back of his neck. Eventually, after about eighteen months of inactivity he became depressed, managed to get hold of a revolver and shot himself pointing the gun inside his mouth; he died from a single shot.

It was a tragic story, sad and depressing but from our, hopefully objective, point of view, it was exceedingly interesting. So many of the reported phenomena fitted the story we had unearthed. The voice of a young man singing; the 'terrible feeling' of depression experienced by one of our team, a young man himself; the sounds, the footsteps (how many times must he have waited for and heard footsteps bringing someone to share his sadness); knocks and raps that he used to attract attention and call to those elsewhere in the house; the dragging sound as the paralysed youth tried to move perhaps; the single shot I had heard in the 'haunted' room; and of course the visible form of a young man in white shirt and trousers with a handkerchief over the back of his neck.

Then there was the attraction that Sandra seemed to have for the haunting entity. Why is it that some tragic happenings leave 'something' behind that can become perceivable to others years later? In some way we do not yet understand it seemed to us that Sandra was the nexus, the focal point, the unconscious attraction, of this particular haunting. It is good to be able to add that Charles Hill and his little family moved into another council house where they were happy and undisturbed in any way and another family moved into the 'haunted' council house and they lived happily there without reporting any disturbances. To us it did seem to point to Sandra as the attraction that sparked off this haunting, unconsciously, unintentionally and involuntarily. A haunting that ceased when she was no longer there.

Old Battersea House

One day, more than thirty years ago now, I was talking to Ghost Club member Alasdair Alpin MacGregor in his Swan Court, Chelsea, flat as he was putting the finishing touches to the second of his 'ghostie' books as he called them, *Phantom Footsteps*, when he chanced to mention his 'quite remarkable' friend Wilhelmena Stirling. She lived not far away at historic Old Battersea House, once the manor house of Battersea, and suddenly dropping the work he had in hand he said, 'Shall we go and see her?' And so off we went.

When she learned that I was interested in ghosts Mrs Stirling said gaily: 'Spooks eh? Well I am on the verge of becoming one myself so come in and we'll talk.' In fact she died in August 1965, a few days before her hundredth birthday, but all thoughts of death or indeed any morbid thoughts were chased from my mind as I eyed the beauty that is Old Battersea House. I saw a house then that had seen better days but happily this fine example of seventeenth-century domestic architecture, certainly the finest in Battersea, has now been wonderfully restored to its distinctive and impressive original character.

The house, formerly known as Terrace House and standing in seven acres of land, has had a chequered history. From the time it was built (a sundial on the south face is dated 1699) until the middle of the nineteenth century, some 150 years, it was the substantial home of various wealthy merchants and men of the professions and, as St John's College for Schoolmasters, it was also an educational training institution at one period.

Twice in this century the mellow old house has been in danger of demolition; in 1930 when it was acquired by Battersea Borough Council and in 1965 when the ownership reverted to Wandsworth Borough Council and it was found to be in a structurally poor condition. Due entirely to the intervention of Mr Malcolm Forbes of the American Forbes Foundation, the house was taken on a ninety-nineyear lease on condition that the property was completely restored. You could look up from the basement and see the sky when Forbes first saw the fine old mansion. But after more than four years' renovation it was turned into a truly elegant and handsome residence – so much so that friends of the Forbes family use it whenever they can. When Ronald Reagan came to London to receive an honorary knighthood from the Queen he stayed there, sleeping in a four-poster bedstead, a bed that Elizabeth Taylor and other distinguished friends and visitors have also occupied during their stays at Old Battersea House.

In 1930, it was suggested that Sir Christopher Wren designed the house for the fiftieth wedding anniversary of

Sir Walter St John but local historians say there is little evidence to support either of these claims and they have found no evidence that any of the St John family ever lived there. Others maintain that it was once the seat of Henry St John, Viscount Bolingbroke (1678–1751) who called it Bolingbroke House. It also seems to have been the occasional home of Alexander Pope (1688–1744) who wrote his *Essays on Man* in the Cedar Room, and Jonathan Swift is numbered among other visitors.

Although 1699 seems a likely date for the present structure some of the brickwork used in the foundations is Tudor and it seems likely that a Tudor building once stood on the site, probably using the same ground plan and foundations. The first recorded resident is Peter DuBois, a City merchant of French Huguenot extraction, and the house is known to have then passed through the hands of the Otgers and the Defishers (both from Flanders) and the Longs, the Petts and the Devissors, all related to each other and all wealthy people of high standing connected with the City, the law, the army, the navy and local government.

The house then passed through other hands, including the original proprietors of the old Battersea Bridge, before a ten-year lease was acquired in 1828 by John George Shaw-Lefevre, a distinguished public servant and Clerk of the Parliament. Afterwards the house stood empty for a while and then Dr James P. Kay used the premises for training schoolmasters, a scheme he transferred to the National Society and as St John's College it continued until 1923 when it was amalgamated with St Mark's College, Chelsea.

Then early in 1930 the whole site was acquired by the

Battersea Borough Council who intended to demolish the building and replace it with council flats. After a public outcry a preservation order was issued, and as various plans to use the house were being considered the Council were approached by Mr and Mrs Stirling (the sister of Evelyn De Morgan) and they succeeded in obtaining a life tenancy on condition that their unique collection of pictures, pottery and porcelain by Evelyn and William De Morgan, contemporaries of William Morris, would be suitably displayed and open to the public by appointment at reasonable times.

By the time of Mrs Stirling's death, her husband having predeceased her, the house was in poor structural condition but provision had been made for the De Morgan Collection to be preserved and displayed at the house. However, Wandsworth Council, who now owned the house, found it impossible to meet the required funds and fortunately Mr Malcolm Forbes offered to restore the house at his own expense, if he could use part as private accommodation. And so it came about that Old Battersea House was restored and refurbished to its former glory.

On that first visit to Old Battersea House I well remember my attention being drawn to a fine carved fifteenth-century Italian armchair and I went to sit down in it but Mrs Stirling stopped me. She had been telling me about the raps she occasionally heard in the house, raps that had no possible rational explanation, but which she said did seem to indicate some personal motive, yet they seemed gentle and kindly and she had almost come to regard them as affectionate. Then, 'No ... No,' she said, firmly but not unkindly. 'Not that chair, dear; I keep it for the ghosts.'

Among others who had asserted that the chair was haunted, I learned, was the late Lady Churchill. On one occasion Mrs Stirling, in Lady Churchill's presence, was about to seat herself in that particular chair when Lady Churchill seized her arm and prevented her from doing so. 'For heaven's sake don't sit there!' she exclaimed. 'Can't you see? There is a man already sitting there! He has a little, pointed beard and a big Elizabethan ruff. He's got a rapier in his hand – and you were about to sit on his lap!'

Since that occasion Mrs Stirling tended to avoid occupying the 'haunted' chair and half-seriously dissuaded her friends from doing so. On another occasion a visitor sat in the chair before she could prevent him doing so, but he jumped up immediately saying the chair was icy cold and he had heard whispering close to his ear. For the rest of his visit to Old Battersea House he could hardly take his eyes off the chair but apparently nothing was visible to him.

Another time when Wilhelmena Stirling was talking to a friend in the Garden Room, her little daughter was playing in the hall when the child suddenly came in and said, 'Who is the man in the chair? He's wearing funny clothes and he won't talk to me . . .' By the time Mrs Stirling and her friend went to see for themselves, they saw only the empty chair and the little girl said, 'Man gone now.'

On yet another occasion Mrs Stirling told me that she was entertaining a friend in the beautiful Garden Room, where in fact we sat chatting, when suddenly her friend, who was facing the arched doorway leading to the hall and stairs, rose from her chair, smiling, as if to welcome someone and then, an astonished look coming over her face, resumed her seat. She said she had plainly seen an elderly lady about to enter the room but as she stood up the figure completely vanished.

Mrs Stirling related another experience involving Lady Churchill with whom she was having tea one Sunday afternoon when they were interrupted and Mrs Stirling left her friend for a moment. When she returned she found Lady Churchill in the hall, curiously silent and pre-occupied. After a moment she asked, 'Do you have a friend here going to a fancy-dress ball?' 'At 4 o'clock on a Sunday afternoon?' replied Mrs Stirling. 'I should hardly think so!'

'Then who could it have been I saw?' asked Lady Churchill and she went on to explain that she had seen a man looking over the banisters and thinking he was looking for her she had come out of the Garden Room. To her surprise she then saw that the man was wearing a plumed hat and a bright coat with rather oddly positioned, diamond-shaped buttons. She also noticed that he was carrying a sword and that he was wearing jackboots, which she saw through the balustrades of the landing. As she gazed at him, wondering who on earth he could be, he turned and slowly walked down the stairs towards her. As he did so Lady Churchill said she distinctly heard the end of his sword strike against the oak stairs step by step. When he reached the bottom of the stairs, he took no notice of Lady Churchill but rudely walked past, almost brushing her as he did so, and then he turned right and disappeared into a closed door!

Thinking back Lady Churchill told Mrs Stirling that the figure much resembled a painting she remembered seeing of the great Duke of Marlborough. In particular she recognised the very odd arrangement of the eight buttons on his coat, two and two on each side and diamond shaped. 'Did the Duke ever visit Old Battersea House?' she asked.

'Tradition has it that he was constantly here,' Mrs Stirling told her. 'You see, he was a great friend of Bolingbroke.' 'So it *was* the Duke!' Lady Churchill exclaimed; 'and he brushed past me because I'm a relative of his!'

As far as I know Mrs Stirling saw no ghosts at Old Battersea House but she certainly heard sounds she could not account for, apart from raps and creaks that are to be expected in any old house. And she did experience definite movement of objects, furniture and heavy paintings and twice she was awakened by a bump in the night, exactly as though a person had thrown himself heavily onto the bed beside her: a most alarming occurrence without any obvious explanation.

In October 1988, while reading over my notes of some thirty years before, it occurred to me that it would be wonderful if I could organise a nocturnal Ghost Club visit to Old Battersea House and I wrote at once to the Administrator explaining my personal involvement and the serious intent of members of the long-established and much respected Ghost Club. A few days later I received a charming letter from the lady Administrator who explained that the house was used by Malcolm Forbes and his family when they visited this country. During the rest of the time, the Administrator lived there alone and she said, 'I am rather concerned that this investigation may upset our "resident" who accepts me totally and I have no wish to cause her distress.' Fortunately, she was willing to discuss the matter and following several telephone conversations and letters, during the course of which I agreed to limit the number of members taking part to twelve, the visit was eventually fixed for Tuesday 2 May 1989. I sent out a preliminary invitation to selected members and the dozen chosen on this occasion comprised Bill Bellars, John and Carole Bellars, Dr Vernon and Elsie Harrison, Ruth Jarvis, Ken Lazenby, Philip Moore, Dennis Moyses, Shirley Shaw and my wife and myself.

In the subsequent usual memorandum and tentative programme I invited members to arrive, as discreetly as possible, between 7 p.m. and 7.30 p.m. and to wear soft-soled shoes, and have with them notebook, pen or pencil, watch, torch and if possible camera, thermometer, tape recorder and any other useful equipment, adding, as ever, 'Please remember at all times that you are a guest in a Private House'.

During the course of introductory remarks the Administrator told us that just three days earlier, a visitor had said she disliked the atmosphere in the hall of Old Battersea House and she could hardly walk across it. On several occasions a number of the very heavy and very valuable paintings had been found carefully leaning against the wall below where they normally hung: there was no broken cord or any obvious reason for these occurrences. Once this had occurred to the picture hanging over the bed in the so-called 'haunted bedroom' and once to the picture over the mantelpiece in the same room. Here, too, lights had been turned on in mysterious and unexplained circumstances.

In one instance a plug leading to an electric lamp was taken out when a four-year-old child was sleeping in the room. In the morning the plug was found to have been inserted and the lamp switched on. Also in the presence of another child, one of the windows was found to have been opened and it was accepted that the child could not possibly have been responsible for these incidents.

On occasions furniture had been found moved and this had apparently been happening in the house for many years. In particular chairs had been found moved right across a room. Once a large mirror was broken although no sound had been heard and it had been undamaged the evening before.

Once at least, in the 'haunted bedroom', the figure of an old lady had been seen standing beside the bed and another time an occupant awoke with the distinct impression that someone was sitting on the bed. In the same room a couple once saw a shape which they were unable to describe. The woman, incidentally, had no knowledge of any happenings at the house, but immediately said she didn't like the hall.

One person who had recently visited the house said she felt a definite presence in the hall and afterwards she claimed to have made contact with the presence who turned out to be an old lady who was not happy with Americans being in possession of the house and making a lot of alterations, such as central heating and extra bedrooms, and she could not settle in her old home with all the changes.

Another visitor asked about the elderly lady they saw looking at the pictures in the passage outside the haunted room and there did seem to be convincing evidence to suggest that the figure of an old lady has haunted the house for the last thirty years (I immediately recalled that

Wilhelmena Stirling, who had lived at the house she passionately loved for over thirty years, had been dead for almost thirty years).

After being conducted over all parts of this exceptionally beautiful house and being given a completely free hand regarding investigation and control of the premises, we set up our apparatus, arranged our rotas of inspection and patrol and generally organised ourselves for the hours ahead.

During the night hours we spent there, using the gorgeous Garden Room as Base Room – was ever ghost hunting conducted in such splendid surroundings? we asked ourselves – two members of our party felt that an elderly woman had come into the room while we were there. One member continued to have this impression and another felt that an animal was present and she seemed to sense the name Margaret Pigg. Once she had the distinct impression that an elderly lady was about to come into the room and she even heard a swishing sound, as of a long dress sweeping the floor, but she said the old lady hovered about the doorway.

Just before 11.30 p.m. one member had the impression of a sweet scent on the top landing but a moment later it had completely gone. Several members felt a drop in temperature in the area of the Study but we did not have a thermometer there at the time. Later there was no apparent drop in temperature and none was recorded. One puzzled member continued, for a quite considerable time, to have the impression of an old lady about to enter the Garden Room; later another member had the impression of the same figure in the Cedar Room.

During one darkness and silence period, between 11.55 p.m. and 12.10 a.m. when members were scattered throughout the whole area under investigation – the hall, stairway, four bedrooms and four ground-floor rooms – there was complete and utter silence everywhere, apart from a clicking sound concerned with lights and the security system. The whole proceedings were recorded by one member on video.

After our visit, owner Malcolm Forbes was anxious to know the identity of the ghost of Old Battersea House and he revealed that one of the pictures inexplicably removed from the wall was Millais' 'Letter to the Squire' which was badly torn, the first picture to be damaged by the ghost – if a ghost was responsible.

I asked one of the investigators present, a former naval man, Bill Bellars, for his thoughts following this private visit and his response was as follows:

I welcomed the prospect of an investigation in this lovely old house where distinguished people had reported seeing the ghost of an Elizabethan man, and the Duke of Marlborough. Furthermore, where the Administrator was conscious of another female 'resident', a friendly one we were enjoined not to upset!

All through our night vigil there was considerable light around the place, particularly from the lighting used to illuminate the many oil paintings the wealthy owner had collected. Contrary to some opinions, light is no bar to people seeing ghosts or experiencing other forms of paranormal activity.

It was in bright daylight conditions that I, myself, once

saw the ghost of a woman in period costume in a house we were living in, in Washington DC. Though light is no barrier to paranormal activity, most phenomena are reported after dark and darkness does tend to produce a state of relaxation conducive to the exercise of any psychic powers people may have. And, of course, legends and ghost stories almost always centre on night time, preferably as the clock strikes midnight!

On the night in question, in Old Battersea House, I spent various periods in different parts of the house, including a reputedly haunted bedroom. Unfortunately I witnessed no ghosts at any time, but then they seldom perform to order! Indeed there is some evidence to suggest that 'they' may resent the appearance of investigators: the ghost hunter's particular 'Murphy's Law' has it that 'when a ghost hunter enters through the front door, the ghosts hurriedly leave through a back window!' Not that this is always the case – far from it.

Though I personally saw nothing, I did feel that there was one spot on the main staircase where there was 'something': an impression, influence, detectable, rather like the beginnings of a shiver down the spine. This I double-checked by passing the spot several times and dismissing from my mind as far as possible the knowledge that it was on the staircase that the ghost of the Duke of Marlborough had been seen.

The whole question of 'atmosphere', 'influence', 'feeling' holds a clue to the explanation of a number of ghosts. It is virtually universal human experience to feel the 'atmosphere' in a house. An Elizabethan mansion in which I used to work was acknowledged by the many people who worked there to have a lovely, friendly atmosphere. This was instinctively put down to the fact that its occupants had, through the centuries, been happy and loving families.

By contrast who has not come across the reverse, where creepy forbidding feelings are felt. I remember once visiting the ruins of Portchester Castle, near Fareham in Hampshire. We were about to descend the steps to the dungeons, when one member of our party stood rigidly still and said she couldn't go down, there was such an unpleasant atmosphere. She was a most outgoing, level-headed, cheerful person but she felt this way at that place at that time. It was in these dungeons that prisoners of war were held in appalling conditions in Napoleonic times. There ought to have been a forbidding 'atmosphere', even if we couldn't all detect it.

'Atmospheres' must be created by previous occupants somehow leaving behind imprints of their emotions, thoughts, personalities. Then surely it is only a small step from experiencing an 'atmosphere' to some people, more sensitive than others, seeing things or hearing sounds – tuning in to the imprint more deeply than just sensing an atmosphere? Indeed this theory suffices to explain some ghosts, but not all. More popular historically, but much more controversial, is the traditional view that ghosts are the spirits of the departed, and usually restless ones.

For me that night at Old Battersea House brought back happy memories and I am quite prepared to accept that Wilhelmena Stirling returns sometimes to the house she knew for so long and always loved, and who can blame her? Her ghost may not have materialised on that particular night but I feel sure she was there, hovering in the wings.

Prestonfield House

Even the staid and justly famous Ward Lock Guide states: 'Edinburgh is a city of ghosts and phantoms of the past' and while this may not be intended to be taken literally, it is nevertheless true that the ghosts of Edinburgh are legion and as varied as they are verified. The Castle, University building, statues, roads, parks, theatres, old and new private houses large and small, even open squares, sections of the Flodden Wall, the claustrophobic closes – all are reputedly haunted with ghosts seen or heard or felt over the years. This is especially true of Prestonfield House, in the south of Edinburgh, the very heart of Scotland.

Prestonfield was opened as a hotel in 1959 with a direct descendant of Sir James Dick, who acquired the property in the seventeenth century, keeping in close contact in an honorary capacity with the running of the hotel. The house, I learn from the hotel booklet, is first recorded in a royal charter in 1153 when it was granted to the monks of Harehope in Northumberland. In 1355, King David II of Scotland, after eleven years of captivity in England, withdrew the grant because the monks had supported his enemy Edward III. As a result Priestfield, as it was then called, reverted to the Scottish Crown. Successive owners, it is said, held it in fee for a pair of gloves rendered annually on St Giles' Day, until 1677 when Sir James Dick acquired the property which remains today in the hands of his descendants.

Sir James, a staunch Roman Catholic, was summoned to London in 1680 by Charles II to attend his brother James, Duke of York. At this time of the Papish Plot, James' uncompromising display of his Catholic convictions, together with his political ineptitude, made him more of a liability than ever to his hard-pressed brother, the King. James was hastily despatched over the border and came to live at the royal palace of Holyroodhouse, where his next-door neighbour was Sir James Dick of Prestonfield. A close friendship developed between the two men, and the Duke, later King James II, was a frequent visitor at Prestonfield, often arriving on foot by a path from the palace which came to be known as Duke's Walk.

The Duke's friendship was not always beneficial, however, to the recipients, as Sir James was to discover. He was at this time Provost of Edinburgh and much battered by the religious storms of the age. His friendship with the dreaded heir to the throne brought him almost universal disapproval on both political and religious grounds and, in 1681, the students of Edinburgh University, thwarted in their ambition to burn an effigy of the Pope – burnt down Prestonfield House instead.

The Duke of York sought to make amends by rebuilding Prestonfield at public expense but the state of the Treasury being what it then was, not more than £800 was ever received by Sir James for this purpose. Yet he did rebuild it, in the form in which it now stands, and the structure was completed in 1687 and the house furnished and ready in 1689, the year in which King James II also set up house anew at St Germain, after a more metaphorical but much more final conflagration.

Two generations later, the two grandsons of the two men again met at Prestonfield when, in 1745, Sir Alexander Dick received Prince Charles Edward Stuart – Bonnie Prince Charlie. Another distinguished guest at Prestonfield in 1759 was Benjamin Franklin, later American ambassador to the Court of Louis XVI when, in 1778, France entered the War of Independence against the English. James Boswell was also a frequent visitor and, on 19 November 1773, in the wake of Dr Samuel Johnson, he dined at Prestonfield. The two guests were returning from their 'journey to the Western Islands of Scotland' and, in 1777, Dr Johnson inscribed a copy of his book to Sir Alexander.

Except for the basement and the old staircase the whole of the present house dates from 1687. In about 1815 the twin dining rooms – one formerly a ballroom – were added and the main hall redesigned to achieve a harmony between the old and the new, and while the black and white marble floor is of the seventeenth century, the Doric columns and pilasters are of this later date. The architect of the seventeenth-century building was Sir William Bruce, who designed the Palace of Holyroodhouse. Prestonfield was his next undertaking and he brought with him the craftsmen he had employed at the royal residence.

The Old Bar, which the visitor will find immediately

upon his left on entering the house, still seems to retain the unhurried calm of a study; this may well be due to the fact that the bar gantry is actually a Sheraton bookcase slightly modified for a more convivial purpose. The sole decoration of the room is a fine set of engravings of Naples and its environs executed in 1770.

Especially attractive are the two dining rooms. These are not quite identical twins, although both are oval in shape and rich in the ornamentation of the early nineteenth century. But to many visitors the Tapestry Room is the most beautiful room in the house: it is certainly the most exciting. The ceiling, rich in ornamentation, with cupids and heraldic beasts rampant and rampaging in high relief, is matched by a fireplace of similar design. The strangely panelled doors were brought from Spain. Here antique furniture, including Chinese porcelain, Persian carpets and Mortlake tapestries, has been accumulated over the years.

Smaller and more intimate than the Tapestry Room, the Leather Room is a perfect sitting room and its four main pieces of antique furniture are of the seventeenth century. Persian rugs on a plain board floor are subdued enough not to detract from the wonder of the rich leather panels, unique in Great Britain, which were bought in Cordova in 1676. Mercifully, these escaped destruction in the fire of 1681, since at that time they were at Sir James's other house in the Lawnmarket.

All the bedrooms are approached by the old stone staircase which has no handrail, and one bedroom, known as the Cupid Room, has as its ceiling the centre-piece of the ceiling of the old main hall and is comparable in style with that of the aforementioned Tapestry Room. The bedrooms are memorable for their comfort, tranquillity and outlook over the lovely grounds, for Prestonfield House stands in some twenty-three acres of its own grounds, approximately ten of these acres being redesigned as a landscape garden. Shadows of trees as old as the seventeenth-century house still trace their patterns across the harled walls. A Scots pine, symbol as far south as Shropshire of a Jacobite refuge for those pursued by the redcoats, stands near the front door. Peacocks step diffidently across the paths, safe in the knowledge that they are all their own, whilst pheasants and partridges still feed on the lawns, unaware that they are within the city's limits. Here the past always seems to be present and I have never forgotten one visit I made to Prestonfield House. It came about when one of my books had its launching at Prestonfield House and Deborah Jarvis, the Press Officer of the publishing house concerned, also stayed at Prestonfield.

Now as to the ghosts: I was informed that there had been not infrequent sightings of the ghostly forms of a man and a woman of the eighteenth century and also a girl dressed in blue. The man is invariably likened to the unmistakable figure of James Boswell who certainly knew and loved this place and may well wish to return, if he has any choice in the matter, or perhaps he has left behind some psychic impression of himself that is seen or sensed by sympathetic visitors two centuries later. The lady has not been identified but her costume and appearance is that of some eighteenth-century visitor or resident; and of the child nothing is known.

Janet Dick-Cunyngham, a previous owner of Prestonfield and who now resides in Spain, tells me that 'some time in the last century a little girl in blue was reported' but neither she nor her mother (who was notoriously psychic) ever saw or heard anything there. A former employee tells me she saw both the male and female ghosts on different occasions and over the years at least eight visitors have told her they have seen one or the other of these friendly and harmless phantoms.

A local resident informs me that he has heard all about ghosts at Prestonfield and may have seen one himself, the little girl in blue. Certainly there were no children answering that description living or visiting Prestonfield at the time. Several of his family and friends assert that they have encountered ghosts at Prestonfield but they too have always felt the presences, seen and unseen, to be benign and friendly.

I do not consider myself especially psychic or susceptible to atmosphere but I have to admit that I felt the old stairway at Prestonfield to be distinctly haunted and Debbie too found this area of the lovely house somewhat disturbing. Since we were not there for the specific purpose of exploring any ghostly activity the fact that we both experienced sights and sounds that we could not explain cannot but be interesting. During the night, Debbie found herself awake several times and she heard footsteps outside her room and the sound of whispering. While these sounds may of course have had perfectly normal explanations, on the last occasion she looked at her watch and found that it was just after 3 o'clock. In the morning she inquired as to the people moving about very late and some of them outside her room at 3 o'clock in the morning, and she was told that she must have been dreaming for everyone in the place had retired before midnight and in any case her room was situated so that only a person occupying that particular room would be in the passage outside. The staff were adamant that no one was in fact in the passage at the time Debbie heard the sounds.

I slept well and without being disturbed at Prestonfield but in the morning as I went downstairs, I glimpsed someone ahead of me on the stairs. It was only a glimpse, a quick impression of a large, elderly man – but then nothing. I was surprised to find no one of that description when I had descended the stairs, or at breakfast, and it was certainly none of the staff.

Prestonfield House has a grace and charm all its own, with its fitting background of peaceful rolling acres and its ghosts, which are gentle shades of its past.

The Queen's House

Visiting The Queen's House, Greenwich, one summer day while on holiday over here from Canada, the Rev. R. W. Hardy and his wife photographed an apparent ghost or ghosts creeping up the circular Tulip Staircase!

This royal residence by the Thames, the first wholly classical building in England, was designed by Inigo Jones in 1616. Over the centuries there have been restorations to both the interior and the exterior and a significant alteration was carried out in the 1930s when the premises were converted from a dwelling house to museum galleries. Then, between 1984 and 1990 considerable attempts were made to restore The Queen's House to its original form. This included repairing the roof and exterior walls and some of the flooring; cleaning surviving original paintwork; replacing such items as shutters and installing humidification and lighting systems. Today the rooms on the first floor look exactly as they would have done when The Queen's House was briefly occupied by the dowager Queen Henrietta Maria in the early 1660s. Some called it the

'White House' and others the 'House of Delight' and either name fitted then and fits today.

In 1614, King James I gave his palace, where Henry VIII and Elizabeth I were both born, and the gardens and park at Greenwich to his extravagant and pleasure-loving Queen, Anne of Denmark. She commissioned Inigo Jones to build a villa near the then private entrance to the park. The original plans show an unusual H-shaped building comprising a block on either side of the public road connected by a central first-floor bridge-room – and already the circular stairway is incorporated, introducing to Britain the cantilevered round stairway, built without any central support. But work on the ambitious project ceased before Queen Anne's death in 1619 with only the basement and walls of the ground floor completed. King James gave Greenwich with its mournful memories to his son, the Prince of Wales.

In 1625, the King was succeeded by this son who became Charles I. He had married that year the quick-witted, vivacious and dark-eyed French princess, Henrietta Maria. Four years later Charles gave the Greenwich estates, including the partly built Queen's House, to Henrietta Maria and Inigo Jones was recommissioned to complete the house without counting the cost. When it was finished the Queen furnished the house sumptuously with ceiling, wall panels and paintings by the leading artists of the day, and she enriched the interior with sculpture from the Royal Collection.

The house escaped damage in the Civil War and was in fact occupied by Cromwell's counsellors. It was sometimes used for odd purposes and certainly in 1653 and again in

1657 it housed the bodies of Commonwealth generals, laying in state in the Great Hall with a gallery running all round it.

After the Restoration of the Stuart monarchy in 1660, Charles II enlarged The Queen's House, changing what had been planned as a villa into a miniature palace for himself and his Queen, Catherine of Braganza. But Charles and Catherine never used The Queen's House although it was occupied for a while by the King's mother, Henrietta Maria.

On her death in France in 1669, The Queen's House passed to Queen Catherine and then to Mary of Modena, consort of King James II, and the premises saw a variety of lodgers over the next few years including Jane Middleton, the 'incomparable beauty' and lover of Charles II. It was also known to John Evelyn and to Samuel Pepys. In 1675 the first Astronomer Royal lived there while the Royal Observatory was being built. Then, in 1689, it became the official residence of the Ranger of Greenwich Park although it remained in royal ownership and William III and Mary used it occasionally. Soon the public roadway, running under the arches of The Queen's House, was closed by the then Ranger, Lord Romney, and with the building of the alternative Romney Road, The Queen's House ceased to be anything to do with Greenwich Park.

In September 1714, Prince George of Hanover held his first reception on British soil in The Queen's House the night before his State entry into London to be crowned King George I. In 1743, the house was much used for entertainment by Lady Catherine Pelham, wife of the Prime Minister of the day. After her death the house was managed or rather mismanaged by a housekeeper and her husband who, in 1792, were accused of making 'a hog-stye of the house and a cow-house of the premises', including using it as a centre for smuggling.

In 1806, the royal connection with The Queen's House finally ended when Caroline, Princess of Wales, purchased it to provide accommodation for the Naval Asylum, a school for the sons and daughters of seamen. In 1873, the Greenwich Hospital buildings became the home of the Royal Naval College and in 1934 the Greenwich Hospital collection of naval relics, mementoes and paintings were transferred to the National Maritime Museum which had already taken over The Queen's House.

The magnificent Great Hall of The Queen's House is a giant forty-foot cube, its ceiling displays reproductions of the marvellous paintings depicting the Arts of Peace by Orazio Gentileschi and his daughter Artemisia of Pisa – the originals having been removed to Marlborough House at the beginning of the eighteenth century. The gallery, with its supporting oak brackets and unique marble floor all combine to make this one of the most beautiful and aesthetically pleasing rooms in England.

By means of a doorway to the east one reaches Inigo Jones' 'grand stairway', the splendid Tulip Staircase, so-called after the motifs on the crafted wrought-iron balustrade. These circular stairs were built for Henrietta Maria as part of the second phase of the construction of The Queen's House in the early 1630s. Originally the stairway ran from the roof to the ground floor but in the nineteenth century stairs were installed down to the basement.

From the Gallery, reached by the Tulip Staircase, access

is obtained to the two principal rooms upstairs. On the west side, with its golden cornice, there is the Queen's sleeping apartment and on the east side the Queen's 'Cabinet' or boudoir, with its ceiling of 'unsurpassed loveliness'. On the southern side the Gallery leads to perhaps the most significant room in the house, 'the Bridge', and from here the residents of the house could watch 'the pageant of the world go by' including the mounted royal messengers and the occasional coach and horses bringing some great lady or gentleman to visit.

The Rev. and Mrs R. W. Hardy, on holiday from White Rock, British Columbia, had no interest whatever in ghosts or haunted houses. After visiting many famous and historic houses in London, they found they had a little time before returning home so, on the spur of the moment, they decided to go to Greenwich, where they visited the *Cutty Sark*, explored the National Maritime Museum and then turned to the beautiful Queen's House where Rubens, the Flemish painter whom they admired, had often stayed. Mrs Hardy had seen pictures of the elegant and symmetrical Tulip Staircase and they would have liked to climb it but they found that the staircase was not accessible to the public. However, they decided to take a photograph which they did. Mr Hardy was a retired United Church Minister and neither he nor his wife previously took the slightest interest in any aspect of psychical research and in fact they were always somewhat sceptical of stories of apparitions.

Back home in Canada the film they had used at The Queen's House and elsewhere in Greenwich was developed and one night the Hardys were entertaining their family and friends with some of the slides they had taken in

England. When the one of the Tulip Staircase was shown, everyone noticed that there appeared to be a shrouded figure on the stairs and clutching the stairway rail! A cousin of the Hardys who was a member of the Ghost Club was shown the transparency and, with the approval of Mr and Mrs Hardy, the facts of the case were placed in my hands for examination and investigation.

The first thing I did when I saw the original transparency was to contact Kodak, the makers of the film used by the Hardys, and ask them for their opinion. Subsequently I contacted other photographic experts, professional and unofficial: the result was always the same. There had been no trickery or manipulation or double-exposure or anything like that as far as the transparency was concerned and the only logical explanation from the photographic point of view was that there must have been someone on the stairway. Against that we have the evidence of the Rev. and Mrs Hardy and the fact that the stairway in question is not open to the public and museum attendants, there to keep an eye on the valuable paintings and the building in general, are understandably strict and firm and would certainly not countenance any dressing-up or playing about in The Queen's House and certainly no climbing the Tulip Staircase.

Optically the photograph is somewhat confusing due to the spirality of the staircase and one has to realise that the vast expanse of staircase that appears on the left-hand side of the picture is the underside of the spiral staircase as it lifts overhead.

Lengthy correspondence on the subject then took place between myself and the helpful Hardys and they were personally interviewed when they were again in London the following year. The gist of the information obtained was that the Hardys' photograph immediately preceding the one of the Tulip Staircase had been of the colonnade at the entrance and the one immediately afterwards had been of the ships' figureheads in the museum; both were quite normal and showed nothing resembling the Tulip Staircase. The Tulip Staircase was, of course, deserted when they took the photograph, which they did in daylight at about 5 o'clock on a Sunday afternoon, aided by the electric candelabra that lights the staircase. No flash was used. The day had been fine but cloudy (and this we subsequently verified with the Meteorological Office at the London Weather Centre). The camera used was a Zeiss Ikon 'Contina' – Prontor SVS Zavar Anastigmat lens 1:3.5f + 45mm with 'skylight' auxiliary haze filter. The film used was Kodachrome X, daylight, 35mm colour film with speed 64. There is no possibility of double exposure with this camera, besides which each picture is accounted for by number. The Hardys were unable to state with certainty the aperture but they thought it was probably about f4 and the shutter speed was also uncertain but they thought probably about four to six seconds. Incidentally one knowledgeable photographer in the club recently questioned the possibility of hand-holding a camera for four to six seconds and obtaining a perfectly static result; this had occurred to me at the time and I put this to the Hardys asking exactly where Mr Hardy had been standing when he took the photograph. They replied that he had stood in the doorway and steadied himself by resting himself and the camera against the door jamb. We also questioned at some length the late Hector MacQueen, the long-standing Ghost Club member who had brought the matter to our attention and his cousin Mrs Joyce Fraser of North Vancouver, B.C. who had first seen the transparency at the Hardys.

Another of the many questions we asked the Hardys was: why had the photograph been taken anyway? The Queen's House has many beautiful rooms and aspects and in particular there was the beautifully proportioned Great Hall with its exquisite ceiling, decorated brackets and frieze, fine mosaic floor and elegant Gallery. All seemed to me to be very photogenic, while the Tulip Staircase, leading off from a doorway in the Hall, would not, I felt, be the feature most likely to attract an amateur photographer. The Hardys' answer I found typically straightforward and acceptable: Mrs Hardy had seen a photograph of the staircase in a book before their visit to England and she really liked it; finding themselves inside The Queen's House, she immediately decided to obtain a photograph of it for herself. She discovered that it was impossible to obtain a photograph at the angle from which the picture she had seen had been taken and she had had to content herself with a shot of a small section of the stairway. At the last moment she decided that her husband should take the photograph.

Interestingly enough the photograph, on first examination, appears to show a figure with an exceptionally long right arm reaching ahead of itself, but close scrutiny establishes that there are two figures and that both the hands on the stair are *left* hands and they both wear a ring on the marriage finger. The higher figure is oddly convincing, since the shadow falls directly across the light rays emitted by the electric chandelier. It is possible to see the shrouded figure leaning forward in a menacing position, apparently in pursuit of the 'shadow' figure as they ascend the stairs. Viewed in this light there is an overwhelmingly malevolent air about the photograph. A plausible explanation would be that the left hands are both those of the same person who is photographed twice mounting the stairway, but the senior museum photographer at the time used yards of film in a futile attempt to obtain a similar photograph by normal means.

The Hardys' story is simple and convincing; listen to Mrs Hardy on another point: 'My husband actually took the picture as his stronger and steadier hands are better than mine at holding a camera steady . . . thus I was free to watch for any possible intrusion of anything visible during the exposure time. Actually a group of people who noticed our preparation apologised and stepped back although I explained that my husband was not quite ready. I mention all this to indicate that no person or visible object could have intervened without my noticing it. Also we had previously tried to ascend the staircase but were blocked by a "No Admittance" sign and rope barrier at the foot of the stairs.'

Considerable efforts were made to identify the ring which the figure in the photograph wears, for it would have been extremely interesting if it could have been established that such a ring was associated with the unpopular Queen Henrietta Maria, who certainly must have known and used the Tulip Staircase. However, all our inquiries, which included consultation with the National Portrait Gallery (where we were permitted to examine pictures not on

313

public view) and the Victoria and Albert Museum, proved unsuccessful.

Next, the Ghost Club contacted Commander W. E. May, then Deputy Director of the National Maritime Museum, who told us he knew of no ghostly associations connected with The Queen's House, although we later learned of one or two vague stories of an unexplained 'figure' in the tunnel under the colonnade and unexplained footsteps and a 'feeling of malevolence' in the vicinity of the Tulip Staircase. We decided to look into the possibility of some members of the Ghost Club spending a night in The Queen's House, especially near the Tulip Staircase, and we found Commander May and his staff most helpful and co-operative.

The Ghost Club investigation team on that occasion was joined by the senior museum photographer at that time, Brian Tremain, and a couple of warders, as agreed. During the night still and cine-photography was employed with special filters and infra-red film; delicate and normal sound recording apparatus were used; various thermometers were used for checking the temperature (especially easy in The Queen's House where the temperature is kept constant to protect the many valuable paintings); a dozen doorways were sealed off with cotton to aid control of the central area; the portion of the Tulip Staircase which appeared on the photograph was smeared with diluted petroleum jelly and periodically checked for fingerprints or other marks; instruments were employed to detect draughts, vibrations and atmospheric variations; objects were distributed over the staircase at set points and ringed to detect possible movement; and during the night various attempts were made to tempt any unseen entities to communicate by various kinds of seances and methods of communication, including automatic writing which Mrs MacQueen had tried on other occasions, with some success.

We did not succeed in scientifically establishing that The Queen's House is or was haunted, but a number of curious sounds were never satisfactorily explained and several members of the investigating team had definite, distinct and inexplicable impressions during the night. Footsteps, which certainly did not originate from any member of the team or officials present were heard on three occasions. They were heard during periods of otherwise complete silence and in total darkness, and they seemed to originate from the direction of the Tulip Staircase, which had been specially opened for us, and where members of the party were stationed at intervals. And there were other sounds; sounds that seemed totally inexplicable and that lasted in the memory.

In May 1993, I asked Mrs MacQueen (now Mrs Margery Skinley) for her memories and recollections of that night and she told me: 'Regarding Greenwich I still have a vivid recollection of hearing a horse trotting outside during that night. The noise was very loud and the clamour was instantly stopped, like switching off a radio. This happened just as it was beginning to get light. It seemed obvious to my mind that the horse was trotting on a hard surface like stone, and on its own, there was no sound of wheels. I noticed afterwards that there was no path adjacent to the building, just grass!'

Also we all heard and recorded, once only, but very

distinctly, the sound of a baby crying. This seemed quite out of place and impossible but much later we learned that a young married couple, living in rooms in The Queen's House many years ago, had become involved in a domestic quarrel and their infant son had been thrown to his death from the Gallery to the mosaic tiled floor below. Certainly, we also found, there have been over the years various people, including staff, who have found the Great Hall and in particular the doorway leading to the Tulip Staircase, uncomfortable and disturbing. Time and again, one experienced and unimaginative attendant told us when we met him the following morning he had found, while on duty in The Queen's House, his attention being drawn in the direction of the little doorway and although he had never seen anything unusual, he had often felt that there was or had been something malevolent about that area of the historic Queen's House.

On a later occasion I took clairvoyant Trixie Allingham, a reliable medium, to The Queen's House and after standing for a few moments in the Great Hall, facing the entrance to the Tulip Staircase she said that clairvoyantly she saw an insanely jealous woman conspiring with a confidant, whom she identified as 'Viscount Kensington', and it seemed to her that they were planning to lure the mistress of the woman's husband to the house and murder her on the Tulip Staircase. Trixie described to me how she could see blood running down those dark stairs.

We had always been puzzled by the fact that the strange photograph seemed to show a cowled figure or possibly two figures, almost like monks, climbing the staircase, for we could not reconcile monks or friars or abbots or priests with

The Queen's House. Then my valued friend Dorothy E. Warren of Chelsea, an archaeological and historical researcher, pointed out to me that the figure could well be some such ecclesiastic (although in that case the ring should be on the *right* hand) for recent archaeological findings at Greenwich show remains of an abbot's house.

When Baldwin II, Count of Flanders, died in 916, his widow, Elstrudis, youngest daughter of Alfred the Great, gave the manors of Greenwich, together with Woolwich and Lewisham, to the Abbey of Ghent as a memorial to her husband and for a long time the Abbots of Ghent received rents and tithes of the priory estates, before they were taken over by the Crown of England in the late fourteenth century. There seems to have been a large medieval house at Greenwich (according to Beryl Platts' *History of Greenwich*) which had an upstairs room grand enough for visiting prelates in the thirteenth century and Miss Warren suggests that this part of the great house may have stood on the site of the later Queen's House and well away from the enclosed parts of the priory. The figures in the photograph do seem to be mounting a staircase extraneous to the present one; a staircase that may have formerly been the stairway to the abbot's guest room. Beryl Platts mentions that in the fourteenth century the abbot let part of his domestic buildings, 'only holding back accommodation for his courts'; so the question of positively identifying the ghosts at this period of time looks like being very difficult indeed, unless more new evidence turns up. Or could the creeping figures go back to the days when smuggling and other nefarious activities took place at The Queen's House?

317

It would be interesting to discover whether any other photographs of The Queen's House include an unexplained figure, or any photographs of the Tulip Staircase show a shrouded or cowled figure creeping up the stairs, its jewelled hand clasping the stair rail as so many hands must have done in the long history of this beautiful house. At all events, given the provenance of this so-called 'Greenwich Ghost Photograph', the people concerned and the views of reliable experts in various fields, I have to say that I consider the Hardys' photograph to be the most remarkable and interesting ghost photograph I have come across in fifty years of serious psychical investigation.

RAF Cosford,
Aerospace Museum

A haunted aircraft? Now that *did* sound different and if reports warranted an investigation I decided it was something that should concern the Ghost Club.

For some time I had been receiving reports concerning a haunted Avro Lincoln bomber, RF 398, housed in the museum hangar at RAF Cosford, Shropshire: reports that recordings had been obtained suggesting a pilot talking to his crew; droning aircraft engines; morse code blips; the sounds of switches and levers being operated; the clanging of hangar doors; and even a spectral airman dressed in battle kit inside the hangar and a figure wearing a flying helmet in the astrodome, the glass dome where the pilot sat in a Lincoln bomber. But this particular Lincoln never saw active war service.

A strange tape recording of the ghostly sounds was said to have been obtained by a freelance broadcaster from Chesterfield, Derbyshire. Many of the noises mentioned above were recorded on the tape. According to reports, the freelancer, Ivan Spenceley, first visited the museum with a local research group and he left his recording machine in the empty cockpit of the bomber that stood in a locked hangar. Unfortunately repeated telephone calls and several letters to Mr Spenceley remain unanswered and I might well have left the curious matter there had I not received independent evidence of something very odd happening in the vicinity of that Lincoln bomber.

The first recorded incidents go back to 1963. The bomber in question, a development of the wartime Lancaster, was completed too late to see active service in the Second World War but it was flown as part of the RAF in various countries, including Africa during tribal disturbances, before being stored at Henlow in 1963. At one period it may have been used to test top-secret equipment. In the late 1970s, it was transported to Cosford where it has been refurbished and maintained by volunteers and helpers. There it has been on continual display among the sixty or so other aircraft together with missiles, engines, uniforms and aviation memorabilia.

The first reported incidents of a possibly paranormal origin occurred when the aeroplane was being renovated. While working on the bomber one man saw a figure approaching the bomber inside the hangar. He thought it was his companion who was working in the cockpit and must have left his work for a moment and was now returning. As he turned to address his friend, the figure disappeared. He then found that his friend had not left the cockpit. Next morning the same two men returned to continue their work on the aeroplane to discover machinery parts underneath the bomber that were certainly not there the night before and they had been the last to leave the hangar and the first to arrive that morning.

Other apparently paranormal happenings included the movement of objects, the sound of whistling inside the aircraft, temperature variations within the bomber, and the appearance of a figure in uniform and wearing a pilot's helmet – an apparition that quickly became known as 'Fred'. Some witnesses have described the phantom airman as wearing a blue battledress jacket and a white polo-neck sweater. Many people have heard footsteps in the immediate vicinity of the Lincoln and then found nothing to account for what they heard.

In 1977, ex-RAF engineer, John Small, was in charge of repairs when he thought he saw an airman he did not recognise near a toolbox inside the bomber. As he approached the 'man' to ask 'him' casually to pass the toolbox the figure suddenly and completely vanished! When he recovered the engineer stooped to unlock the toolbox but could not find the key, although he felt certain he had left it beside the box the night before. There was simply no sign of it anywhere and thinking he must have left it in the crew room, he went and looked. When he could find no sign of the key and no one seemed to know anything about it, the engineer decided that it must be beside the toolbox and he returned to the aircraft. There he saw the face of a man, dressed in a pilot's helmet, seemingly watching him from the astrodome. On reaching the toolbox he immediately found the key lying beside it but as he bent to pick it up, the key moved by itself under the toolbox! He then lifted the box, picked up the key, unlocked the box and took out the tools he was seeking. Looking back towards the cockpit he saw no sign of the 'man' he had seen seconds earlier.

A visitor to the museum in 1980, Mrs Graves of Cannock, Staffordshire, reported seeing a fair-haired man wearing a white polo-neck sweater and a forage cap in the cockpit of the Lincoln; a figure who had completely disappeared a second later. The figure was obviously not a member of the museum staff and there was no visitor answering such a description in the museum at the time. He was dressed too informally to be a serving officer but could well have been an officer off duty, she thought.

In 1984, the phantom pilot was reportedly seen during the filming of a television travel programme in the *Wish You Were Here* series for an item dealing with holidays in the West Midlands. Chris Kelly, the popular producer, writer and presenter of television programmes was sitting in the cockpit of the Lincoln bomber when the cameraman on the ground beneath the front of the nose of the aircraft called up and said he needed the chap behind Chris Kelly to move – he was right in the shot. Chris Kelly turned round; he was quite alone in the aircraft at the time and told the cameraman there was no one else in the cockpit or anywhere near him. The cameraman again insisted that he could see someone very clearly through the camera sights and with his naked eye. Chris Kelly again checked that he was alone and said, 'There's still nobody here!' His colleague then conceded that the figure had disappeared and he could see only Chris Kelly but he was adamant that there had previously been someone sitting behind the presenter.

322

At one stage a visiting vicar, hearing about the mysterious happenings and ghostly appearances, offered to exorcise the aeroplane but the team responsible for looking after the aircraft always felt the ghost or entity was very friendly and not in the least frightening and they rejected the vicar's kind proposal.

In 1985, the Aerospace Museum was visited by five members of a Research Group, who incidentally now reject the tape with its various sounds since they are convinced that the equipment used had no screening against extraneous radio signals which the particular recording machine in question was notorious for picking up. Furthermore, the final tape had been heard by only two of the six people present when it was obtained, and a report concerning the tape and submitted to Cosford was, they believe, demonstrably inaccurate in some respects. At one time the curious sounds were thought to be due to temperature fluctuations causing expanding and contracting sounds as the hangar cooled during the night but the technical curator of the museum, Bill Roseby, is on record as conceding that the noises are completely different from temperature-related sounds.

Ivan Spenceley has visited the museum many times and has spent eight nights there, mainly in the cockpit of the Lincoln. On two occasions he was accompanied by Gwyn Richards, a radio producer, and they reported rapid drops in temperature and diminutive moving lights. Once Ivan Spenceley and Gwyn Richards stated they saw a 'murky apparition' accompanied by a sudden drop in temperature and their companion Peter Thornycroft began to shake uncontrollably. All the lights were switched on and an immediate search was carried out but no one was found. On another occasion Ivan Spenceley saw the legs of a man walking by, his body obscured by an aeroplane – yet no living person, other than Spenceley himself, was in the area at the time. Spenceley also claimed that he and a colleague saw a 'wartime pilot opening a door' in the hangar.

The visiting Research Group were given free access to the Lincoln bomber, under the supervision of two members of the museum staff. Their observations and conclusions included the discovery of several 'cold spots' in the vicinity of the aircraft not consistent with the admitted areas of shade. Inside the bomber two female members of the group, both of whom claim some degree of psychic sensitivity, reported independently feelings of incoherence and light-headedness in the cockpit at the front of the aircraft, where the phantom pilot has reportedly been seen.

One member of the group was making an exit from the rear turret after taking some photographs when a noise attracted her attention. The sound seemed to come from behind her and when she turned round she saw a small handle revolving. As she watched the handle made several complete revolutions and experimentation seemed to preclude the possibility that this could have been the result of being touched by accident.

At one point all the members of the group vacated the vicinity of the Lincoln leaving two tape recorders aboard, one near the tail and one on the navigation table. They also left four cameras about the aircraft, and then locked all the doors. When they returned they found the back of one of the cameras open but otherwise there was no disturbance and nothing was recorded on tape.

Two years later seven members of the same Research Group spent a June night in the hangar containing the Lincoln. They left a tape recorder running that would record for two hours and they then boarded the aircraft to observe events from within the aeroplane. The first hour's recording was spoilt by the machine malfunctioning but the second recording contained a number of unexplained sounds: 'morse code blips, ghostly hangar doors opening and closing, Merlin engines running out of synchronisation' and much more. This is the tape that is now in contention.

Author Francis Marshall says that he spoke to a part-time cleaner at the museum who stated that she and a colleague have been in the hangar on many occasions and have heard sounds like the crackle of radio messages breaking up. They added that because of all the stories associated with the Lincoln RF 398, they always avoided going near it as much as they could.

Other apparent phenomena reported at Cosford includes a strange sleepy sensation that affects some people inside the aircraft; a sweet perfume that wafts past near the bomber; and a sensation of 'peaceful disapproval' but nothing really frightening. Reports of a figure resembling a man in flying gear, especially in the cockpit area of the aeroplane, seemed to be increasing and I set about exploring the possibility of a party of Ghost Club investigators spending a night in the hangar.

Early on I had come across a story associated with the bomber suggesting that one pilot so loved the aeroplane that he said he would never leave it, even after death. He was killed in a flying accident soon after making that statement in the presence of several of his fellow officers.

325

Among the later theories to account for the appearance of the phantom airman at Cosford is the idea that it may be the ghost of an engineer who killed himself when the bomber he was responsible for crashed in the 1940s killing all the crew; some parts of the crashed bomber finding their way into the haunted hangar at the Aerospace Museum. I understand that RAF Cosford opened in 1938 and during the last war some 70,000 engineers and mechanics and armourers passed through the station which housed an important maintenance unit and handled many kinds of aircraft, including Spitfires and Wellingtons. Furthermore an RAF Hospital was established at Cosford during the war so there are many, perhaps too many, possible candidates for the ghost airman.

Mr L. Woodgate, T.Eng (CEI), AMIRTE, AMIISO, the Museum Curator replied to my approach for a Ghost Club visit by informing us that the happenings at Cosford had prompted a host of similar requests. He had felt it necessary to refuse any more recordings inside the aircraft because it meant leaving the hangar unsecured. Fortunately, however, he investigated the Ghost Club and, finding it to be 'a serious research group', felt able to reconsider our request. Consequently, I soon got together a small investigative team. The introductory information for the team on this occasion included a description of the curious tape recording made by Ivan Spenceley and the other odd events, such as the changes in temperature experienced, the fact the bomber always seems polished while others became dusty and the sightings of the ghostly airman in battle kit – although the 'haunted' aeroplane had never seen active service.

We arranged to meet on Friday 19 May between 7.30 and 8 p.m. After some discussion about the known facts and the setting up of the investigative equipment, we planned to start our vigil at 10.45 p.m. for a period of two hours. If, at 12.45 a.m., nothing of any interest had transpired, we planned to leave the museum. We were also hoping to listen to Ivan Spenceley's tape recording, but in the event we were not able to hear it and I have not heard it to this day.

Having explored the whole premises and in particular the enormous hangar in which the 'haunted' Lincoln bomber was only one exhibit and which we had completely to ourselves throughout the investigation, we sorted ourselves out just behind the aircraft and agreed the placing of various apparatus, rotas, patrolling, etc. Seven thermometers were distributed inside the aeroplane: two in the cockpit, and one each in the areas once frequented by the bomb aimer, the navigator, the radio operator and the tail gunner. The seventh thermometer we placed in the exact centre of the airplane and an eighth thermometer was placed underneath the cockpit, outside the aircraft but not on concrete. We also distributed and ringed 'trigger' objects in and around the aircraft including a brass paper knife in the form of a dagger; four service badges; three 1940s' coins; a crystal ball; a key; an ashtray; a book; a Second World War postcard; a set of playing cards; and a pair of binoculars.

The thermometer readings showed no abnormality although the one in the tail was consistently 4°F lower than the temperature elsewhere in the aeroplane and the one underneath the cockpit, outside the airplane, was 6°F lower than inside the bomber. During periodical intervals of silence and darkness members were settled in various parts of the aircraft. Once, at 8.40 p.m., one member became aware of a curious and unpleasant feeling inside the bomber and at 9.15 p.m., when all the team were having a break for refreshments, one member caught a glimpse of something or someone outside the bomber. Another member described the atmosphere at one time inside the aeroplane as 'charged with some sort of force, energy perhaps; it was almost like meeting an invisible wall in there...' Among the 'trigger' objects that were found moved were the pack of playing cards, recorded to have moved twice out of their chalk circle, at 11 p.m. and again at 11.15 p.m. The binoculars were also found moved a full two inches at 11.15 p.m. and the three service badges in the cockpit were also found moved a full two inches outside their chalked circle.

Twice members of the team thought they caught sight of the figure of a man in the hangar and later three different members had the same impression. It was the sort of thing that is so difficult to establish satisfactorily as objective and real but the fact that five different members of the experienced team reported this cannot be treated lightly. On one occasion a shadowy figure was reported and seen in one place from two different vantage points that were wide apart. But perhaps the most interesting result of the visit was the photograph taken by Philip Moore. In a letter to me soon after the visit he enclosed the photograph which showed the centre window of the cockpit. He asked, 'Is there a face looking through the glass?' At first he thought it was his imagination, but looking carefully with a magnifying glass he thought he could discern someone wearing flying headgear and possibly an oxygen mask. He assured me that there was no one anywhere near the cockpit at the time. Later he sent me another photograph from a film that he'd just had developed. He wrote, 'There does seem to be someone in flying gear seated in the front observation dome of the bomber . . .'

Subsequently Philip Moore wrote up an account of his visit to the RAF Aerospace Museum for the Ghost Club *Newsletter* during the course of which he said: 'My particular experience occurred midway through the vigil. It was reported that the atmosphere near the bomber had altered. I climbed the ladder at the rear of the plane and entered the aircraft to be immediately confronted with a sudden wave of static electricity. It felt as though a wall had been erected and the air was alive, and although I could see nothing the feeling of expectancy remained. The experience lasted for about two minutes before everything returned to normal. I cannot explain this experience, maybe it was part imagination, but the feeling was so strong and vivid that I believe the event could be classed as supernatural, certainly something that cannot be easily explained.'

Altogether an interesting and well-worthwhile investigation that will long be remembered by those taking part. At more than one time during that calm May night it really seemed that we were standing at the very edge of the unknown; that some force or entity was in the hangar with us; was perhaps inside that great Lincoln and only needed the right conditions and the right environment to come out . . .

The Rookery

One day during the spring of 1988 I read a snippet in a newspaper referring to psychic manifestations including the sound of clashing swords, the movement of objects, unaccountable scents, and apparitions at the home of Mary Knox-Johnston, mother of round-the-world yachtsman Robin. The only clue to the address of Mrs Knox-Johnston was 'a Georgian house on the outskirts of London'. I decided a little detective work was called for.

My *Who's Who* informed me that Robin Knox-Johnston CBE was the only son of the late David Robert Knox-Johnston and Elizabeth Mary; that he was the first person to sail single-handed non-stop around the world; that he had won many sailing races and broken many sailing records and that he had been made a Freeman of the Borough of Bromley, Kent – could that, I wondered, have been because he had been born somewhere in the area? I looked at the appropriate telephone directory and there was Mrs E. M. Knox-Johnston, The Rookery, Rookery Lane, Downe, Farnborough, Kent. Farnborough is within the London Borough of Bromley.

The Rookery was even marked on my 1:100000 map, north of Downe House where Charles Darwin once lived and died in a house that is now haunted. To the south I saw Biggin Hill, the most famous fighter airfield in the world – and still haunted by the sound of a Spitfire coming home. I wrote at once to Mrs Knox-Johnston telling her something about the Ghost Club and expressing our wish to spend a night in her home. She was kind enough to reply saying she had no objection whatever to our visiting and trying to find an explanation for the sightings and sounds experienced by her and her housekeeper; indeed she said she would be only too delighted if we could discover an explanation for her. We fixed on a mutually convenient date and soon a confidential memo went out to selected members which described the odd happenings at the house. There had been sounds of clashing swords at night; objects had been moved; several apparitions had been reportedly seen; and there had been unexplained smells of oranges and cigars.

The Ghost Club team, having been selected, arranged to meet at The Rookery between 6.30 and 7 p.m. on a Friday evening for an all-night vigil at the house. As usual, each member received an itinerary for the night's proceedings which detailed the standard preparations such as choosing a Base Room, familiarising ourselves with the house and establishing the known facts of the case with the owner.

There followed the usual personal notes for participation in such events including simple equipment to be brought by each member and instructions should anything apparently paranormal be experienced. Finally there was a note: 'Mrs Knox-Johnston is the mother of round-the-world yachtsman Robin Knox-Johnston.

Among the disturbances reported by Mrs Knox-Johnston and her housekeeper are being awakened at night by the sound of shouting and the apparent clashing of swords; movement of objects – especially on the landing; the sighting of apparitions – sometimes ethereal but also a child, seemingly real and solid. Inexplicable scents have also been experienced in certain parts of the house.'

On arrival the investigative team was shown into an enormous reception room which was placed at our disposal for the night and after brief introductions Mrs Knox-Johnston related something of the history of the house and her experiences.

Mrs Knox-Johnston moved into the house in December 1963 and on 1 January 1964 she was awakened in the early hours by a considerable racket: loud noises that seemed to be centred in the hall in the vicinity of the front door. She leaned over the banister of the landing at the head of the stairs and felt she was looking at the centre of the sounds but she saw nothing. The really loud sounds seemed to her to resemble the clashing of weapon upon weapon, almost as though a fight was going on with primitive weapons, swords perhaps. Later she heard that there was a story that three Cavaliers, a man and his two sons, had been surprised here by Roundheads and murdered during the Civil War – and she almost expected to see something of the sort as she leaned over the banister but she saw nothing at all.

The main part of The Rookery, the middle, was built in 1729 and later parts were added in the early twentieth century so no part of the present building would have existed during the Civil Wars of 1642–51 but it is possible that there was a former structure on the site of the present house or that the desperate fight to the death took place on the spot where the front door and hall of The Rookery now stands. Mrs Knox-Johnston stated that a medium, visiting the house, with no knowledge of its history or knowing anything about any of the curious happenings that had been reported, said on arrival and without being told anything that she felt 'an atmosphere' outside the front of the house which seemed to be centred on the great yew tree facing the front door. The story goes that the three Cavaliers were eventually hanged from this yew tree. It does seem to have an oppressive atmosphere, as some very old trees have, and there have been several 'unaccountable' accidents in the vicinity of the tree. Once, Mrs Knox-Johnston said, her car seemed to literally be 'taken over' and she hit the wall near the tree; she was not hurt but the car was a mess. Another time a car being driven by a young man smashed into the wall at the same place; he had no explanation but he was quite badly hurt. The yew tree could well be nearly 500 years old.

In the hall a former companion-help witnessed with Mrs Knox-Johnston some money slowly rise into the air from a table without anyone being near it, then slowly sink down again. Another time some paper money disappeared from the ottoman at the top of the stairs and was later found rolled up like a cigarette in a doorway that led into the hall.

When Mrs Knox-Johnston's mother was staying at The Rookery on one occasion she said each night she saw a ghostly little boy in the Red Bedroom where she was sleeping. He appeared to be quite solid and real and she described his flannel trousers and striped shirt. Her description seemed to be that of a contemporary child and a former occupant of The Rookery, Colonel Daniels, always felt that his grown-up grandson Robert visited his home when he was a child and asleep. Could this happening have become impressed on the atmosphere and resulted in a 'ghost', we wondered. The child ghost at The Rookery has been nicknamed 'Roger'. Also in the Red Bedroom a silver purse went missing and was later discovered inside the bedclothes. Money also reportedly disappeared in the same room; once £25 disappeared and, some time later, was found under the eiderdown on the bed.

Mrs Knox-Johnston's husband died in the Yellow Bedroom nearby and once a Professor friend spent the night in this room, knowing nothing of the circumstances or manner of David Robert Knox-Johnston's death but in the morning the Professor stated that he had had the most frightening experience during the night, having had all the symptoms of a fatal heart attack. David Robert Knox-Johnston died in the Yellow Room of a fatal heart attack.

Although the clashing sounds, as of fighting men, had certainly been heard several times over the years, recently it seemed all had been comparatively quiet. Doris Crawford, a later companion and help to Mrs Knox-Johnston, related her experiences and said she too had once heard the most appalling sounds of quarrelling and fighting one summer night in the early hours. It certainly came from the direction of the front of the hall, near the front door, but nothing was visible to account for the sounds. Her two sons were young at the time and were fast asleep in bed. Two older boys also heard the sounds and were very frightened. Once in the Red Bedroom a duster 'disappeared' while Doris Crawford was dusting and she later found it underneath the bed; how it got there she could not imagine. She also verified the disappearance from the ottoman of money which she in fact found standing upright, rolled up like a cigarette, in the hall, in a doorway.

In the back garden it had been noticed that dogs always seemed uneasy on the left-hand side, looking from the house. There is an extensive lawn at the back bordered by trees and shrubs. On the landing at the top of the stairs, leading into the Red Bedroom and near to the Yellow Bedroom and Mrs Knox-Johnston's bedroom and a bathroom, and where there were also stairs leading up to the third storey, Doris Crawford stated that she occasionally felt quite certain that someone was immediately behind her, but there was never anybody there. This did not frighten her (although she was inclined to be nervous of thunderstorms and such like). Sometimes the feeling was overwhelmingly evil and she had to stop what she was doing and go to another part of the house; when she returned to the landing it would be all right.

Once or twice strange smells, cigars or perfume, had been noticed in the house, completely inexplicable but nevertheless very strong and unmistakable. Also a mysterious coldness was sometimes noticed near the window in the living room, which adjoined the reception room used as a Base Room during the investigative visit.

During the night seven thermometers were placed in strategic places: in the living room where coldness had been reported; on the left-hand side of the front door; in the hall on the right-hand side of the front door; at the bottom of the stairs; on the ottoman on the landing; in the Red

Bedroom and in the Yellow Bedroom. 'Control' or 'trigger' objects were also placed about the allegedly haunted areas: a glass paperweight in the living room by the window; some money (a £5 note and a 50p coin) on a table in the middle of the hall; a horsebrass on a chair on the right-hand side of the front door; a ball on the ottoman on the landing; a crucifix in the Red Bedroom; a doll in the Yellow Bedroom and also a paper and crayon – in the hope of a paranormal message! All these objects were carefully ringed with chalk and checked at twenty-minute intervals between 11 p.m. and 7 a.m., apart from an hour rest period between 3.30 a.m. and 4.30 a.m. This checking was slotted between the checking of all thermometers – also each twenty minutes – and a leisurely 'patrol' was instituted of the whole relevant area at half-hour intervals throughout the night. All checking and patrolling was carried out by two people working together.

Although nothing of great moment seemed to happen during the period under observation several small incidents were reported. Thermometer readings showed no abnormality and there was no significant fluctuation, the temperature being in fact remarkably consistent; only the thermometers at the bottom of the stairs registering a much lower temperature than anywhere else in the house. At 11.20 p.m., while taking flash photographs alone, one member reported seeing a 'black shape' in the Yellow Bedroom. At 11.35 p.m. the same room seemed warm to two members on patrol while the Red Bedroom seemed very cold and one member felt a cold draught on his person on the side *away* from the window where no draught was registered.

At 11.40 p.m. two members heard what sounded like footsteps tripping down the stairway which was under their observation and deserted. At 11.55 p.m. two different members reported a distinct coldness in the centre of the living room and at 12.07 a.m. (during a period of total darkness) a curious 'splat' noise was heard in the hall by six members. Also during this period of darkness three members mentioned independently that one of the pillars on the landing overlooking the hall seemed to light up; this was just possibly the result of reflection of the full moon through an upper window but all three members felt it was rather strange. At 12.20 a.m. two members said the Yellow Bedroom 'felt warm' – contrary to the thermometer readings in the room. One of the members had the distinct feeling of being followed when he crossed the landing between the top of the stairs and the Red Bedroom at 1.13 a.m., and at 1.30 a.m. a 'cold spot' seemed to be noticed in the living room; so noticeable in fact that an extra thermometer was placed to monitor the temperature but no abnormality was revealed. At 5.30 a.m. two patrolling members reported a slight movement from its chalked circle of one 'trigger' object which was replaced and did not move again; interestingly enough it was beside the front door but this fact suggested that the object could possibly have been accidentally moved by normal means. Perhaps the most significant event of the night was revealed when a recording was played back. It comprised an attempted seance with glass and letters, held in the hall and later in the Red Bedroom by eight members. In between questions, a sound resembling a babble of voices is distinctly discernible and at one stage a voice is heard to say 'wipe the table'. These sounds are very puzzling in the circumstances under which they appeared on the tape but it has been suggested that the odd sounds are those of the glass moving over the table and the voice may be that of an observer at the seance. The sounds were later enhanced but it was still not possible to decide exactly what they were.

At one point during the seances two entities seemed to be trying to get through; one connected with the present house, The Rookery, and one not having any such connections. The first gave a very definite 'Yes' twice when asked whether they had lived at the house, adding 'long ago'. When asked the name of the communicating entity, 'it' replied, 'Why?' Later a Roundhead purported to communicate and said he died by the tree outside the house, but by and large the answers received did not make a lot of sense.

After a snack breakfast in the great dining room, a small presentation was made to Mrs Knox-Johnston for her hospitality and kindness (she even laid a fire for the party in case we were cold during the night) and the party left The Rookery about 8 a.m.

In 1993 I asked Mrs Knox-Johnston, who had impressed each and everyone as a 'good, solid person who doesn't imagine things', whether there had been any odd happenings since our visit and in reply she said, 'There has been nothing new to report – due perhaps to the fact that for more than fifteen months we have been in utter chaos with the house being treated for dry rot! But one odd thing did occur: one of the workmen refused to work in the cellar, he said there was someone behind him all the time.' On that note – an independent witness describing an experience which has been experienced elsewhere in the house and even during the Ghost Club investigative visit – we will leave The Rookery and its ghosts.

Rushbrooke Hall

At the time of the last war, during the course of service with the Suffolk Regiment, I was in hospital at Bury St Edmunds and from there went to nearby Rushbrooke Hall for convalescence.

This mid-Tudor, red-brick mansion, empty but in reasonable condition in 1947 was derelict by 1961 and the Lord Rothschild of the day couldn't give it away. He ordered its demolition but it caught fire while being demolished and although the fire was put out, it was then relit as the most effective way of destroying the house and today there is little to show where it once stood, a proud house where Elizabeth I once held court.

The history of Rushbrooke is the history of the Jermyns; one of whom built Jermyn Street, Haymarket in 1667, a street where Louis Napoleon lived in 1846 and a street well known to Sir Walter Scott, Sir Isaac Newton, the Duke of Marlborough, Gladstone and Thackeray for they all lived in Jermyn Street at one time or another. One Sir Thomas Jermyn (who died in 1504) planned and built Rushbrooke and it remained in the Jermyn family, sometimes used as a farm, until early in the nineteenth century when it passed through marriage to Lord Bristol who sold it to Robert Rushbrooke. After being in the Rushbrooke family for a century the Hall saw one or two quick changes in ownership and then, after the First World War, it was purchased by Lord Islington and sold by his widow to Lord Rothschild in 1938.

In the first Elizabethan age the Hall must have been the scene of great splendour. Scores of people lived within its walls. There were lights that showed up the lovely furniture and fine pillars; music for the beautifully dressed ladies and gentlemen to dance to; and tables groaning with food and wine. Elizabeth herself watched the great bell for Rushbrooke being cast in the bell foundry at Bury St Edmunds where she knighted Robert Jermyn after he had feasted the French ambassador and herself: everyone was 'marvellously contented' it is recorded.

In 1578, Queen Elizabeth held court at the sixty-room mansion owned by the unwaveringly loyal Jermyns; and on the same night a murder took place at Rushbrooke Hall. Details are few and far between but a lady of some rank was done to death and the gruesome fact had to be hushed up. At dead of night the body was weighted and hurled from a high window into the deep moat where it sank and probably remained undiscovered for years, if it is not still there. Some of this grim story is said to have been re-enacted annually on the anniversary of the murder.

In the years that followed Elizabeth's reign the only troubles that seem to have touched Rushbrooke were religious ones. Sir Robert Jermyn was a staunch Protestant and associated himself with a band of Puritans who were in the habit of meeting at nearby Bury St Edmunds. A long succession of Jermyns became Members of Parliament and with the coming of the Stuarts one became Comptroller of the Household, another Groom of the Bedchamber to Prince Charles, later Charles II and yet another Vice-Chamberlain to Queen Henrietta Maria and when the Civil War came they fought with the Cavaliers, one following the young prince abroad and only returning to England after the execution of the King. Another was entrusted with the protection of the Queen, Henrietta Maria, and went with her to France. During the years of the Protectorate the glory of the Jermyns diminished to some extent, impoverished by taxes and fines, but they continued to live at Rushbrooke Hall, encouraged by frequent royalist gatherings there and looking forward to better times.

In 1660, one Henry Jermyn returned to England, after years of exile, bringing with him silver gilt communion plate, made in France, which he presented to Rushbrooke Hall. He was created Earl of St Albans, a title formerly held by Francis Bacon. Later he became a Knight of the Garter and enjoyed considerable success, living for a time at Somerset House on the Embankment, then the residence of Henrietta Maria, and he was responsible for some of the fine buildings in Pall Mall. He died in 1684, the year the Thames froze over, and he left his many treasures to Rushbrooke, including two cabinets with the monograms of Henrietta Maria and a chest with the initials of Charles I; inside the chest were two shirts and a nightcap that had belonged to the unhappy King. This furniture can now be seen in the Vandyke Room at Windsor.

But the Jermyns' long story was almost over and for one

of the nephews of the Earl of St Albans, Lord Jermyn, his last years were full of sorrow. Of his thirteen children, seven died in infancy and were buried side by side at Rushbrooke and one son, Thomas, was killed in an accident at the age of fifteen in 1692. Can all this history and sorrow have left its mark at Rushbrooke and provided the atmosphere conducive to recurring psychic activity? With only five daughters left and his brother Lord Dover having no children, Lord Jermyn's death in 1701 brought to an end 500 years of the Jermyns at Rushbrooke. The estate passed to a daughter who had married Sir Robert Davers, a rich sugar planter, and Rushbrooke began its slow but sure decline into oblivion 259 years later.

When I was at Rushbrooke the air was full of history. We had professors from Cambridge to lecture to us and even a visit from the then owner, Lord Rothschild, and still the air pulsated with the past and I and three of my army friends sought to hear all there was to learn about Rushbrooke and its inhabitants of long ago, of its history, its happy days and its tragedies.

So we came to hear about the murder and we visited the 'murder room', long unused. We heard several versions of the murder and several reasons for the murder: jealousy, greed, lust, anger, envy – most of the seven deadly sins in fact but a few facts were common to all the stories: the murder had happened in that room; the body had been hurled from the window into the moat below and the date – a date that was fast approaching!

These were early ghost hunting days for me but I still took such precautions as I could. The four of us told no one of our plans and only at the last possible moment did we seek and obtain the necessary permission to spend the night in the 'haunted room' or 'murder room'. It was agreed this would be a strictly confidential arrangement; we would on no account be disturbed; we had the only keys to the room; we prepared ourselves for the night with adequate rest beforehand and food and drink (not alcoholic – even then!). My companions were aware of the considerable circumstantial evidence for the annual haunting but details of the actual alleged experiences varied from a full visual image to a sound-only re-enactment but that *something* happened there each year on that particular date seemed fairly well established.

At the appointed time on the appointed night we quietly gathered in an upstairs corridor (it had been circulated that we had all-night passes) and we cautiously made our way to the 'haunted room'. All was quiet and still as we unlocked the door, entered the room, relocked the door, and prepared for our vigil. The night was still, in fact there was hardly a breath of wind but a bright moon shone through the tall windows and onto the moat below.

Having ascertained that the room was deserted we made sure all the windows were closed and fastened and then we made ourselves as comfortable as we could. After an hour or so, at 10.45 p.m. to be precise, we found the moonlight very bright and we carefully closed the heavy shutters on the windows and resumed our previous relaxed positions. I do recall that we were most careful to see that the shutters were tightly fastened as we were aware that any movement of the shutters would cause sounds and it was sounds, as well as sightings, that we were waiting for – although the night was exceptionally still and there was no wind.

All was very quiet but we passed the time with quiet chatter and ensuring that none of us dozed off! We mused on the people who had used that room over the centuries and the uses to which the room had been put; had a murder *really* taken place there? Could the air still be charged with the trauma of such a moment? What were we doing there instead of being comfortably in bed?

Suddenly, just before 2 o'clock in the morning, when there was total silence in the room we were occupying and outside, and still there was no breath of wind, abruptly and without any kind of warning, the shutters on one window slammed back against the wall and the window opened! As the moonlight streamed into the room we were all alert, ears cocked, eyes wide, waiting for the next move, the least sound. None of us moved. We all knew that the window and the shutters had been securely fastened but had they not been, the fact was they had remained closed and silent for over three hours where now one window swung open, rattling in the night air.

After a moment we all gingerly approached the window and looked out. Everything seemed to be still and quiet inside and outside and in the dark moat below. As we crouched over the sill, peering down, we suddenly felt, all four of us, an icy draught over our heads and, as we looked at each other to ensure that each of us had in fact noticed the sudden coldness, we all felt that something flew past our heads and we all heard a dull 'plop' from the direction of the moat below us. Looking down we thought we could distinguish a disturbance in the water and, silent and wondering, we watched the ever-increasing circles of water in the clear moonlight and we asked ourselves what had come out of that 'haunted' room, passed over our crouched heads and dropped into the moat to cause those ripples? Had it anything to do with the icy draught we had experienced? Had it anything to do with the story of murder in that room four centuries earlier?

Sandwood Bay

Sandwood Bay, Cape Wrath, on the north-western tip of Scotland is a strange and isolated place where one can still walk for a whole day among the rocky hills and great lumps of stone slowly disintegrating through the ages, without meeting another living soul. But, by all accounts, one might encounter a ghost.

The late MacDonald Robertson, who was no stranger to mysterious encounters, has written about a disused fisherman's hut long reputed to be haunted and how a crew of fishermen, beached in the bay after a day's fishing was over, set off to walk home to their crofts leaving one of their number in charge of the boat and fishing gear and saying they would return in the morning.

That night, sheltering in the hut, this fisherman was startled to hear, outside the desolate hut in that lonely place to which there was no road or pathway, the tramp of footsteps on the shingle, coming ever closer. Soon he saw a huge man in a long black cloak ... a ghostly visitor who later disappeared in the direction of the beach.

Sometime afterwards another fisherman, a member of

the same crew, had a similar experience while alone one night in the same hut and, writing in 1985, MacDonald Robertson says there are local folk who can vouch for the accuracy of these and other unexplained incidents in the area of that haunted hut.

Antony Hippisley Coxe describes Sandwood Bay as 'a very haunted spot', and the ghost a figure in sea boots, reefer jacket and sailor's cap. 'It has been seen,' he says, 'on many occasions in 1949 and 1953 and sometimes inside a cottage facing Cape Wrath lighthouse.' Legend has it that a Polish ship was driven ashore here some 300 years ago and the spectre of one of the crew that perished searches for his lost shipmates. This theory of the ghost being a long-dead sailor is the one that most accurately fits all the sightings. Apparently, this bearded figure has been seen on the beach and near the hut. Poltergeist activity has also been reported which may possibly be caused by him. However, there doesn't seem to be any evidence to corroborate that this ghost is of Polish origin, nor is there any information about the ship in which he supposedly met his death.

Another theory is that the ghost is that of an Irish sailor. Apparently, early in the 1940s, Sandy Gunn, George McKay and William MacLeod saw a bearded man walk behind some rocks and disappear. Fourteen days later they claimed that an Irish sailor who had drowned in a shipwreck was the same man!

In the late 1940s, a crofter and his son were out with their pony gathering driftwood when they suddenly encountered a large and bearded man, standing beside them on the sands. Their pony, normally a quiet and docile creature, became extremely restive and as they sought to calm the animal, the figure disappeared as mysteriously as it had appeared but not before both father and son had noticed the brass buttons on the tunic, the worn sea-boots, the faded sailor's cap and the dark, weather-beaten clothing.

Not long afterwards a farmer was searching the area for stray sheep when he saw the outline of a tall man among the nearby rocks. Thinking it must be a local man he called out and walked towards the figure but as he drew near he saw the figure was a sailor and unfamiliar to him. A few steps closer and the figure completely vanished.

Also in 1949, early one afternoon, all the members of a fishing party from Kinlochbervie, who were rounding one of the big sand dunes that dot the beach of Sandwood Bay, clearly saw a figure striding along the crest of a sandy knoll – a figure wearing a sailor's cap and clothing, and they caught a glimpse of brass buttons glinting in the sunlight as the figure disappeared behind a hillock. One of the party was a local gillie who saw the figure with his stalking-glass and thinking it might be a poacher, he set off to track the man down, only to return, ashen-faced and puzzled, to report that there was no sign of anyone at all anywhere in the bay, except themselves; nor were there any footmarks or other indications that there had been anyone where everyone in the party had clearly seen the figure.

One afternoon in the summer of 1953 a party of picnickers from Edinburgh suddenly noticed a tall, bearded sailor gazing at them from the crest of a nearby hillock. They all saw the figure and watched 'him' for some minutes before 'he' appeared to take a step backwards and completely disappeared. When they searched the area they could find no trace of the figure they had seen and there were no footprints in the sand where 'he' had stood.

About a mile from the sand dunes of the bay, stand the remains of Sandwood Cottage, unoccupied now for many years and probably the most remote and solitary habitation on the mainland of Scotland – a deserted fisherman's hut that is also reputed to be haunted.

A tired old shepherd decided to sleep in the empty cottage one night (possibly Sandy Gunn in the early 1940s) and later related that after he had retired and was almost asleep he suddenly thought he heard the footsteps of someone padding about downstairs inside the cottage. He got up and listened as the sounds seemed to move from one room to the other and then back again, time after time. At length he lit a candle, quietly opened the door and proceeded to search every inch of the cottage. He found nothing to account for the sounds he had heard and went back to bed and was not disturbed again but nothing could ever convince the hard-headed old shepherd but that something 'not of this world' had entered the cottage that night.

Years before, it is said, a wealthy Australian had fallen under the spell of Sandwood Bay and he had visited the place and the cottage year after year, each time more loath to leave. After his last visit he had died in Australia and the old shepherd believed that his spirit returned to the place he loved so much.

Some time later, but before 1961, an Edinburgh woman received part of the broken wooden staircase (no longer existing) from Sandwood Cottage, and strange happenings occurred in her house, such as crockery falling to the floor;

there was a strong smell of alcohol; the piece of staircase rattled occasionally; and she saw the ghost of a bearded sailor.

Some years later, in the late 1970s, an old fisherman found himself in the bay late one night and he decided to stay the night in Sandwood Cottage. He made himself as comfortable as possible on the ground floor. Around midnight he was awakened by his dog barking and he then heard distinct and firm footsteps approaching the cottage. There followed a knock on the window and looking in that direction he clearly saw, in the bright moonlight, the face of a bearded sailor looking into the cottage. As the figure retreated the fisherman noted the short black coat with brass buttons and peaked cap that the figure wore. When he opened the door he could find no trace of any living soul. Accompanied by his dog he searched the whole cottage inside and outside but found nothing to account for the figure he had seen and the dog had heard.

Also, in September 1970, two walkers from Surrey were making their way from Durness to the Cape Wrath light-house and thence, following the coast, to Kinlochbervie to catch a bus to Lairg. But the sun was going down as they reached Sandwood Cottage and they decided to spend the night there and continue in the morning.

Next day they fled the cottage at dawn and told the local postmaster, the first person they met, about the ghastly night they had spent in Sandwood Cottage. In the middle of the night they had heard a fearful noise, as though the whole place was being smashed up – the cottage vibrating as if in a violent storm except that the night was calm and dry. Then, after the rocking and crashing sounds ceased they heard a noise like a horse stamping and pawing the ground and this sound seemed to come from within the cottage, above them. This frightening sound lasted perhaps four or five minutes and then ceased. The walkers sat, huddled together in the darkness, dreading further disturbances, until dawn broke and they, like others before them and after them, fled from the haunted cottage at Sandwood Bay, the cottage that does not like to be visited.

A valued and experienced Ghost Club member, John Fraser, visited Sandwood Bay and spent a night in the haunted cottage. He has kindly allowed me to use information and quote from his subsequent report. He visited the cottage on the morning of 4 April 1988 to take some initial photographs and ascertain what he would need to take with him for his all-night vigil. It is impossible to park a car closer than two miles from the cottage as the surrounding terrain is mostly moorland. Furthermore, because of quicksand on the beach and the boggy overland route, he realised he would be unable to return to the car until morning. Therefore he had to decide upon necessary equipment and what could be comfortably carried. He sorted out two cameras (one with infra-red film), a tape recorder, a torch and a few other items as essential requisites.

John decided to have his evening meal at the Old School House Restaurant where he learned about an old hermit who frequently visited the cottage and could possibly be mistaken for a ghost. Unfortunately, he left his powerful torch behind at the restaurant having its batteries recharged.

Feeling somewhat apprehensive, he set out from his car

to walk to the cottage at about 7.15 p.m. It was only a two-mile walk, but he lost his way ~~and it was well~~ into dusk by the time he arrived at the bothy. In his report he states: 'As night falls it gives the impression of being one of the most lonely and desolate places you can imagine ... if one wished to return to the safety of civilisation, forget it before morning... For these reasons there is a certain feeling of comparison with those old horror movies where one is trapped inside the haunted house until dawn!'

John Fraser had found the cottage to be a two-roomed shell (the second storey no longer existing). He now checked the building for the hermit or any other signs of activity, then identified any persistent rattles so that he wouldn't be disturbed by them during the night. As it was now getting quite dark, he tried to light a fire. For some reason he was 'singularly unsuccessful', so he decided to position his equipment instead but misfortune struck again. The camera containing the infra-red film had been knocked and was damaged beyond repair, while the tape recorder not only refused to record but the brand-new high-powered batteries seemed to drain within five minutes. Furthermore, because he had forgotten his torch he was now completely in the dark.

However, despite the atmosphere being seemingly 'right' for something strange to happen, nothing of consequence occurred during the night and the next morning he quickly made his way back to civilisation.

John decided to do some more research into the matter and visited Sally Tyszko in the craft shop at Kinlochbervie who, according to the restaurant, was knowledgeable about the local area. Sally told John that the hermit was an

355

old Glaswegian by the name of James MacRory Smith whose description matched well that of the ghostly sailor, down to his bushy beard and peaked sailor-type cap. He did not actually use Sandwood Cottage, but apparently he had been using nearby Strathchailleach Bothy – which was in better condition – for some twenty years as a summer residence.

Sally also suggested that John visit Bridgit, the postmistress at Oldshoremore who might have more information. Bridgit turned out to be most helpful in pointing out the house in which Sandy Gunn (one of the best witnesses) used to live and informing John that next door to this house there still lived an elderly lady who would certainly have some interesting recollections. This old lady kindly offered John hospitality and some useful information: that as far as she could remember Sandwood Cottage had never been inhabited by an Australian; that Sandy Gunn had been known as a man who never told a lie, but she clearly remembered that Sandy had claimed to see a mermaid and not a sailor; and that MacDonald Robertson, the writer of local folklore, had lived in a house between Oldshoremore and Sheigra, which might be a good source of more information.

John followed the old lady's directions to Robertson's house and there was shown a copy of Robertson's long out-of-print book *Scottish Highland Folktales*. He discovered that most of the original information about the ghost had come from this source and that later writers had, in some cases, just copied from the book.

After his visit and subsequent inquiries, John Fraser had a number of conclusions about this case. It seems that most of the earlier sightings were originally recorded by MacDonald Robertson, a local resident who probably got most of his information first hand. Apart from its age and the fact that Sandy Gunn's old neighbour contradicts Robertson's report (being positive that Gunn saw a mermaid and not a ghostly sailor), John felt that it was very good evidence. Of the later sightings, John commented 'there are absolutely no grounds on which to think of these as being anything other than accurate reports of claimed experiences', although he acknowledged the possibility of fake reports occurring when a haunting becomes well known.

John also acknowledged the theory that the ghost could be the hermit James MacRory Smith, but he has only been frequenting the area for twenty years – after the earlier sightings in the 1940s and 1950s – and, as John points out, 'nor does our hermit have the ability to disappear into thin air'. Perhaps Smith's presence has influenced the reported haunting of Strathchailleach Bothy which is where he lives during the summer? As John states, 'In short, while MacRory Smith may be able to cast light on some aspects of the haunting, his presence does not offer a complete explanation.' John also discounted the Australian ghost theory completely as he found no evidence to corroborate it.

Finally, despite the technical problems John suffered (which he put down to not testing the equipment properly rather than anything more unusual), he did take some photographs in total darkness using the other camera containing ordinary film. On one of the photographs, once it has been pointed out, there is a clear outline of the head of a bearded man which resembles the head of a statue. However, as John explains 'it is often not noticed by people told to look for "something unusual" ... and as it is surrounded by flash reflection it seems likely to assume that it is merely a clever trick of the flashlight. This, however, has as yet not been confirmed and until this is done the photograph remains interesting.' To sum up, John Fraser stated in his report: 'Several questions still remain unanswered in my conclusions and therefore further investigation may yet find a more definitive answer to this puzzle.'

Interesting stories of ghosts at Sandwood Cottage and in the vicinity of Cape Wrath cried out for investigation and John Fraser answered that call. I shall be most interested to hear from anyone else who is brave enough to follow his example.

Slaybrook Hall

The successive families who have lived at Slaybrook, a small hall house near Hythe, have always lived happily with the ghosts of ages past. 'It really is a lovely old house,' one told me, and the present occupant added: 'Slaybrook Hall has a reputation for being the most haunted house in the area; but that is an exaggeration. All I can say is that Slaybrook Hall is a happy place now, ghosts and all.'

It is a charming house, full of memories and associations of the past. Sir Gerald du Maurier (father of Daphne du Maurier) once owned the house and Sir Noel Coward was a frequent visitor at one time – a man who was no stranger to ghosts.

The present occupant is Brigadier J. A. MacKenzie, CBE, DSO, MC, and what a wonderful house he lives in, nestling in the fold of a hill in a beautiful part of England. Originally it was a medieval hall house, rectangular with dragon beams and moulded windows, and the main structure and façade of the house dates from the fifteenth century although alterations were made to the house in the sixteenth century and a new section was added in the 1930s.

Original pillars in the hall suggest there may well have been a building here as long ago as the twelfth century and this gives credence to the story, long associated with Slaybrook, that the four knights who came across from France to murder Thomas à Becket at Canterbury stayed the night at a nearby castle, their servants and horses spending the night at the hostelry which is thought to have stood on the site where Slaybrook Hall stands today.

The previous occupants, Mr and Mrs Reginald Hoskins and their children Zoe, Adrian and Howard, were aware of the ghosts that frequent Slaybrook and at first they all felt that they were resented but after a while all was well. As Vicky Hoskins said, 'We always liked the house but we had to find out if the house liked us. For those first few months it definitely did not but later we made our peace with it.'

There was the phantom form of an old man who on occasions left a strong aroma of alcohol in Zoe's bedroom; there was the ghost of an old lady in flowing robes who stood on the bridge in the garden; and then there were the unexplained figures who occasionally walked through closed doors and the inexplicable sounds and voices that occurred from time to time.

As I began to make plans for some kind of investigation at Slaybrook Hall, Brigadier J. A. MacKenzie was kind enough to tell me about some of the reported paranormal manifestations, and among the ghostly happenings I learned that there are still echoes from Roman times when there were frequent skirmishes hereabouts and a particularly bloody battle once took place at Slaybrook, ending in a massacre of all the local Britons. It is said the brook here ran with blood for a week and hence the name

Slaybrook. There were strange flickering lights in the garden at certain times each year; there were also happy ghosts at Slaybrook; something powerful and icy cold thoroughly frightened a sane and sensible painter and decorator while he was in the study; and there was a very puzzling incident that happened when the MacKenzies first moved into the house. The Brigadier told me, 'The first morning it was noticed that what seemed to be drops of blood appeared on our "Elizabethan" dining table which were exceptionally difficult to shift and can still be seen. Naturally I was amazed and my first thought was that the roofing contractors had not done their job properly and so let the rain seep down the old timbers. This was thoroughly checked and the roof was proved to be watertight. One can only surmise that perhaps the knights did dine in that room after the murder.'

Understandably, the curious blood-like stain on the oaken table revived memories of the knights responsible for the murder of Thomas à Becket. Actually there is a table in existence which, according to legend, rejected the swords of the knights who had foully slain the archbishop. It is preserved in the Anne of Cleves Museum at Lewes and Fiona Marsden, Head of Research there, tells me: 'The Knights' Table is actually a hefty eight-sided slab of Sussex marble forty-six inches wide and three and a quarter inches thick. An early photograph of it in the museum shows it resting on an eight-sided painted wooden base in Gothic style but now it is supported by a cluster of four staddle stones. It came to us from Malling House and we have an old photograph showing it in situ in a gazebo that still stands in the grounds. Our museum label reads as follows:

361

"Of Sussex Marble which is similar to Purbeck Marble containing small fossil shells. The base has been constructed recently from stone granary supports. The table top was formerly at Old Malling House, Lewes, and has the following legend: 'Reginald Fitzhurse, Hugh de Moreville, William de Tracey and Richard le Bret slew St Thomas à Becket on Tuesday 29 December 1170 in Canterbury. On December the 31st they rode to South Malling near Lewes. On entering the house they threw off their arms and trappings onto the table which stood in the hall, and after supper gathered round the blazing hearth. Suddenly the table started back and threw its burden to the ground. The attendants replaced the arms, but soon a still louder crash was heard, and the various articles were thrown still further off. Soldiers and servants then searched in vain under the solid table to find the cause of its convulsions till one of the conscience-stricken knights suggested that it was indignantly refusing to bear the sacrilegious burden of their arms.'" I regret to say that I do not know precisely where the information comes from but the table is an interesting piece of local folk lore.'

All things considered it seemed Slaybrook Hall warranted our attention and Brigadier MacKenzie and his wife readily agreed to an investigative visit. Dealing in more detail with some of the happenings, Brigadier MacKenzie informed me that he had always been sceptical of ghost stories but having owned in his time a large number of houses, including one of the oldest timber-framed medieval houses in Kent, Eastling Manor near Faversham, dating from 1250, he had come to the conclusion that there is something of the unexplained about some houses. In fact he believed that 'old houses, like recording tapes, absorb the crises, emotions and happenings of the families that own and occupy them over the centuries; and then in their own mysterious way and at times best known to them, these scenes are played back, perhaps to make people aware of past events in the history of the house – and why not? This is no more unusual than putting a man on the moon, outer space exploration, television, computers, robots, etc. The past reminds us of our heritage.'

Brigadier MacKenzie went on, 'There is a sixth sense in all of us that lies dormant in our highly civilised way of life and comfort. But in times of stress and danger the sixth sense is activated to a high degree, as when life itself is threatened. This animal instinct is in all of us, but more so in some than in others. I found this in the many battle experiences in the last war and also in my many tours overseas. This instinct also manifests itself even in the mundane problem of buying a house.

'When viewing an old house with the prospect of buying it, my wife and I always ask the question: "Is this a happy house?" If the atmosphere is right, we buy. There have been houses where the atmosphere has been all wrong, and afterwards we learn that a suicide or some ghastly event had taken place there . . . however, I can say that Slaybrook is a happy place to own, ghosts and all.'

On the question of the story dating from the days of the murder of Thomas à Becket, the Archbishop of Canterbury, Brigadier MacKenzie tells me that at that time, 1170, Slaybrook was a hostelry less than a mile from Saltwood Castle and when nobles, bishops and other dignitaries stayed at the castle, it was usual for their retainers, grooms and servants to be lodged at Slaybrook while fresh horses were procured. Such people preferred the relaxed atmosphere of the hostelry to the restrictions and strict discipline of the castle garrison and in any case the merry and buxom Slaybrook wenches serving at the hostelry were renowned for giving 'good value for money': perhaps they are some of the happy ghosts of Slaybrook.

The murder of Thomas à Becket is well recorded and the four knights responsible plotted the murder in Saltwood Castle. Local legend has it that after the murder the knights were warned not to return to the castle but to spend the night at the hostelry nearby before departing the country the next day.

Then there were the visitations of the so-called Grey Lady that have been reported here on innumerable occasions. She seems to have been seen only in the area of the small courtyard between the house and the brook. There have also been reports of an old lady standing on the bridge over the brook as we have seen – a figure seen by a passing bus driver on one occasion – and another female figure in flowing robes seen on the lawn behind the house. The latter may be the ghost of Lilly Elsie, a music-hall star at the turn of the century who lived at Slaybrook Hall and was in the habit of dancing on the lawn.

One afternoon Brigadier MacKenzie was mowing his front lawn and had just stopped to adjust the cutting blades of the mower when his attention was drawn to the figure of a woman who was bending over his rhododendron plants about fifteen yards away and adjacent to the courtyard. She was dressed in a long blue and white striped dress with a high ruff collar round the neck. Then like a flash she disappeared! He doubted at first whether it could have been the mysterious Grey Lady (no one knows who she was) but then his wife pointed out that blue and white, at a distance, could well merge into the colour of grey; so perhaps it was the Grey Lady of Slaybrook Hall he saw in the garden that sunny day. If so Brigadier MacKenzie thinks that perhaps she is one of the many owners who loved the house and especially the attractive walk round the courtyard beside the brook.

Enlarging a little on the incident in his study involving the painter and decorator, the Brigadier said this man, who he had not previously found to be perturbed by anything, was badly startled by his experience in the study, one of the rooms in the house long reputed to be haunted. Without warning and hearing no sound the door on the workman's left opened and then he found himself thrust against the wall by an icy-cold presence which then immediately left by the door leading to the kitchen. This hard-headed, no-nonsense man refused to work alone in that room again or to work in the house at all when no one was at home. No explanation was ever found for this incident.

Within recent memory mysterious lights have been seen in the grounds of Slaybrook Hall and a dark figure has been seen in the garden. Passing pedestrians are among the witnesses – people who had never heard of Slaybrook Hall or its ghosts.

Nine of us spent a summer night at Slaybrook and our usual investigative procedures, surveillance and attempts at holding seances, met with little success and there were only three things of real interest that occurred. First, at three different seances, at 12.10 a.m., 1.30 a.m. and

5.10 a.m., the initials of one of our keenest members came through repeatedly; a member who was present but not taking part in the seances. Secondly, there was a difference of several degrees in the temperature readings at each end of the heavy table with the 'irremovable blood-stains' at one reading, a difference that was checked by another member – yet from one end of the table to the other was a matter of feet. Thirdly, and most interesting of all perhaps, one lady member, while situated in the 'haunted' study, reported hearing sounds from outside the house that she likened to Roman soldiers passing by: marching footsteps, the clank of armour and the clash of weapons.

Brigadier MacKenzie told us that in Roman times the area around Slaybrook was a tribal settlement of Britons who were scattered deep into the forests surrounding the Roman port of Lemanis (now Lympne). Through the forest ran the Roman route Stone Street, leading to Canterbury. These Britons were in the habit of plundering the Roman supply wagons that journeyed between Lemanis and Canterbury and these raids became so bad that the Romans were forced to take punitive action by sending two legions of Roman soldiers to the settlement at the place later to become Slaybrook. A very bloody battle ensued which gave the place its name, ending in the complete massacre of all the Britons and, for good measure, their homes were destroyed by fire. It is said the dying tribal chief of the Britons laid a curse on the Romans for this massacre and said that all future generations would be reminded of the ghastly deed.

Every year, we were told, between the months of December and January, strange flickering lights are to be seen in the vicinity of the trees and in the gardens of Slaybrook. Brigadier MacKenzie told us that when he and his wife first saw the lights they thought it might be lightning but there was no sound of thunder or normal lightning and no storm anywhere in the vicinity. Could it really be a reminder of the great massacre, Brigadier MacKenzie wondered, and could some of the past owners of Slaybrook have caught a fleeting glimpse of Roman soldiers near the brook?

Interestingly enough, on this particular visit female members of the Ghost Club exceeded the number of males present and perhaps this was significant and played a part in the manifestations we did experience. At all events the memory of the sounds of clanking armour and marching soldiers passing the house at dead of night remains vivid for the person concerned and a puzzle for the rest of those present on that haunting visit to a haunted house.

In August 1993, Brigadier MacKenzie informed me that he had nothing new to report but he did tell me that it was as long ago as around 1903 that Slaybrook Hall became known to villagers as 'the haunted house'. After nearly 100 years it seems an apt description.

Woodfield

When I learned that a house in Bedfordshire was to be 'officially' investigated to see whether or not it was haunted – because the owner was trying to get his rates reduced because of the 'haunted' reputation the house had acquired – I felt I had to see whether I could be present. So it came about that I took part in the first official investigation into a haunting. The official status was warranted, it seemed, because the local borough council was setting up the investigation.

Councillor H. W. Richards of Luton Area Assessment Committee and another Councillor contacted me immediately and said they would be delighted to have me join the investigating party and I was very welcome to bring with me a fellow investigator. I contacted Tom Brown and together we travelled to Woodfield, a house in Weathercock Lane, Aspley Guise, to meet the rest of the investigating team and to learn something of the story of the house and the haunting.

Dusk was fast falling as we approached Woodfield, a gloomy and forbidding structure it seemed that autumn evening, and we found a crowd of people outside the house clamouring to get in. The investigation had become news and the narrow lane outside the high hedge was crowded with a motley collection of people: reporters from far and wide, local people, gaping sight-seers and several police-men. With our Gladstone bags containing a minimum of investigation equipment and rather obviously invited and prepared to spend the night in the house, we were the immediate centre of attention and the way the news media behaved that night resulted in my choosing to avoid them whenever possible in the years that followed.

With some difficulty we reached the porch of the house, tall and unfriendly in the uncertain light, and there the door was opened by the owner of the house, Mr Blaney Key, who lived on Eel Pie Island, Twickenham, in a house called The Pie Crust. We were ushered inside and introduced to the aged and crippled occupant, Mrs Amy Dickinson, Councillor H. W. Richards, Dr Donald J. West, Mrs Florence Thompson, a medium and her assistant Peter Craven, Leslie B. Howard, a spiritualist journalist, Tom Sheen, a freelance photographer, and his wife Helen Nichols of the local *Luton News* and Doreen Price, a fifteen-year-old girl from London who was living tem-porarily at the house. There were other journalists from national and local papers who were gradually escorted from the premises before the business of the evening began. A seance had been arranged.

Woodfield is not an old house, probably Victorian with later additions, but there is evidence of an earlier building, possibly an inn, once occupying the site. There was a persistent local legend, we learned, long accepted by many people for miles around which accounted for the haunting of Woodfield and which dated back perhaps 250 years. It was a story of thwarted lovers.

The inn that then stood on the site was occupied by a widower and his teenage daughter. This girl had a sweetheart or secret lover who used to visit the inn when the girl's father was absent. One night he returned unexpectedly and in a panic the pair just had time to secrete themselves in one of the large cupboards in the kitchen before the father entered. We examined the cupboards which were certainly large enough to accommodate two people. Unknown to them, however, the father had seen the guilty pair through the window and he had watched them enter their hiding place. In his anger he pushed heavy furniture against the cupboard door, imprisoning the couple, and left them to die.

Some time later the notorious highwayman Dick Turpin is reputed to have broken into Woodfield and accidentally discovered the bodies of the girl and her sweetheart. Realising that he had stumbled upon some ghastly secret, he awakened the startled father of the murdered couple who blurted out the whole story to the highwayman. Turpin agreed to remain silent about the affair on condition that he could use the house as a hideout and to this the old man agreed. The bodies were taken from the cupboard and buried in the cellar which was reached from the room in which the seances were to be held. Blaney Key told me he believed there was irrefutable evidence that Dick Turpin did in fact visit Woodfield or the inn that once stood there on more than one occasion, and the cupboards, he maintained, were incorporated into the later building.

At various times the ghosts of the murdered lovers were reportedly seen at Woodfield, both inside the house and in the garden; the hooves of Turpin's horse were said to have been heard galloping down the hill towards the house and safety, and his ghostly form had been seen dismounting and hurriedly entering the grounds at a spot no longer used as an entrance.

Doreen Price claimed to have seen the phantom couple in the room where the seances were held. The girl appeared to have her arms outstretched as though appealing for something – but what?

On that first visit, having examined the house and some of the grounds, Brown and I adjourned to the room where the seances were to take place. It was a spacious room with two bay windows. Against these windows Mrs Dickinson, who had lived at the house for four or five years, told us she had heard loud flapping noises which she had at first put down to birds or bats, but on more than one occasion she had arranged for someone to be outside and they could see nothing to account for the noises – but she said she didn't believe in ghosts. The noises continued to be heard occasionally but only from *inside* the house. The room was normally used more as a store room than anything else and it was crowded with glass, china and bric-a-brac. We arranged eight chairs in a circle and took our places with Councillor Richards' chauffeur on guard at the door to see that we were not disturbed.

Just as the seance was about to begin we were interrupted by two newspaper men who claimed to have been promised admission to the seance room, but after a somewhat lengthy and heated argument, they departed.

The medium, who was just going into trance, and her assistant attributed the failure of the first seance to this interruption.

When at length Florence Thompson did succeed in apparently entering the trance state, just before midnight, she appeared to be acutely distressed; she leaned forwards and backwards, rubbing her head and moaning and groaning. After a while she murmured faintly, 'Red Wings' (the name of one of her spirit guides) and then emitted spasmodically, and sometimes with an appreciable lapse of silence between the outbursts, in a high-pitched voice allegedly of the dead girl, such phrases as: 'Oh! my head, I've been shot'; 'Let me go'; 'Oh! my head'; 'Let me go, you're killing me'; 'Why can't you let me go?'; 'You've tied me up'; 'I want to go away'; 'Let me go'.

There was a good deal of distressed moaning between the expressions, the medium holding her head, especially the right side. Peter Craven meanwhile tried to obtain the name of the entity manifesting through the medium but Florence Thompson simply turned her head towards a corner of the room where there was an alcove that could have once contained a cupboard.

Little further transpired and after the medium had returned to her normal self just before 2 a.m., she asserted that some tragic happening, possibly a murder, had taken place in the room in which we were all seated. She stated that the tragedy had happened in one corner of the room, that which she had indicated. She believed Woodfield to be haunted by two entities, probably lovers, and that one or possibly both of them had been murdered. She suggested that another seance, preferably with an additional medium who was used to 'rescue work', would probably clear the house. There seemed to be some confusion here, for the present house, being only 100 years old at most, could not be associated with the traditional story involving Dick Turpin who was hanged in 1739.

Peter Craven told me that from his knowledge of Florence Thompson in the trance state, he would say that she had been under the influence of a very distressed young woman (the medium gave her age as not older than twenty-two) who had almost certainly been murdered, possibly after having been tied up and raped. When someone suggested a double tragedy, as had happened if we accept the legend, Mrs Thompson opined that the girl had been raped and shot, her lover being forced to witness the act before he too was murdered. This hardly fits in with the legend, unless we assume that the girl's father first raped her and then shot them both. After further discussion we left Woodfield as a distant church clock chimed 4 a.m.

The second visit to Woodfield took place a fortnight later. This time Tom Brown and I arrived at the haunted house at 8.15 p.m. and again we thoroughly examined the twelve-room house from attic to cellars. As I entered the kitchen, Mr George Kenneth, a London medium, declared that in his opinion this was not the room in which the tragedy had taken place. Mr Key, evidently forgetting that the present house could not have been the one visited by Dick Turpin, told George Kenneth that one of the cupboards in the kitchen had always been assumed to be the one in which the couple had hidden, but the medium repeated that in his opinion no tragedy had happened there – which was probably true. To be fair to Blaney Key there was talk of the cupboards in question being originally in the property that formerly occupied the site and being rebuilt into the present structure.

Next we entered the room with the bay windows, the seance room, and there George Kenneth declared that a tragedy certainly *had* taken place in the room. Blaney Key pointed out that there was no cupboard in the room and said that, as far as he knew (and the house had been in his family for the best part of a hundred years), there had never been a cupboard in this room as large as those in the kitchen. We verified that the kitchen cupboards were in fact large enough to secrete two people, for it seemed to us that two separate crimes might be associated with the house. George Kenneth pointed to the large alcove in the seance room and suggested that a cupboard had once occupied the space; this was the alcove twice pointed out as the scene of the tragedy by Florence Thompson on the previous visit.

We questioned Blaney Key regarding the cellar, under the floor of which the bodies of the lovers were reputed to have been buried and he led us to the trapdoor in the floor of the seance room. I descended and explored the shallow cellar and found it to be some four feet deep, five feet wide and ten feet long. By careful measurement we ascertained that there was now a wall, or two walls, with a total width of just under three feet between *two* cellars!

At 9.15 p.m. we assembled for another seance, again held in the room with the bay windows, with both mediums, Florence Thompson and George Kenneth (who knew each other) taking part. As Florence Thompson was going into trance, George Kenneth remarked, 'There was a loud shriek in this room.' Mrs Thompson was considerably quicker in sinking into a trance on this occasion and then again we heard the high-pitched voice which could have belonged to a young woman. After some coaxing from Peter Craven, the following words came from the medium's mouth in a distressed, half-frightened tone: 'I've been here a long time – a long time – who are all these people? – You won't hurt me will you?'

Peter Craven reassured 'her', by saying that we were all friends and had come to help. He then asked the entity to tell us 'her' name and what had happened to 'her'. The voice replied: 'They call me Bessie – pray for me, won't you? Pray for both of us – John and me – we were going away together and my father found out – he hurt me – you will help us won't you?'

Gradually the voice appeared to grow weaker but after a little while 'she' was speaking again; and then I noticed Peter Craven, on my left, trying to attract my attention. While talking intermittently to 'Bessie', he at last managed to whisper in my ear, 'I keep seeing a face over there' and he pointed towards George Kenneth on the opposite side of the circle. I immediately looked to where he pointed and in the dim light over George Kenneth's right shoulder I seemed to see a grey-white face which might have belonged to an old man. I could discern no semblance of a body. As I watched, peering to convince myself of its reality and attempting to distinguish the features, the face moved slowly behind George Kenneth's head only to reappear over the other shoulder; then it disappeared. I shall always regret that time and circumstances did not allow me to attract the attention of other people present in the room to this apparent manifestation. At least three independent witnesses are desirable before such a vision can be put down to anything other than imagination or some trick of the light. I feel on reflection that some such logical explanation is probably the answer, but it is interesting that Peter Craven remarked only that he could see 'a face'. When I asked him afterwards to describe the face he had seen, he said: 'An old man's face, definitely; it appeared to be moving from one side to the other of George Kenneth's head, almost as though trying to whisper something in his ear' – which was exactly what I had seen.

Shortly after this episode, 'Bessie' ceased talking and Florence Thompson returned to her normal self. After a few moments George Kenneth said there was a crowd of spirit people in the room and he could pick out a dark girl of about twenty with a dark young man. There was also an old man, dressed like a farmer, who was insistently trying to 'get through'. George Kenneth announced that he would like to go into trance to see whether the old man would manifest. Mr Leslie B. Howard was in charge of a small red lamp and George asked him to shine the lamp on him after giving him a few minutes in which to enter the trance state.

George Kenneth lay back in his chair and relaxed for a short while and then appeared to go into a trance. Slowly and menacingly he sat up, at the same time raising his arms with clutching fingers and reaching out towards the lamp. As his face came into the dim light we saw that it had taken on a hateful and wicked expression. His eyes remained closed and a number of gurgling and snarling noises emanated from his throat. Although Florence Thompson tried to help him to speak, no words came; he just kept bending over the red lamp with clutching hands held menacingly high. Suddenly he appeared nearly to choke; he then coughed and quickly returned to his normal self.

George Kenneth appeared to be surprised to learn that he had said nothing while in trance and said that he felt as though he had been arguing with all of us a great deal. He also said there was a big black horse in the room (!) and everyone immediately thought of Dick Turpin's Black Bess.

While George Kenneth was in trance both Florence Thompson and Peter Craven said they felt suddenly cold. Two other members of the circle intimated that they too had had the same sensation. I asked each member of the circle whether they had anything to relate. Councillor Richards said he had experienced nothing at all; Helen Nichols had had the impression of a cross with a little 'c' on it over the head of Mrs Thompson. George Kenneth said the old man was still in the room and was still anxious to 'come through', Leslie B. Howard told of having twice had the impression of a bright light shining behind him; and Peter Craven said he had impressions of stars or small bright lights shining behind Florence Thompson, in addition to having seen the face of an old man. Of the other four people in the room, only the chauffeur by the door had anything to report: he said that he too had felt suddenly cold at what appeared to be the same time as the four members of the circle.

After somewhat lengthy discussion on various hauntings as well as the case in hand, we all prepared to leave Woodfield. After some hesitation, Tom Brown and I decided to go to Bletchley Station as he had to get back to north Hertfordshire and I had made arrangements to visit a haunted house in the vicinity of Watford the following morning, or rather, later the same morning, for the time was about 1.30 a.m.

On our way to Fenny Stratford we passed only one human being, a man on foot hurrying in the opposite direction to ourselves. As we passed through the town we were surprised to see many police, both on foot and in cars, patrolling the sleeping streets. It was not long before a hawk-eyed officer of the law approached us and I asked him for directions to Bletchley Station. He obliged, pointing to a street branching away to the north as the first step; then, as he caught sight of the Gladstone-style ghost-hunting bags, he added suspiciously: 'You're about rather late, sirs, aren't you?' After he had examined our credentials we were allowed to continue on our way, the way which he had pointed out to us – which was fortunate as, after perhaps half a mile, a torch suddenly appeared in the gloom ahead and behind it, our friend the constable! He did no more than give us further directions, and as we left him we both wondered why he had checked on our movements. Arriving at Bletchley we learned that the whole countryside was being combed for a man who had shot his wife the night before, a few miles away at Leighton Buzzard. Could he perhaps have been the lone man we had met earlier?

We read accounts of the latest 'investigations' at Woodfield in the morning papers before we left the district and returned about a fortnight later for the third and final visit to the haunted house. Meanwhile we made a number of inquiries and discovered that originally there had been an entrance to Woodfield where now a high hedge grew but it was here that three witnesses claimed they had seen a mounted horseman disappear.

At Woodfield this time the seance commenced at 9 p.m. and those forming the circle included Florence Thompson and her assistant Peter Craven; Councillor Richards, Tom Brown and myself. Others in the room included three press representatives and again the chauffeur at the door. After nearly twenty minutes' silence, the medium showed signs of being in the trance state and we caught the following words, whispered at first but gradually becoming louder: 'It's Bessie – who are all these people?' Here Peter Craven again assured the entity that we were all gathered to help her and John. 'Bessie' then continued: 'You all came before, didn't you? John's here too and a whole crowd of people – we've been waiting for you to come again – it's lighter now – I'm tied up – why am I tied up?'

Florence Thompson wriggled and squirmed as though trying to rid herself of invisible bonds. 'Bessie' was told she was no longer bound and that she was in fact what we call dead and was living in another world which meant that she had no body now and was free. Asked why she was haunting Woodfield, 'Bessie' replied: 'I belong here – but I want to go away – it's much lighter now—' At this point Leslie B. Howard interrupted to ask Peter Craven to try and establish her identity. The immediate answer was 'Bessie'. On being asked her surname, the answer was, 'I can't remember'. Howard asked whether the names Brander or Grant meant anything to her. 'Bessie' answered, 'I – I can't remember – Grant was my father's name – I can't remember – I want to forget.'

Leslie B. Howard subsequently informed us that he had discovered that two doctors had once resided at Woodfield and that as far as he knew no other person at the seances was aware of this fact and any information concerning these names might therefore have been of some importance. He went on to say that he was unable to accept the remark that Grant was 'Bessie's' father, as this did not fit in with the information he had obtained during an afternoon spent making discreet inquiries in the locality; his informant claimed to have known the Grants during their tenancy and to have been in close association with the house for over fifty years.

The entity 'Bessie' continued: 'It's getting lighter now – there's a nun here – I want to go away – we are both going away now – we won't haunt this place any more.' On being told by Peter Craven to go with the nun, the entity replied: 'Yes, we are going now – you have all helped us – we thank you.'

After the alleged voice of 'Bessie' had faded away, to be heard by the assembled company no more, we questioned members of the circle as to what experiences the sitters claimed at this seance. Councillor Richards remarked that a small round patch of red light had been visible from time to time between Peter Craven and the medium. I immediately glanced at the red-fronted stove in the room and I feel that it was probably some reflection of this that provided Councillor Richards with his sole experience during the series of seances. The red light had also been seen by two other members of the circle. The next sitter asserted that she had seen the figure of a skeleton sitting by my side during the seance! Peter Craven reported having felt a heavy blow on the back of his neck, just as the seance began; he had also seen a number of 'spirit' lights. He added that he was definitely under the impression that the house did not feel as hostile as it had done before the first seance; he especially felt an oppressive feeling in this particular room had cleared. The chauffeur, on guard as usual at the door, did not agree; he said he felt the room to be considerably more hostile and frightening, much more so than at the previous seance. He also said he had seen a number of stars in the shape of a swastika over the sitters' heads during the seance.

As we left Councillor Richards told us he felt able to report to Luton Area Assessment Committee that 'he was satisfied on the evidence that the place was haunted'. In fact there can be little doubt but that the seances were unconvincing and I have no knowledge that anything further was ever done in an attempt to establish the reality of the haunting. At length Mr Blaney Key's appeal took place at the Shire Hall, Bedford, but still the affair did not end conclusively for, after the chairman of Bedfordshire Quarter Sessions Appeals Committee, Mr C. L. Henderson, Q.C., and the council had discussed the matter privately, the appeal was withdrawn.

A year later, Mr Key tried again to get the rate assessment reduced; he told the Bedfordshire Quarter Sessions Appeals Committee on that occasion that no one would rent the place and claimed that people still heard the sound of galloping hooves down Weathercock Lane and saw a horseman disappear through a hedge, and he produced other reasons for reducing the assessment. But his appeal was dismissed by Mr Henderson who said that

Mr Key's reasons were 'devoid of merit and without point or substance'.

The loss of the appeal was included in a BBC news broadcast and provided one of the few occasions when a reputedly haunted house has been mentioned seriously in a news bulletin. Tom Brown and I subsequently visited Blaney Key at his home on Eel Pie Island. He was still convinced of the reality of the haunting of Woodfield but on the evidence both Tom Brown and I agreed that we would have to consider the haunting, long thought to be 'the first official investigation into a haunting' to be 'not proven'. I never heard any more about ghosts at Woodfield, Aspley Guise.

Appendix
The places and the people

Practically every investigative visit included a Ghost Club Society Council Member.

Borley Cottage, Borley, Essex
P. I. Thomas Brown
Peter Underwood

Bovey House, Branscombe, Devon
Freda and Steuart Kiarnander
Joyce and Peter Underwood

Bramshill House, Eversley, Basingstoke, Hampshire
Sidney Scott
Peter Underwood
Toby Underwood

Bretforton Manor, Worcestershire
Bill and John Bellars
Godfrey Goolden

Elsie and Vernon Harrison
Mary Hartshorn
Paddy and Stan Hughes
Ruth Jarvis
Marilyn and Trevor Kenward
Tony Kerwin
Ken Lazenby
Keith Morbey
Dennis Moyses
Alan Roper
Shirley Shaw
Joyce and Peter Underwood
Paul Went

Bromfield Manor, Shropshire
Mary Hartshorn
Ruth and Sarah Jarvis
Marilyn and Trevor Kenward
Jennie Newland
Shirley Shaw
Margery and John Skinley
Joyce and Peter Underwood

The Bull, Long Melford, Suffolk
P. I. Thomas Brown
Mavis Don
Rosemary and Stewart P. Evans
Godfrey Goolden
Peter Hilton-Rowe
Rose Holt
Philip Moore
Dennis Moyses
Joyce and Peter Underwood
Melvyn J. Willin

Chingle Hall, Goosnargh, Lancashire
Michael J. Brett
Godfrey Goolden
Elsie and Vernon Harrison
Freda and Steuart Kiernander
Ken Lazenby
Joyce and Peter Underwood

Curry Mallet Manor House, Somerset
Bob Cato
Mavis Don
Ruth Jarvis
Marilyn and Trevor Kenward
Tim Miller
Philip Moore
Dennis Moyses
Lynda Randall
Shirley Shaw
Michael Sweetman
Joyce and Peter Underwood
Michael Williams

Eton Vicarage, Berkshire
Elsie and Vernon Harrison
Freda and Steuart Kiernander
Frances Jones
Ken Lazenby
Joyce and Peter Underwood

Farnham Castle, Farnham, Surrey
Tony Broughall
Geoffrey Jordan
Alan Roper
Joyce and Peter Underwood

Glamis Castle, Angus, Scotland
James Wentworth Day
Joyce and Peter Underwood

Gosling Hall, Occold, Suffolk
Bill, John and Carole Bellars
Mary Hartshorn
Angela and Kevin Hore
Ruth Jarvis
Trevor Kenward
Philip Moore
Shirley Shaw
Joyce and Peter Underwood

Harlaxton Manor, Grantham, Lincolnshire
Joyce and Peter Underwood

Knowle Farm, Weston on the Green, Oxfordshire
Michael J. Brett
Steuart Kiernander
Joyce and Peter Underwood

Langenhoe Church, near Colchester, Essex
John Dening
Tommy Frankland
Peter Hilton-Rowe
P. H. Skelton
Joyce and Peter Underwood

Loventor Manor and Berry Pomeroy Castle, Devon
Adele Butler
Eileen C. Coapes
Bob Daulby

Godfrey Goolden
Mary Hartshorn
Jack Hazzard
Rose Holt
Angela and Kevin Hore
Marilyn and Trevor Kenward
Freda and Steuart Kiernander
Jennie Newland
Deryck Seymour
Margery and John Skinley
Joyce and Peter Underwood

Mermaid Inn and Lamb House, Rye, East Sussex
Bill, John and Carole Bellars
Pamela and John Calder
Mavis Don
Linda and Joe Goodman
Mary Hartshorn
Angela and Kevin Hore
Philip Moore
Tom Perrott
Shirley Shaw
Joyce and Peter Underwood
Janice and Philip Wilson

Newark Park, Ozleworth, Wooton-under-Edge, Gloucestershire
Bill Bellars
Michael J. Brett
Adele Butler
Henry Curtis
Catherine Duval
Godfrey Goolden
Elsie and Vernon Harrison

Mary Hartshorn
Steuart Kiernander
Pauline Langfield
Ken Lazenby
Moira Maxwell-Heron
Alan Roper
Joyce and Peter Underwood

Nottingham Council House, Bilborough Estate, Nottingham
Dennis Bardens
David Cuttler
Richard Howard
Steuart Kiernander
Ralph Morris
Alan Roper
Maxine M. T. Overgaard
Peter Underwood

Old Battersea House, Vicarage Crescent, London
Bill, John and Carole Bellars
Elsie and Vernon Harrison
Ruth Jarvis
Ken Lazenby
Philip Moore
Dennis Moyses
Shirley Shaw
Joyce and Peter Underwood

Prestonfield House, Edinburgh
Deborah Jarvis
Peter Underwood

The Queen's House, Greenwich, London
Trixie Allingham
Peter Hilton-Rowe
Richard Howard
Margery and Hector McQueen
Peter Underwood

RAF Cosford Aerospace Museum, Shropshire
John Fraser
Trevor Kenward
Philip Moore
Dennis Moyses
Alan Roper
Joyce and Peter Underwood

The Rookery, Downe, Kent
Bill, John and Carole Bellars
Elsie and Vernon Harrison
Ruth Jarvis
Marilyn and Trevor Kenward
Ken Lazenby
Philip Moore
Keith Morbey
Dennis Moyses
Lynda Randall
Alan Roper
Heidi Shakleton
Shirley Shaw
Michael Sweetman
Joyce and Peter Underwood

Rushbrooke Hall, Bury St Edmunds, Suffolk
Peter Underwood

Sandwood Bay, Cape Wrath, Sutherland, Scotland
John Fraser

Slaybrook Hall, Saltwood, Kent
Bill Bellars
Elsie and Vernon Harrison
Mary Hartshorn
Ruth and Sarah Jarvis
Dennis Moyses
Joyce and Peter Underwood

Woodfield, Aspley Guise, Bedfordshire
P. I. Thomas Brown
Peter Craven
Amy Dickinson
Leslie B. Howard
Helen Nicholls
Doreen Price
H. W. Richards
Tom Sheen
Florence Thompson
Peter Underwood
Donald J. West

Select Bibliography

Dennis Bardens, *Ghosts and Hauntings*, Robert Hale, 1965; *Mysterious Worlds*, Robert Hale, 1970

Harry Bell, *Guide to the Haunted Castles of Scotland*, Leyline Publications, 1981

John Blashford-Snell, *Mysteries*, Bodley Head, 1983

A. J. Chapple, *Beer in Time and Tide*, A. J. Chapple, 1993

Antony Hippisley Coxe, *Haunted Britain*, Hutchinson, 1973

James Wentworth Day, *A Ghost Hunter's Game Book*, Muller, 1958; *In Search of Ghosts*, Muller, 1969

Martin Ebon, *True Experiences with Ghosts*, New American Library, 1968

Charles Gatty, *The Incredible Mrs Van der Elst*, Frewin, 1972

Rumer Godden, *A House with Four Walls*, Macmillan, 1989

Christina Hole, *Haunted England*, Batsford, 1940

R. Thurston Hopkins, *Ghosts Over England*, Meridian Books, 1953

H. Montgomery Hyde, *The Story of Lamb House*, Adams of Rye, 1966

Henry James, *The Turn of the Screw*, Routledge, 1898

Alasdair Alpin MacGregor, *The Ghost Book*, Robert Hale, 1955; *Phantom Footsteps*, Robert Hale, 1959

Diana Norman, *The Stately Ghosts of England*, Frederick Muller, 1963

Harry Price, '*The Most Haunted House in England*', Longmans, 1940; *Search for Truth*, Collins, 1942; *The End of Borley Rectory*, Harrap, 1946

Deryck Seymour, *Berry Pomeroy Castle*, D. Seymour, 1982; *The Ghosts of Berry Pomeroy Castle*, Obelisk Publications, 1990

Doris Stokes, *Voices in My Ear*, Futura, 1979

John and Anne Spencer, *The Encyclopedia of Ghosts and Spirits*, Headline, 1992

A. M. W. Stirling, *Ghosts Vivisected*, Robert Hale, 1957

James Turner, *Ghosts in the South West*, David & Charles, 1973

Sally Wallbank, *Chingle: Britain's Most Haunted House*, Owl Books, 1992

Colin Wilson, *Poltergeist!*, New English Library, 1981

Index

More True Crime from Headline:

ROCKY STOCKMAN
THE
HANGMAN'S DIARY

A CALENDAR OF JUDICIAL HANGINGS
Introduction by Colin Wilson

**An extraordinary calendar of judicial hangings from around
the world and through the ages…**

3 January
1946 THE END OF LORD HAW-HAW
William Joyce (40), dubbed 'Lord Haw-Haw', hanged at Wandsworth Prison for
treason. *Hangman: Albert Pierrepoint*

23 February
1885 THE 'MAN THEY COULD NOT HANG'
John Lee (19) was the 'Man They Could Not Hang' at Exeter Gaol. He had been
sentenced for the murder of his employer Emma Keyse (68). *Hangman: James Berry*

28 May
1686 HANGMAN HANGED
Pascha Rose, butcher and public hangman, hanged at Tyburn Tree for house-
breaking and theft. *Hangman: Jack Ketch*

19 August
1692 SALEM WITCHES
Reverend George Burroughs (42), and others, hanged at Gallows Hill, Salem,
Massachusetts, USA, for witchcraft. *Hangman: Sheriff John Corwin*

23 November
1910 'THE MURDER OF THE CENTURY'
Dr Hawley Harvey Crippen (48) hanged at Pentonville Prison for the murder and
dismemberment of his wife Cora Crippen (37). *Hangman: John Ellis*

24 December
1867 THE MURDER AND MUTILATION OF SWEET FANNY ADAMS
Frederick Baker (29) publicly hanged at Winchester Prison for the ghastly murder
of Fanny Adams (8). *Hangman: William Calcraft*

NON-FICTION/TRUE CRIME   0 7472 4015 9

More Non-fiction from Headline:

THE UFO ENCYCLOPEDIA

THE MOST COMPREHENSIVE BOOK ON UFOLOGY EVER WRITTEN

COMPILED AND EDITED BY

JOHN SPENCER

FOR THE BRITISH UFO RESEARCH ASSOCIATION

Compiled by one of the world's leading authorities
on the subject, THE UFO ENCYCLOPEDIA is an
authoritative, level-headed and witty reference book
covering all aspects of the UFO phenomenon.
It includes:

* Over 1,000 entries and over 70 colour and black
and white photos

* In-depth analyses of celebrated cases including the
Gulf Breeze Sightings, the Pascagoula Abduction
and the Trindade Island photographs

* First-hand accounts of alien abductions

* Rare photographs and previously unknown cases

* The latest information on related phenomena
including corn circles and the Bermuda Triangle

THE UFO ENCYCLOPEDIA

- a comprehensive manual for professionals and
amateurs alike.

NON-FICTION/REFERENCE   0 7472 3494 9

More True Crime from Headline:

FRANK JONES

MURDEROUS WOMEN

TRUE TALES OF WOMEN WHO KILLED

As Madame Fahmy stalked and killed her husband in cold blood at the elegant Savoy Hotel, what thoughts were in her mind? Could Louise Masset have thought that murder would open the way to a respectable marriage? What led Myra Hindley to participate in the grisly torture and murder of ten-year-old Lesley Ann Downey, photographing and tape-recording her death agonies?

In *Murderous Women* Frank Jones delves into the psyches of fifteen notorious females, from Victorian times to the present. With wit, insight, suspense and compassion he grippingly reconstructs their gruesome crimes from beginning to end.

NON-FICTION/TRUE CRIME   0 7472 3798 0

A selection of non-fiction from Headline

THE DRACULA SYNDROME	Richard Monaco & William Burt	£5.99	☐
DEADLY JEALOUSY	Martin Fido	£5.99	☐
WHITE COLLAR KILLERS	Frank Jones	£4.99	☐
THE MURDER YEARBOOK 1994	Brian Lane	£5.99	☐
THE PLAYFAIR CRICKET ANNUAL	Bill Frindall	£3.99	☐
ROD STEWART	Stafford Hildred & Tim Ewbank	£5.99	☐
THE JACK THE RIPPER A–Z	Paul Begg, Martin Fido & Keith Skinner	£7.99	☐
THE *DAILY EXPRESS* HOW TO WIN ON THE HORSES	Danny Hall	£4.99	☐
COUPLE SEXUAL AWARENESS	Barry & Emily McCarthy	£5.99	☐
GRAPEVINE: THE COMPLETE WINEBUYERS HANDBOOK	Anthony Rose & Tim Atkins	£5.99	☐
ROBERT LOUIS STEVENSON: DREAMS OF EXILE	Ian Bell	£7.99	☐

All Headline books are available at your local bookshop or newsagent, or can be ordered direct from the publisher. Just tick the titles you want and fill in the form below. Prices and availability subject to change without notice.

Headline Book Publishing, Cash Sales Department, Bookpoint, 39 Milton Park, Abingdon, OXON, OX14 4TD, UK. If you have a credit card you may order by telephone – 0235 400400.

Please enclose a cheque or postal order made payable to Bookpoint Ltd to the value of the cover price and allow the following for postage and packing:
UK & BFPO: £1.00 for the first book, 50p for the second book and 30p for each additional book ordered up to a maximum charge of £3.00.
OVERSEAS & EIRE: £2.00 for the first book, £1.00 for the second book and 50p for each additional book.

Name ....

Address ....

....

....

If you would prefer to pay by credit card, please complete:
Please debit my Visa/Access/Diner's Card/American Express (delete as applicable) card no:

Signature .... Expiry Date ....